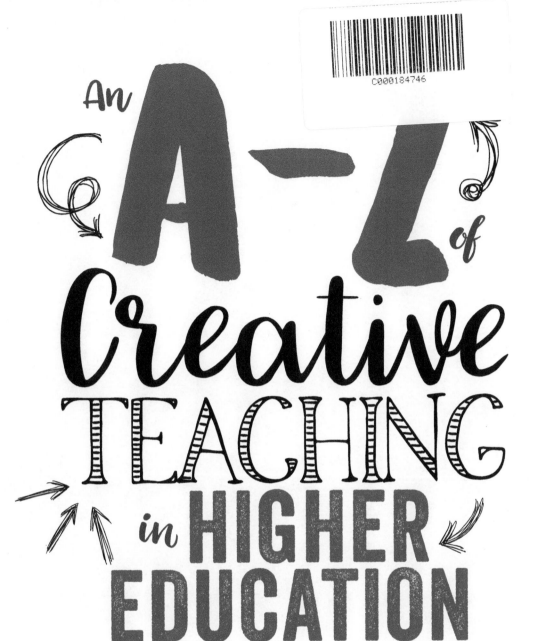

An **A-Z** of

Creative
TEACHING
in HIGHER
EDUCATION

Sara Miller McCune founded SAGE Publishing in 1965 to support the dissemination of usable knowledge and educate a global community. SAGE publishes more than 1000 journals and over 800 new books each year, spanning a wide range of subject areas. Our growing selection of library products includes archives, data, case studies and video. SAGE remains majority owned by our founder and after her lifetime will become owned by a charitable trust that secures the company's continued independence.

Los Angeles | London | New Delhi | Singapore | Washington DC | Melbourne

An A-Z of Creative TEACHING in HIGHER EDUCATION

★ SYLVIA ASHTON & RACHEL STONE ★

Los Angeles | London | New Delhi
Singapore | Washington DC | Melbourne

Los Angeles | London | New Delhi
Singapore | Washington DC | Melbourne

SAGE Publications Ltd
1 Oliver's Yard
55 City Road
London EC1Y 1SP

SAGE Publications Inc.
2455 Teller Road
Thousand Oaks, California 91320

SAGE Publications India Pvt Ltd
B 1/I 1 Mohan Cooperative Industrial Area
Mathura Road
New Delhi 110 044

SAGE Publications Asia-Pacific Pte Ltd
3 Church Street
#10-04 Samsung Hub
Singapore 049483

Editor: Amy Thornton
Development editor: Geoff Barker
Production Editor: Chris Marke
Marketing manager: Lorna Patkai
Cover design: Wendy Scott
Typeset by: C&M Digitals (P) Ltd, Chennai, India
Printed in the UK

First published in 2018 by SAGE Publications Inc

Library of Congress Control Number: 2017954833

British Library Cataloguing in Publication Data

A catalogue record for this book is available from the
British Library

ISBN: 978-1-5264-0102-1 (hbk)
978-1-5264-0103-8 (pbk)

At SAGE we take sustainability seriously. Most of our products are printed in the UK using FSC papers and boards.
When we print overseas we ensure sustainable papers are used as measured by the PREPS grading system.
We undertake an annual audit to monitor our sustainability.

To our mums.
We hope we would have made them proud.

Elizabeth Ashton (1919-88)
Susheila Stone (1930-97)

CONTENTS

LIST OF ILLUSTRATIONS

MEET THE AUTHORS

Rachel on Sylvia

Sylvia is one of the most principled – and joyous – people I've ever known. When we first met, she was a teacher educator specialising in Teaching English to Speakers of Other Languages at Sheffield Hallam University. I remember discussing her research with her – really exciting stuff about creating empowering contexts with multilingual students of the English language.

Later, I had the privilege of working with Sylvia on the Postgraduate Certificate in Learning and Teaching in HE (Pg Cert LTHE), where she was Course Leader. It's largely our creative development on this programme that has formed the basis of this book.

Sylvia has worked in a range of contexts, including the Open College Network awarding body, adult and community education, and secondary and primary schools. She approaches her teaching with playfulness and integrity (the 'A–Z' format was her idea), something she carries into her current role as an independent education consultant. Her most enviable traits are being able to silence a room without raising her voice and her quiet, calm teaching presence.

Sylvia on Rachel

Rachel came to Sheffield Hallam University from LLU+ at London South Bank University, an organisation whose creative approaches to teaching I very much admired. We share a history of working with adults on what used to be called 'Basic Skills' courses and learning from their resourcefulness as learners in really challenging circumstances.

As well as a career as an independent maths education consultant, Rachel has taught in a variety of sectors, including schools, offender learning and further education. She is the co-editor of a book on *Adult Numeracy Teaching* and previously worked in the public and voluntary sectors.

Teaching together on the Pg Cert LTHE, we discovered that we shared a deep commitment to the principles of inclusive practice (an area reflected in Rachel's current research interests). Rachel still teaches on the course and in addition leads a Foundation Award in Education and Learning Support. She is a model for me of academic integrity and critically reflective practice, as well as being a superb designer and facilitator of online learning.

ACKNOWLEDGEMENTS

We would like to thank all our students from the Postgraduate Certificate in Learning and Teaching in Higher Education at Sheffield Hallam University for being such an inspiring set of practitioners. Special thanks go to Danny Allwood, Catrin Andersson, Alex Hamilton, Sarah Holland, Jamie Hufford, Mark Marshall (and his colleague Andy Dearden), Andy Mills, Diane Rodgers, Joe Stone, Sukey Tarr, Collette Turner and Drew Woodhouse, as well as to those who asked not to be named, for agreeing to let us draw on their work. Thanks also to Graham Griffiths and Herine Otieno for allowing us to refer to their examples of good practice.

We would also like to thank the following colleagues and friends who took the time to review our work and give us valuable suggestions to improve it: Ian Glover, Susanna Grace, Lisa McGrath, Karen Nichols, Sinead O'Toole, John Plowright, Kent Roach, Jacqueline Stevenson, Roberta Taylor, Viv Thom, Krassimira Teneva, Linda Wilson, the careers team at Sheffield Hallam University and Sarah Woodall; also Catherine Burchell, Gill Greenwood and Laura Church.

Thanks too to Derek Dawson for believing in us over the years, and to Geoff, Chris and Amy at Sage for their encouragement and positive feedback.

Finally, thanks to Sylv's partner Val for her support, and to our families, particularly Reuben, Jonah, Matthew, Michael, Margaret, Shona, Oisin and Calum for their patience and help as we wrote this book.

PRAISE FOR THIS BOOK

'A book filled with tips for becoming an inspirational teacher. A must read for all teachers, junior and experienced.'

Mari Sako, Professor of Management Studies,
University of Oxford

'I found the methods and techniques presented in *An A-Z of Creative Teaching in Higher Education* inspiring and extremely helpful. Its focus on the activity and experience of the students themselves is mirrored in the style and presentation of the book itself. I would recommend the book highly for anyone looking to bring more thought and engagement to their higher education teaching.'

Patrick Ball, Graduate Teaching Assistant,
University of Pennsylvania

'This book should be of interest to experienced and staff new to teaching in higher education alike. It introduces concepts in a way which makes the reader stop and think about their own practice and values, but also challenges the reader to go beyond their comfort zone and try something new. The authors have clearly built on their years of experience working with staff new to teaching in higher education and offer vignettes of practice to stimulate discussion, reflection and further reading. It is a book which can be dipped into and stimulates you to find out more, whilst being interspersed with relevant literature without intimidating the reader.'

Professor Sally Bradley, Academic Lead – Professional Learning and
Development, Higher Education Academy

'This book is a must-read for anyone teaching in higher education (and other contexts), offering excellent ideas and practical strategies that are evidence-based and empowering for both students and teachers. It has an easy-to-read format and it imbues the reader with the authors' evident enthusiasm for teaching and learning. Perfect when starting a new course or when looking for creative ideas to refresh old formats.'

Vera Hutchinson, Professional Development Manager,
UCL Institute of Education

INTRODUCTION

AN INTERVIEW WITH THE AUTHORS

Who is this book for?

We've written the book for academics in higher education who want to develop their teaching in imaginative and creative ways in order to support all of their students to learn.

And how will it help?

The chapters are packed full of suggestions and examples of creative teaching practices. We've drawn from a range of contexts, and we've included reflective prompts for you to evaluate and apply them to your own teaching.

So, it's a practical book, then, rather than an academic, theoretical one?

It's both. Our intention here is to blur the boundaries between research, theory and practice so closely that you can't see the join. We want teachers in HE to be able to practise their principles. Teaching is a professional endeavour, and to do it effectively we need to approach it creatively, reflectively and collegially, with practices that are rooted in theory, research and professional values.

This means that what it's *not* is a simply a 'pocket guide of hints and tips' – we've included a strong theoretical and research base for the teaching approaches described and we write from a critical perspective. But, on the other hand, this isn't a thesis – where we've used references and citations they are illustrative and illuminative rather than exhaustive. We also draw on our combined wisdom and experience from many years of working in educational contexts, and on some of the excellent practices we've observed in our roles as teacher educators. You'll also find that we've used a range of genres in our writing – these vary from one chapter to another. Our intention was to 'disturb' some of the more traditional conventions of academic texts.

Is it for teachers from particular subject disciplines?

We've designed the book for any teacher of any subject. There are examples from a very broad range of disciplines and much of the theory is applicable across subject areas. However, we have restricted ourselves in the main to teaching that occurs in seminar rooms, computer labs, lecture theatres and online. We don't, in this volume, include field trips, work-based learning or specialist environments, although some of the content would be applicable in such settings.

Is the book largely for those who are new to teaching in HE?

We think that there's something in the book for everyone, novice and expert alike, even those who've been teaching in the sector for years. There's always room to share ideas, since, as Professor Diana Laurillard says:

> *Teaching is not rocket science. It's much, much harder than that. Rocket science is about moving atoms from a to b; teaching is about moving minds.*
>
> (2012: 5)

For early career practitioners in HE, we hope this might be the first book on teaching they pick up and that it gives them some ideas to try out in practice and some directions for future reading, but we've deliberately avoided a traditional approach to teaching and learning (planning, methods, assessment, learning theory, inclusion, etc.) in order to examine practice afresh. So we're confident that 'old hands' in higher education teaching will find something new, too.

Why A–Z? Must the reader start at A and finish at Z?

The chapters can be read in any order. It's the sort of book you can dip in and out of – great for busy professionals. We signpost other chapters within chapters, so you may find that one chapter leads to another (or to several others).

Why did we use the alphabet? Well, we came together to write because, having worked together for many years, we've found that we share a particular philosophy of teaching and have common values. We see education as a holistic practice rather than a series of linear processes. Just like the people it involves, it can't be divided into separate components – even the idea of teaching, learning and assessment is an artificial set of headings. However, a book with no chapters is hard to digest and we hit upon the alphabet as a playful way to present the material.

And why 'creative'?

The word 'creative' is there because we feel passionately that teaching is a vibrant, dynamic and unpredictable process that draws on all your faculties. As a teacher, you're committed to enabling your students to learn, but that might mean coming at the subject in a whole new way, trying out a number of approaches, listening to what the learners have to say or simply pausing and thinking 'how can we do this differently?' Dunn (2017) describes this as a sort of alchemy, *a power or process that changes or transforms something in a mysterious or impressive way*. We're not just trying to move minds, but hearts too, and not just the students', but our own.

The sandwich-in-a-can was a creative invention, but that doesn't mean it was any good, does it?

Excellent point! Kara (2015) points out that creativity means different things in different cultures, ranging from how people can help society to the solving of individual problems. In the book we suggest that all creative teaching practices are assessed for authenticity, integrity and effectiveness.

Can you tell me more about your areas of expertise?

You can read more about us in the author biographies, but, in brief, we've both been teacher educators for a number of years, working mostly with practitioners in the further education and higher education sectors. Before that, we each worked in a range of contexts, including primary, secondary, FE, HE, secure unit, and adult and community settings. We've also taught on undergraduate and postgraduate education programmes. In our respective roles, between us we've observed and discussed hundreds of teaching and learning sessions across the full range of subject disciplines, and at different times we've each researched a variety of aspects of the education process.

The book is a celebration of our collective knowledge, experience and scholarship, drawing particularly on our work with the HE teachers who have given us the privilege of observing them teach and reflecting with them afterwards, thus helping to develop their and our practice.

Why do you keep on saying 'teachers'? Don't you mean 'lecturers'?

There are certain academic conventions that we try to disrupt in the book. One example is our avoidance of the word 'lecturer', as this has connotations of a very dry, traditional, didactic form of teaching. Other examples include the adoption of 'large group and small group teaching' instead of 'lectures and seminars' or 'facilitation' instead of 'delivery'. The reason we want to disrupt these ideas is because we believe that the associations that we make with such expressions can block creativity. De Bono (1977 in Mason, 2002: 36) talks of avoiding technical terms such as these in case they eclipse possible alternatives.

Are you against the use of lectures?

It depends what you do with them! To find out more, we suggest you read our chapters P is for Presentations, F is for Flexible and V is for Visuals.

Also, I notice you use the word 'teaching' on its own. Oughtn't you to be saying 'learning-teaching-and-assessment'?

We use 'teaching' as a concept in its own right, rather than marrying it with learning and assessment, thereby upending what has been the cultural norm in the sector for the last few years. As far as we're concerned, if the students aren't learning, then you're not teaching. And if you're not assessing them, you don't know whether they're learning. 'Learning' and 'assessment' are part and parcel of teaching in any case, so why list them as add-ons?

Where's the chapter on technology-enhanced learning?

There are a number of cross-cutting themes that weave in and out of the chapters. Technology-enhanced learning is one such example.

What other themes are there?

N is for No One Excluded looks at some of the discourses around attainment gaps and 'disadvantaged' students, but in fact the principles of inclusion and diversity form the cornerstone of every chapter.

Sociocultural theories of learning, where students play an active role in their learning, are at the heart of our work and our writing. We teach in the belief that learning happens through social interaction (Vygotsky, 1978) and that knowledge is constructed through the forming of communities of practice. Communities of practice are *groups of people who share a concern or a passion about a topic, and who deepen their knowledge and expertise in this area by interacting on an ongoing basis* (Wenger *et al.*, 2002: 4). Three key characteristics of members of these communities are that they are all committed to their shared interest, that they form a supportive and developmental community, and that they are practitioners.

Another theme is that of curriculum as praxis – that is, *reflection and action upon the world in order to transform it* (Freire, 1970: 6). We aim to model transformative learning (*a process of changing our taken-for-granted assumptions to make them more inclusive and truthful* (Mezirow, 2000 in Butterwick and Lipson Lawrence, 2009: 35).

Are the characters in the book and the case studies 'real'?

We've drawn on our experiences of working in several different contexts and institutions. We've observed or been part of all the good practice we describe and this is used with the kind permission of our colleagues, although some names have been changed. The examples of poor practice are creations of our imagination. There are also a few fictional characters in the book. We hope you enjoy meeting them.

Will reading this book make the reader an excellent teacher?

All of us have different ideas about what 'excellent' teaching might look like. In our view, 'excellence' is another one of those conceptual 'packages' that is so loaded with particular assumptions and values that there is a danger of it preventing meaningful discussion about what goes on in actual teaching and learning practices (see, for example, Burke *et al.*, 2015). In a way, this book sets out to redress that balance. We certainly hope that engaging with the ideas in the book will make you a more enquiring, reflective, creative and 'inclusive' teacher and that this will benefit each of your students.

So it's about all the things teachers must do to improve their teaching?

No – it's definitely not an instruction manual. We want readers to question everything we say. We want the book to open a dialogue with teachers. We can't tell you how to be creative – it doesn't work like that, and anyway, we don't know your learning environment like you do.

But we do want you to reflect on the chapters you read, and to try out some ideas – however, you need to do this with an open, critical and enquiring mind. We were originally going to write a 'quality checklist' for experimenting with new approaches in teaching, but then we decided that 'quality' was yet another of those conceptual packages that tends to blot out all meaningful alternatives, so we decided to talk instead about 'authentic teaching' that is 'rooted in the principles of good practice'. The metaphor of the root is a very powerful one:

> *Rootedness is a primary, organizing trope that accommodates the need to feel connected to something outside the self.*
>
> (Wampole, 2016: 2)

For a teacher considering their own professional practice, rootedness means being part of a community of practitioners as described above. This community can be formed of immediate colleagues and more distant contacts, as well as authors whose literature or research has informed the field of practice. If you're planning to try out a new approach or activity in your teaching, we suggest that you use the principles below to assess the extent to which your approach is rooted in principles of good practice within this professional community. This means that teaching and learning approaches are:

1. designed to support students in achieving the aims and outcomes of the session/module/course;
2. audited so that no student's physical or mental wellbeing will be put at risk;
3. screened for any unreasonable assumptions about students;
4. student-centred and interactive, with opportunities for collaborative learning;
5. accessible to all, with support and challenges built in;
6. created with critical thinking and reflective practice at the heart of the learning;
7. planned so that opportunities to evidence learning are threaded throughout so that teaching can be adjusted accordingly;
8. built upon an evidence-base for activities of this sort in your subject discipline, with firm theoretical underpinnings;

9. clearly aligned to student learning experiences as a whole – for example, prior and later learning, or affective responses; and
10. related to the rest of the world – for example, employment or the global context, including reflecting and celebrating the diversity of the environment.

Is it just about universities or will it have relevance for other HE providers too? What about internationally?

We use the word 'university' frequently in the book, but we intend this to encompass all providers of higher education. Feedback from readers suggests that people from other areas of education and related disciplines are finding the content helpful, too. Although the book is written from a UK perspective, we feel that the chapters are highly relevant to the international context.

There's so much packed into each chapter, won't teachers start to feel a bit overwhelmed – after all, they've got exam scripts to mark and funding bids to put in and papers to review?

We know how you feel! That's why we've tried to make the book as accessible as possible, for example by writing short chapters. We suggest that you use the book to make small changes over time. We'd be the last people to want to overload teachers with the idea that they need to change the world by tomorrow. And it's a non-linear, continuous process. We're still learning and changing too.

Another point is that for the most part we've written very much from the perspective of an individual teacher rather than discussing whole organisation strategies or institutional policies (except where directly relevant). We recognise that there's only so much you can do as an individual – hence the reason we keep mentioning communities of practice.

Was there anything you wanted to include in the book but didn't?

Of course. As reflective practitioners, we realise that we have things left out that we would have loved to explore, but we had a word limit and made some hard choices. They will have to wait until we collaborate again.

is for
ACTION

HOW TO MAKE LEARNING MORE ACTIVE

CHAPTER SUMMARY

Why promote 'active' learning, and what does it mean?

In our call to action, this chapter seeks to place active learning at the heart of our practice. We look at why this really works to enhance learning and what it can look like in different contexts. Addressing some common concerns about active learning, we unpick these to reveal the full extent of the teacher's role in this work. Finally, we offer some 'dos and don'ts' when facilitating activities for learning.

You can't cross the sea merely by standing and staring at the water.

(Rabrindranath Tagore, in Sen, 1968)

TASK 1

Think of an occasion where you learnt something effectively – not necessarily in an academic context.

What did you learn and how did you learn it? What was helpful about this way of learning? What barriers were there?

REFLECTIONS

Maybe you felt you learned well because you were so motivated, maybe because the teacher was passionate about her subject or maybe because it touched your experience. We look at all these aspects of learning in other chapters. Did you respond to the above by describing learning by 'doing' – like tying shoelaces or cooking a particular dish? That's what we're looking at in A is for Action. It can sometimes be tricky to say exactly how such learning took place and what role was played by the 'teacher' if there was even one involved. Later in the chapter, we suggest ways to facilitate such active learning.

Why a chapter on active learning?

For us, to learn is to construct, to reconstruct, to observe with a view to changing.

(Freire, 1998)

This book is predicated on the idea that learners should be involved in their learning. It is tied not only to the theory that *conscious learning emerges from activity* (Jonassen and Rohrer-Murphy, 1999: 61), but also to the political notion that learning is about change and empowerment that can only come about when we are all actively involved in the process.

It's important to note that direct learner–learner or teacher–learner interaction is not the only way in which learning can be active. Even listening to a lecture, you can still be actively constructing and reconstructing knowledge (we look at this in P is for Presentations). Here, however, we focus on using activity as a tool for learning.

TASK 2

Read the following story, then answer the two questions posed.

In an undergraduate session on Healthcare Policy, Kiran presents some slides that critically analyse government strategy on alcohol consumption in the UK. She assumes that the students are familiar with the arguments in this area, so she talks through the slides quite fast. Afterwards, she asks for questions. There is a long and embarrassing silence. Kiran doesn't know if this is because the students have understood everything so well that they feel no need to ask questions (though she doubts this, from the expressions on their faces), or if it is because they have understood so little that they don't even know where to begin in terms of asking questions.

1. What might be the issue here?
2. How could Kiran actively engage the students, to assess their understanding of the topic?

REFLECTIONS

Active learning and formative assessment are closely intertwined. Kiran could have asked her students to spend one minute (or longer) working in pairs sharing what they already know about alcohol consumption in the UK and listing any questions they have. She could also have set them an open-book, collaborative quiz on the subject – in fact, regular use of this approach has been shown to increase conceptual learning and raise student performance (Rezaei, 2015). See C is for Communicating for more on quizzes.

The teacher's role here may be to circulate, or to stand back and observe, or even to allow the students a few moments of space and privacy to get on with the task (or a combination of these). The time could be used to see who has material which will take the topic further in the plenary or to build the confidence of the quiet student and encourage them to contribute later in the whole group. There is an excellent opportunity to differentiate between students here by discussing more complex

(Continued)

(Continued)

ideas with some pairings and revisiting more basic building blocks with others as they work in their pairs. In terms of assessment, this task offers a chance to see how close the students are to addressing the session learning outcomes – or indeed, in some cases, whether they are ready to move beyond these.

Kiran would also need to decide whether the whole group would benefit from a plenary and what this would be for – this could be different each time. Maybe every pair came up with similar questions and there is a need to recap some material; maybe it's to look at new and unexpected ideas generated. It could be simply to get learners more confident at hearing their own voices in the room. One of the advantages – and challenges – of active learning is that it is unpredictable. As the teacher, you must act responsively, constantly adjusting your session to your learners while at the same time supporting them to progress towards the intended learning outcomes. Such an approach is an exemplification of inclusive, or enabling, practice – much more so than a 'one-size-fits-all' approach of delivering from a predetermined script. It is where the *interests, needs and curiosity of the student interact with the knowledge, resources and facilitative attitudes of the teacher* (Rogers et al., 2014: 61).

In our experiences of observing teaching in learning in HE, a number of teachers appear to be reluctant to use active learning approaches. In the next section, we examine some of the reasons why.

Common concerns about active learning

The problem is, there's simply no room in this approach for sharing the knowledge and experience of the teacher.

You need to be sure in your planning that any activities in the session will provide time both for the learners to construct knowledge for themselves and for you to build on this by filling the gaps or extending knowledge using your own subject expertise. You may need to synthesise new material offered by your learners on the spot rather than just deliver material you have prepared and answer questions to which you know the answers (Cowan, 2006).

Also, it's not really teaching, is it? I mean, the teacher's role in activities is passive, and you don't need preparation.

The teacher's role includes assessing learning, monitoring engagement and progress, deciding when and how to intervene or prompt, asking questions to develop or consolidate understanding and much more.

Active learning also requires that you ensure that both you and the learners are interacting in an inclusive and enabling way. This means, among other things, being alert to oppressive behaviour, being prepared to intervene and challenge this, finding ways to engage reluctant learners and being watchful for any prior assumptions that you are making about the learners.

Yes, but at the end of the day active learning is basically a waste of precious time which could be spent 'covering material'. Right?

It is indeed true that you can fit lots of slides and presentation into an hour and maybe in this time you can only do one activity, but let's go back to the underpinning philosophy of active learning and look at formative assessment, which shifts the focus from teaching to learning.

Learning can be defined as being a change that has taken place in your learners. What can they do, what do they know, what have they created that is different from when they joined you for that session? The key question then becomes not what *you* can cover but what the *students* have learnt. And you may just find that the more you 'cover', the less they 'learn'. Besides which, part of the content can be flipped into directed study outside the session (see F is for Flexible).

What if students refuse to cooperate with activities?

Students who have not been used to being active participants in their own learning may find it hard at first to see the value of this approach. Normalise activity. You can establish from the beginning an ethos where learning is seen as a joint venture. That's what we are trying to model through the tasks that occur throughout this book. Make sure that students do not get used to sitting in the same place, working with the same people, experiencing the same passive format in every session. Add a question to your evaluations that asks 'what was your contribution to the learning?' rather than focusing entirely on teacher performance. Talk to the students about the benefits of active learning (see M is for Metalearning), including graduate attributes and the employability agenda (O is for Occupations). However, be aware of students with identified needs and of any sensitivities within a group (see Q is for Quiet).

I feel like I might lose control of the group if I'm not standing at the front, lecturing.

If students are carrying out activities, then you may find that they go off-task, that they complete tasks more quickly or more slowly than planned, that something goes wrong or that they simply lose interest.

However, if you lecture from the front, your students may disengage, fail to keep up or become bored without you even being aware of it. In one sense, you have less control teaching from the front, because if you're not giving them opportunities to evidence their learning, you can't adjust your teaching appropriately. You can also use active learning for part of a session rather than the whole session, gradually increasing the amount of time devoted to interactivity.

This is all very well in small groups, but what about large group teaching?

Some research suggests that active learning is 'easier' to do with smaller cohorts of students (e.g. Alexander, 2004 in Blatchford *et al.*, 2016: 278). However, this does not mean that you can't build some active learning strategies into a large group teaching situation – e.g. in a lecture theatre. Examples that we've observed which can apply to small or large groups include the following.

- A Computer Science teacher introducing her students to flow charts and asking them each to design such a chart mapping out their respective journeys into university that morning. She checks and feeds back on random examples before showing them one she did earlier.
- An Early Years teacher educator getting his students to play with modelling dough, to experience its benefits for young children. In a large group this could be done by passing a tub along each row.
- A Law teacher asking students to answer questions and collating their responses using a student response system ('voting' technology). Such approaches have been found to increase student engagement and enjoyment in large group settings (Heaslip *et al.*, 2014).
- A Psychology teacher encouraging students to take part in mini-psychology experiments on themselves during a lecture.

Note that in these examples there is an emphasis on self-assessment by the students, since it is not always practical for the teacher to assess everyone. This means creating opportunities for students to check their progress.

Dos and don'ts when facilitating learning activities

Do have a strategy to ensure that your activity instructions are understood. Make them available in another format (on screen, board or paper). Ask students to explain the instructions back to you and invite questions. Observe students to see if they are following the instructions as intended (Fedesco, 2014).

Don't assume that students will be happy to carry out an activity without a clear rationale for doing so. Make links to assessments, employability, other parts of the module/course and research evidence that promotes the use and benefits of active learning. This links with the principles of 'andragogy' (Knowles, 1980), where adult learners need to know why they are learning something.

Do prepare some 'differentiation' strategies in advance and make sure that the activity aligns with the outcomes for the session. This could mean making support material available to 'scaffold' the learning for those who might struggle (Vygotsky and Cole, 1978), a further task to challenge those who've sailed easily through the first part, or encouraging groups to compare results and discuss any differences.

Don't get caught up with one group of students and ignore the rest. Scan the room regularly to check that everyone is on task. Reassure students you'll come back to them shortly and move on to another group.

Do try to ensure that the students know more after a plenary than they did before. Avoid simply asking each group to repeat their task in front of the others. Time the feedback – for example, three minutes per group to identify key points. Ask and encourage questions to deepen learning. You could give groups different tasks so that they have a reason to present to each other. In this way, active learning opportunities are planned not only to encourage *the activation of prior knowledge in the small-group setting* but also to provide *opportunities for elaboration on that knowledge* (Schmidt *et al.*, 2011: 792).

Don't simply disregard the results of an activity with students. Refer to their work later in the session/module. Encourage them to 'capture' their responses – for example, via online message boards, taking photos or typing up results. Create a shared group resource using online presentation slides. Value the results of activities as an authentic piece of work that all have contributed to and all can benefit from, and students will do the same (as evidenced in Cavanagh, 2011).

Do ensure that students don't leave the session thinking, 'Well, that was fun, but did we actually learn anything?'. A well-planned activity should support progress in learning. Leave enough time to summarise the key outcomes and link them to the intended aims of the session, and for students to reflect on what they've learned from the activity.

Conclusion

A final word about A is for Action: as well as being a reference to active learning, it evokes thoughts about a call to action. In a sense, this book is just that – a call to act, to create ways of teaching that are emancipatory and empowering for student and teacher alike.

B is for
BLUE SKIES

HOW WOULD YOU *REALLY* LIKE TO TEACH YOUR SUBJECT?

CHAPTER SUMMARY

This chapter is based on the following principles: that as a teacher in HE it's important not to lose sight of your ideals in relation to learning and teaching (here referred to as your Blue Skies curriculum); that unpacking these ideals can reveal much about your own principles and values; that it's essential to authenticate such principles and approaches against available evidence and the views of others within the community of practice of HE, and that, however constrained your current practice, there is usually a tiny gap to be found where your Blue Skies curriculum can shine through.

... and then, in dreaming

The clouds methought would open and show riches

Ready to drop upon me; that, when I waked

I cried to dream again.

(Caliban in Shakespeare's *The Tempest*, Act III, Scene ii)

(Shakespeare, Wells and Taylor, 1997: 347)

Have you ever dreamt of how you might teach if you had no constraints whatsoever on your working practice? A no-limits budget, and a curriculum where you get to choose when, where and how teaching occurs? What might it look like?

As teachers in the system of higher education, by routinely and unthinkingly performing our everyday practices we can find ourselves subconsciously colluding with our departmental, institutional and sector cultures whether we agree with them or not (Mason, 2002). How can we give ourselves enough distance from our working contexts to be able to question the assumptions that underpin the ways in which we teach and support learning in our students? How far, do you think, your teaching practice might have deviated from what you feel is an authentic approach to your subject?

One way to do this, we suggest, is to start with a vision, where imagination and creativity can fly free, and the clouds draw back to reveal a rich store of possibilities. It's this very envisioning that can begin to awaken us from the deadening effect of everyday, institutional constraints.

The following task is designed to support you to think 'outside the box' about teaching and learning in your subject area, beyond the daily routines and accepted practices within your professional context, and beyond merely preserving the status quo within your specialist field and wider society.

TASK 1

Your Blue Skies curriculum

Think of your subject specialism. Imagine that you could teach it any way you wanted, with no limits on resources and no one saying, 'No, that contravenes the assessment regulations and is impossible to administer'.

(Continued)

(Continued)

- What would the overall aims and content of your imagined curriculum look like? (Would there even be any overall aims or predetermined content?)
- What teaching and learning strategies would be used?
- How would learning and progress be assessed (if at all)?
- Where and when might learning take place?

Bear in mind that you are free even to reject the premises of our guiding questions. For example, perhaps in your Blue Skies curriculum the distinction between teacher and learner or the boundary between one subject discipline and another is blurred.

It is also important to note that your students are still your students in this exercise. They are who they are. If your Blue Skies curriculum can only exist by altering your students to fit into it, then this needs some careful reflection. We believe that teaching is not about the learners having to conform to the teacher's expectations, but about the teacher placing the learners at the centre of their practice to support them to progress towards their goals and beyond. This might mean blue-sky changes that would usually be beyond your control: a 'bridging year' prior to your course; non-traditional settings; smaller group sizes, and so on. It's your dream curriculum – you can create it however you want. The sky's the limit.

Take a moment and allow yourself to dream.

Make some notes on your Blue Skies curriculum. If you like, you can draw a fluffy cloud to hold your thoughts and ideas, and use diagrams, images, keywords, and so on.

REFLECTIONS

'Blue sky thinking' can be thought of as *creative ideas free from practical constraints* (Davidson, 2016). No idea generated through Blue Sky thinking can be rejected as *too silly* (BBC, 2014). The term is thought to originate from business management, but has been applied to other areas, including research.

Often, when we use the Blue Skies curriculum activity with HE teachers, the energy levels in the room lift and it's as if the sun has come out and the clouds have drifted away. What's left is a sky full of dreams, a rainbow of possibilities bursting with creativity, imagination and innovation.

What we find is that generally there is a move *away* from didactic, knowledge-based models, and *towards* process-based, experiential and reflective models. For example, the Blue Skies curricula of the historians on our courses regularly feature time machines, the sports physios have cutting-edge technology for the students to play with and the business management specialists have exciting, unlimited workplace learning opportunities, placements and field trips. The transformation is thus towards students learning by 'doing', rather than being the passive recipients of uncontestable, transmitted knowledge. Notably, the university also plays an important role in these models, perhaps as a space for developing critical and theoretical perspectives with students. This links to constructivist notions of learning, as discussed in the introduction to this book (and also in P is for Presentation), and the suggestion that knowledge is fluid and centred in communities of practice, as described in K is for Knowledge.

Others may be more conservative in their thinking, the rituals and traditions of centuries of higher education proving too hard to breach, and yet even here we sense a shift towards a more dynamic, interactive way of teaching and learning.

What does *your* Blue Skies curriculum look like? How different or similar is it to what already happens in current teaching and learning practices in your subject area?

So what's the point?

Why should it matter what your Blue Skies curriculum looks like? The answer is that if you don't know what your ideals are, how can you position yourself as an educator and how can you innovate change? How can you teach with passion and enjoy what you are doing because you believe in it? The alternative is to risk becoming absorbed into the standard practices and policies of teaching and learning in HE in your subject discipline to the extent that you forget to believe that it could ever be any different.

Various social theorists have attempted to analyse this phenomenon – for example, Pierre Bourdieu, whose ideas help us to *draw out those institutional processes and structural relations that lurk behind every action made within the educational field* (Webb *et al.*, 2002: 141). Of course, it could be argued that even one's Blue Skies curriculum is subject to unseen forces and constraints of which we ourselves are unaware. And yet, the very process of articulating how things *might be* could be the beginning of an awareness of the influence of such forces. Indeed,

> *There are moments in life where the question of knowing whether one might think otherwise than one thinks and perceive otherwise than one sees is indispensable if one is to continue to observe or reflect.*
>
> (Foucault, 1998: 15)

This is not to reject or undermine all current academic practices in HE – of course, there are highly reflective and effective innovations going on in all sorts of areas. But the exercise of imagining how education in your subject would look if you had the power to change it at a strategic level is not only enabling but provides a useful window into your own assumptions and principles about how and why students learn, and what you believe the purpose of studying in your subject area is. This reflexivity can then provide an opportunity for critical dialogue both within yourself and with others in your community of practice, and thus a starting point for making changes to practice, even tiny ones.

An example of Blue Skies curricula

Figure B1 shows us what Caitlin, a Design Crafts (jewellery) teacher in HE, had to say about how she would teach if she could. If this is not your own specialism, please stay with this example. It may have relevance, and there are others to follow.

Figure B1   Example of a Blue Skies curriculum

Caitlin's approach, values and principles

These are closely tied to Caitlin's subject specialism. Her approach is organic and student-centred, but not entirely self-directed; support exists in the form of help with technical skills and input on the theme to be explored, along with its historical and cultural context. There is an emphasis on space and environment – physical, temporal and personal (in fact, 'haystack' or 'straw bale' classrooms do exist in various parts of the world, some in truly beautiful settings, such as the Haystack Mountain School of Crafts in Maine).

Project-based learning in Arts education encourages creativity and divergent thinking (Clews, 2010). Caitlin's self-appointed role as a facilitator positions her in the humanist paradigm, where learning is about personal involvement, transformation and, essentially, meaning (Rogers and Freiburg, 1994). Caitlin also attends to the 'affective' domain (Krathwol *et al.*, 1964), with emotion and aesthetics playing integral roles in the learning process. And her chosen learning environment offers multisensory stimulation. We inhabit a world where our senses are constantly stimulated, which suggests that the learning process is at its most optimal when introducing multisensory interactions (see V is for Visuals for more on this). This doesn't have to mean bombarding your students with information in different media, but paying attention to the whole environment and its sensory stimuli. This then supports the students to 'carefully observe and select potential starting points from the myriad of possibilities around them' (Caitlin's own words).

Regarding the content of Caitlin's curriculum, the UK Quality Assurance Agency benchmark statement for Art and Design talks of *historical, theoretical, socio-political, economic and environmental dimensions* (QAA, 2016: 10). Situating the subject in time, space and culture enables students to question their own assumptions and reflect critically. This resonates with the principles of transformative learning such as Mezirow and Taylor (2009).

Finally, by offering creative and technical support as and when needed, Caitlin is providing some 'scaffolding' for the students to enable them to reach their potential – that is, to move through their *zones of proximal development* (Vygotsky in Connery *et al.*, 2010).

How can Caitlin integrate aspects of her forest-based, haystack curriculum into her everyday practice?

In fact, she already is, to some considerable extent, particularly in her role as a facilitator of learning. Much of Caitlin's Blue Skies curriculum is about allowing students time and space to achieve their potential, so further steps might be taken to enable access to workshop space out of class time, while technical support could be 'on demand' via the use of videos and animations as well as in-class support. The students already take part in field trips, which could include rural as well as urban settings. Students could share artefacts from their own cultural contexts for others to see or touch, including examples of music or sounds, thus providing stimuli for new concepts and ideas, and moving towards an even more student 'owned' and multisensory curriculum. Finally, Caitlin's personal principles of attending to emotion and creating a metaphorical space for self-direction also deserve further consideration within her current setting.

Other examples

As mentioned, some of this will already be happening, while other suggestions need further development. This is where you can innovate in collaboration with your students, and obtain their feedback to inform future planning.

In fact, the Blue Skies curricula that have been produced by our students vary widely in their nature. Bereket, who teaches accountancy, would like to encourage deeper learning (Entwistle, 2001) but, even in clear blue skies, feels constrained by the expectations of his students and by the requirements of his professional awarding body. James, a maths teacher, wants to throw out the prescribed curriculum and see what the students come up with themselves – an approach underpinned by constructivist theories of learning. Many colleagues express a desire for more work-based learning in authentic contexts, not just in vocational/professional subject areas, but also in disciplines such as the humanities, where students can conduct their own research, a type of learning that is situated in culture, context and 'doing' (Lave and Wenger, 1991).

How might such ideals gain purchase in the 'real' world of resource constraints, assessment demands and cultural expectations? If you look, there is usually some way to let some light and air in, no matter how small. Developments such as the Student Voice (Kidd and Czerniawski, 2011), or Students as Producers (Neary *et al.*, 2014) are placing control of the curriculum at least partly back in the hands of the students and supporting authentic, undergraduate-centred research, while the phenomenon of the flipped classroom means that more opportunities for deep learning can be planned into taught sessions (see F is for Flexible for more on this).

TASK 2

Making your dreams come true

Return to your own Blue Skies curriculum from Task 1 and consider the questions below.

---

1. Look back at what your Blue Skies curriculum says about you as a teacher, including your own professional values and views of teaching and learning. To what extent are these views reflected in the wider professional community – for example, in pedagogical theory or research, within your subject discipline or in relation to sector standards for HE teaching?
2. How can you enable some small aspect of your learning and teaching ideals to find its way into your current practice?
3. How will you evaluate and assure the integrity of your intervention? Our advice here is to read the comments on being rooted in good practice section in the Introduction to this book.

We recommend that you discuss your thoughts with colleagues.

Help needed?

If you've found the tasks in this chapter challenging – for example, it's possible that someone might struggle to conceive of what 'thinking out of the box' might look like in relation to their own practice or context – we suggest that you read some of the other chapters in this book and revisit this one later. What we hope is that the content of each chapter will support the reader to further develop their vision of a rich, creative, living curriculum, one that not only challenges those norms and rituals that are unconducive to learning, but creates innovative ways of supporting students to engage and learn.

is for
COMMUNICATIONS

HOW TO CONNECT WITH YOUR STUDENTS

CHAPTER SUMMARY

Communication is at the root of all we do as teachers and is also a skill that we seek to develop in our students. Without this, we can't build the community of practice we seek in order to foster learning. Developing students' subject knowledge alone is insufficient. Students need to be able to communicate about their subject effectively in a wide a range of contexts. The poignant poem, *On Studying English*, captures the joy of communication, as it talks of *a tongue lying frozen* released to *grasp the words and dance* (Maley and Mukundan, 2007: 66). In this chapter we will look at creative ways in which we can dance with our students – and support them to dance with each other.

TASK 1

Think of a session you have taught and list the ways in which you communicated with your students.

REFLECTIONS

It's likely that you have spoken with the students and used some form of text, perhaps with images, perhaps via a technological medium. However, we also communicate through our social practices as we present or create a learning community and expect our students to learn to become members. If we talk about students as passive consumers, there's a danger they will converse with us as suppliers of goods. Similarly, if we position ourselves purely as experts and assessors, we are likely to stem any communication from them which challenges what we say and takes agency of learning. Foucault looks in more detail at the way in which discourses of power operate through language (Piro, 2008: 39).

Other things also influence the communication received by students: your body language, the types of words and images you use, the 'register' in which you are speaking, the way you dress or whether you are using specialist discourse can all make a difference, as can dialects, accents, and the way in which you use the space available to you. For example, clear messages are sent: if you always let the same few people answer your questions; if all your case study examples are of a particular gender, sexuality, social class, disability status, age or ethnicity, or if you 'other' certain groups of people in your narratives (see N is for No One Excluded for more on this).

Is what's received the same as what's delivered?

In our comments above, we referred to our social practice as a form of communication.

> *The nature of pedagogical practice in higher education and its dependence on the identities, experience and interactions of multiple players means that the interrelation between student–staff collaboration and individual participants' development as learners will be complex.*
>
> (Dickerson *et al.*, 2016: 262)

In other parts of the book we look at what students bring to the classroom – and their prior experiences will both colour the way they receive information and add new knowledge to the classroom. There will be barriers formed to communication because of the differences between the backgrounds of those studying there and it will always be important to establish from the beginning that communication is two-way, partly so that you know what has been received.

How can we improve our communication?

Some suggestions are made to support student contributions to sessions in Q is for Quiet. Many of these focus on reducing the volume of 'teacher talk'. Here we present some further strategies at departmental and individual level for improving student–teacher communication.

Collaboration of staff and students in research or course design

One way to create a more egalitarian community that enhances communication is to initiate projects that are done in collaboration with students who are viewed as 'co-producers'. Dickerson *et al.* report (2006) on some such projects: one student was concerned to learn that there would be staff in the team, but after the project said, 'that changed – you feel valued – anything you say is noted and taken seriously'.

The use of questions

In language teaching, the process of *eliciting* involves fostering *students' habit of asking questions* (Guo, 1994). The advantages of using elicitation as a teaching approach across a range of subject disciplines are many, one being the way that questions create the opportunity to communicate. Steve Darn (2010), in a blog post on the British Council website, points out that students arrive on courses with existing knowledge which needs to be *activated* in order for new knowledge to be assimilated or accommodated (Piaget, 1952); information is more memorable if one discovers it for oneself, and elicitation is an effective means of diagnosing learners' starting points, leading to more flexible and responsive teaching. Guo contrasts elicitation with *cramming*, comparing the former to lighting a candle, as opposed to the latter, which is *filling a jug* (1994).

Table C1 gives some examples of how information-heavy slides might be turned into questions designed to elicit student knowledge.

Table C1   Eliciting student knowledge

Transmission approach	Questioning and communicative approach
Here's what we covered last week	What did we learn in last week's session? Raise your hand if you can tell me even one thing you can remember.
The definition of health, according to the *BMJ*, is ... And according to the WHO is ...	How would you define 'health'? Take a couple of minutes, then post your responses... We'll discuss them and then compare them with what the *British Medical Journal* and the World Health Organisation have to say.
The principles of Boolean algebra are ...	What do you know about Boolean algebra? Call out some key words 'And' – great! 'Not' – wonderful! Any more? 'Gate'? Let me write these on the board. Anyone not met these terms before? What do these words mean? Can you explain a bit more? What is Boolean algebra used for?

Quizzes are another way of eliciting knowledge from students. Table C2 shows some of the different ways in which quizzes can be designed, depending on the desired learning outcomes.

Questioning can be about far more than recall, however. Phillipson and Wegerif (2016) categorise questions that can be used in a Socratic-style dialogue in order to promote critical thinking, paraphrased here as:

- *clarification questions* ('Can you say that again but in a different way?', 'Can you give an example?');
- *justification questions* ('Why?', 'What evidence do you have?', 'How did you reach that conclusion?');
- *experimental questions* ('Can you find a counter-example?', 'What happens if we double x?', 'How could we find out?');
- *metalevel questions* ('Why did you start from here?', 'What are you assuming when you say ... ', 'How did you approach that problem?').

As you use questions, you model an enquiry-based approach to learning, which, hopefully, your students will adopt too.

Online communication

Traditional learning spaces often privilege the use of one type of language, an academic form of English which is not always necessary to create and explore ideas in every (or any?) subject area, and which can act as a barrier to creative learning and teaching. Ryan and Viete (2009: 305) describe the use of *thirdspace learning environments* such as online discussions that *require fundamental shifts in the ways that teaching and learning are mediated, including through dialogic interactions that are shared, respectful, and multivoiced.*

Table C2 100 things to consider when creating a quiz

100 things to consider when creating a quiz

Medium	*Content*	*Purpose*
Paper-based, spoken Q+A, mini whiteboards, technology (for example, online quizzes, polling software/hardware, mobile phone apps)	Factual, open/closed questions, opinion, info gathering, MCQ, images, sounds, problem-solving scenarios, creative stimuli	Diagnostic/formative, summative, self-assessment, assessment as learning, wake-up call, fun, collaborative, peer-learning
How	*Responses*	*Assessing answers*
Open book, closed book, individual, paired, teams, pub quiz style, 'race to the finish', competitive, non-competitive, formal, informal, follow popular TV format, games, for example matching, ordering, treasure hunt	Hands up, buzzers, electronic – e.g. voting technology, other MCQ software, written, spoken, typed, texted, drawn, acted, targeted questions to individuals, conferring as a team, first to answer, take turns to answer	On the spot, afterwards, automated, panel, give out answers for self-assessment, peer assessment (mark each other's)
Feedback	*Support*	*Extensions*
After each question, after the whole thing, on a handout, electronically, individually	No scaffolding, some scaffolding – e.g. clues, phone a friend, 50/50, team conferring allowed, open book, level of difficulty of questions, type of questions, crib sheet	Bonus questions, some questions open book, some closed, some collaborative, some not, choice of follow-on tasks depending on results, questions that require critical thinking skills, asking the students to write their own questions
Safeguarding and accessibility	*Rewards*	*When*
Confidential responses, anonymous responses, avoid putting vulnerable individuals on the spot, emphasise a low score is informative (as opposed to evidence of failure), signpost students to follow up support, ensure materials are accessible and that they represent diversity	Prizes, no prizes, badging, certificates, medals, tokens, food (check for allergies, diet choices or restrictions, cultural norms – e.g. gelatine in sweets)	Start and/or end of session/module/ course, asynchronous or synchronous, flipped or in class

Online communication can take many different forms and, as with all communication, will need protocols setting up to ensure that it is inclusive. Discussions online can be linear, with one comment following another, or non-linear, where individuals post comments, images and so on, and others comment on selected posts. It's important for you as teacher to have an online presence in these discussions, and for you to refer to them in face-to-face sessions, not only to highlight their existence to those who have not communicated via the medium, but to integrate the content into the planned curriculum, giving the online contributions purpose and authenticity.

Much has been written about the differences between formal discussion spaces that are teacher-initiated, and informal ones initiated by students (see, for example, O'Connor *et al.*, 2016). Whether or not to moderate content is also an important question. One teacher we know moderated an online discussion forum which she had set up for a cohort of students, censoring what she felt was inappropriate language. The students responded by abandoning the forum, setting up their own one via an alternative platform and then inviting the staff team to join – as participants but not as administrators.

Assessment feedback

Much has been written about how to give feedback to students – slightly less about how to receive it. Weller (2016: 87) suggests that we capture the potential of feedback as a way of communicating which is two-way and engages students by

> *building on the development of active, discursive and formative approaches within the student-engaged classroom, developing a dialogue-based approach.*

Feedback can compound feelings of failure or resentment ...

> *This is the lowest grade I've ever had. No other tutor on this course has graded me so low.*
>
> *Why did she get a 2:1 when I got a third?*
>
> *I put so much effort into this, I nearly cried when I saw your feedback.*

These anecdotal examples of student responses to assessment feedback show how emotionally fraught the whole process can be. Two areas of research are key here.

First, Lipnevich and Smith, in a study of college students, found that *Overall, detailed, descriptive feedback was found to be most effective when given alone, unaccompanied by grades or praise* (2009: 319).

Second, work done in neuroscience suggests that our brains are hard-wired to look for negatives, perhaps as a survival technique (Hanson, 2009). The fixation by students on their grades is difficult to overcome without a whole-course redesign. The focus on negatives, however, is somewhat easier to address. Here are some possible strategies:

1. Phrase feedback as 'feedforward' (for example, 'You should have included more explanation' could be rephrased as 'Next time, make sure you include more …').
2. Model oneself as a student. Tracey, a colleague, showed one of her self-critical but high-achieving Level 6 students an example of her own academic work, scribbled all over by her doctoral supervisor. 'I wanted to show that receiving challenging feedback doesn't mean you're a failure – it's just part of the process,' she explained. A similar example could be a teacher sharing with their students feedback from a reviewer for a journal article they have drafted.
3. Rather than exemplars, give students an example of a draft, with feedback and the subsequent changes carried out. This makes the process of drafting, reviewing and revising more transparent.

Other suggestions to include the feedback process are as follows.

- It's useful to talk about how and when you will give feedback in your inductions and throughout courses so that everyone knows what to expect and when. You can also link this conversation to the development of critical thinking and reflection as these are skills needed to use it effectively.
- Explain the use of formative feedback as assessment for or as learning, and also that summative feedback can feed forward to subsequent modules.
- Do a 'feedback' newsletter following a batch of drafts that focuses on common issues (like referencing skills, for example – this could also include some signposting to further support).
- Use lots of ways to feed back – self and peer feedback, recorded or videoed comments, tutorials – work out the best way for your students and your workload within your assessment regulations. Biggs and Tang (2011: 65) talk of creating a *Theory Y climate* where errors are publicly debated in a spirit of support and enquiry.

Supporting students to communicate with each other

Modelling good communication with our students is a helpful start, but what other ways can we use to develop this key skill?

Protocols

In Maslow's theory of motivation, he mentions the idea that learners need to feel safe, to feel loved and to belong before they will want to learn properly (Maslow, 1970). One way to establish a safe place in a group is to encourage them to negotiate a way of working together. Some people refer to these as ground rules, but these can quickly be reduced to superficial statements such as 'no mobile phones on in sessions'. We are suggesting a deeper, more inclusive conversation that will be unique to a group and, while most of the resulting statements will include the requirement for confidentiality, they may also suggest more creative ideas based on the experience of one particular group's interaction. Examples may include the request that speakers use the first person, that there is 'real listening' or that those who dominate the conversation can be interrupted.

Giving space to practise communication

It's possible to give lots of opportunities for students to practise communication with each other using different media. For example, if they have done some group work to present to the whole class, ask them to share their findings creatively – e.g. as a poster, a role-play, a short video or a blog (we have even experienced students presenting to their peers in the form of a rap). Other examples might be:

- to provide a live video recording of a taught session for those who cannot be present, with a function for them to join in in real time;
- having students create their own podcasts, blogs and video blogs to share online, supported by a function to comment on each other's contributions (see, for example, Lazzari, 2009).

We have looked at a few ways in which we can support our communication with our students and some ways in which we can support the development of their communication skills. What we haven't had time to cover is communication with colleagues. With this in mind, we urge you to use this book as a starting point for discussions and, if you have the time, informal peer observations relating to your professional practice as a teacher in higher education. Reflecting on your teaching – with colleagues as well as individually – and supporting your students to reflect on their learning can help to connect students and teachers alike.

is for DESIGN

HOW TO PLAN LEARNING FOR ALL

CHAPTER SUMMARY

In this chapter, we first explore the meaning of 'design' in teaching and learning in HE. We critique the universal design for learning approach, we look at the concept of the learning environment, and finally we provide a checklist to consider when designing bespoke teaching within your context.

What do we mean by design?

Ever wanted to be an architect? Maybe you *are* an architect, having moved from 'industry' to become an academic. Well this chapter is for you – this is where you can look at the ways you might apply the skills of design to teaching. And if you've been longing to treat education more as a science, you'll also find something joyful here about design science to try out. And, even if you've never yearned to do either of the above, you still need to read this one. It's about more than planning. It's about realising that if we want learners to be active and teaching to be 'inclusive', we have to start designing our work to facilitate this. It's about using research in our practice so that we refine theory 'on the ground' by testing, redesigning, evaluating in the complexity of the real classroom. Maybe it's about developing principles – you can decide when you've read about the models below. However you choose to use the idea, it chimes with the *collaborative, experiential, inquiry-based, problem based approaches citing theories of constructionism, social constructivism and situated learning* (Laurillard in Beetham and Sharpe, 2013: xvi) celebrated throughout this book.

While engaged in learning, students need to be analytical, experiential and experimental. They may bring all kinds of knowledge to the table that disrupt your lovely plans – it's a messy business that depends very much on the practitioner to deal with the unpredictable. This chapter is about the active role you need to play to plan as much as possible for everyone in advance and the tools you can use when designing your teaching.

As we write, we can hear you saying 'and where does the time come for this?' We could not agree more. But it is part of the job and while we are in Blue Skies mode, we'll suggest it's worth looking for funding for small-scale research work to support you.

In this section, as an introduction to thinking about design, we'll look briefly at three concepts in this field: design science, learning design and, finally, universal design for learning.

Teaching as a Design Science

A design science uses and contributes to theoretical science, but it builds design principles rather than theories, and the heuristics of practice rather than explanations, although like both the sciences and the arts, it uses what has gone before as a platform or inspiration for what it creates. Teaching is more like a design science because it uses what is known about teaching to attain the goal of student learning, and uses the implementation of its designs to keep improving them.

(Laurillard, 2012: 1)

So Diana Laurillard begins her book entitled *Teaching as a Design Science*. She goes on to explain that, particularly with the advent of technology-enhanced learning, we need to start engaging with design so that education drives technology rather than the reverse. She makes a useful point about technology potentially stifling transformation and supporting 'traditional' teaching. We've seen the danger, for example, of power-point slides taking us backwards to the yawning days of 'chalk and talk' (of course, design is not dependent on the use of technology).

We need to create an iterative and collaborative process whereby we plan new educational environments with our learners and other stakeholders while negotiating the minefield of their different desires and intentions for higher education. A key feature is the involvement of learners as *the exploration of a greater equality of control over the design of learning could be a significant shift for pedagogy* (Laurillard in Beetham and Sharpe, 2013: xviii).

Learning design

This is a concept that some claim is inseparable from creativity: *Design can be, simultaneously, the application of 'systematic principles and methods' and 'a creative activity that cannot be fully reduced to standard steps'* (Winograd, 1996: xx, xxii in Masterman, 2013: 66).

Masterman gives some examples that show how design can have different starting points.

- One teacher treats design as a puzzle to be solved. The puzzle may consist of trying to create a 'logical fit' when teaching a seminar following someone else's lecture, using a third-party compiled reading list.
- Another begins their design with learner-negotiated activities.
- A third starts with a circle, with the topic in the middle (2013: 67) before drilling down to linear outcomes.

Universal Design for Learning (UDL)

UDL has its origins in architecture (hence our comment at the beginning of the chapter). Universal Design, to which it is linked, was conceived by Ron Mace at North Carolina State University to look at meeting the needs of disabled people at the design stage of buildings, communication networks, etc. As with many adaptations, these often proved useful for everybody. One example given by Hall *et al.* (2012: 5) is that of closed captioning on television originally *intended for people with hearing impairments … now benefits … also exercisers in health clubs, [and] travellers in airports.*

According to the Higher Education Opportunity Act (2008), UDL is defined as follows.

A scientifically valid framework for guiding educational practice that –

(A) provides flexibility in the ways information is presented, in the ways students respond or demonstrate knowledge or skills, and in the ways students are engaged; and

(B) reduces barriers in instruction, provides appropriate accommodations, supports, and challenges, and maintains high achievement expectations for all students, including students with disabilities and students who are limited English proficient.

(HEOA, 2008)

This framework looks at providing flexible ways to represent what is learnt, multiple ways to support how it is learnt and many options to support engagement and motivation with why it is learnt. The idea is to design in advance using set principles in order to avoid having to 'retrofit' to accommodate students' needs. Hall *et al.* (2012: 93) give an example in the context of history where digital multimedia are used to enable students to actively engage with history in a variety of ways.

A few notes of caution

The following cautions may be helpful in working with UDL.

- You may well have limited control over the design of the physical spaces in which you teach. Classrooms beautifully designed for one subject area may prove hard to use for others. We once taught an active session on assessment design which involved skirting a 6-foot Gruffalo and a toy kitchen – a stimulating area for one bunch of learners perhaps, but a potential nightmare for others who needed peace and space.
- When designing assessment tasks to meet the needs of all, we still need to honour the purpose of the module or the course and consider the development of 'graduate attributes' (for more on this, see O is for Occupations). So – if a module seeks to ensure that learners can organise, interpret and articulate project findings, the student with anxiety issues, rather than present their findings to their peers, can be supported to evidence this in a different way (a video, a one-to-one presentation) but opportunities could be designed for the student to gain confidence in presenting in informal contexts as part of the course as a whole.
- The idea of not having to 'retrofit' looks great at first glance but we don't get to meet all our learners before we do our designs, so, taking architecture as our metaphor, some of the 'building' can be designed in advance, but some will be deconstructed and reconstructed or 'tweaked'

as you go along – this is because the students will shape the curriculum too. The stronger (and the more 'universal') the design, the less adapting you will need to do, but maybe the process of a certain amount of adaptation is necessary – it's the difference between a building, which is a fixed entity, and teaching and learning, which is a process.

What is a learning environment?

Attention was being paid by enlightened theorists to the importance of designing a whole environment for learning way back in 1915 by, for example, Dewey and Dewey, who rejected the education of the day.

> [Its main function is to] *train children to docility and obedience, to the careful performance of imposed tasks because they are imposed, regardless of where they lead – a purpose suited only to autocratic societies.*
>
> (Dewey and Dewey, 1915: 303)

Dewey (1966) also noted that *the environment consists of those conditions that promote or hinder, stimulate or inhibit, the characteristics of a human being.* Those characteristics will be not only cognitive but also emotional, psychological, physical and social. Thanks to theorists such as Bruner, Vygotsky and John and Evelyn Dewey, we have moved from the silent lecture theatre to the interactive learning seminar – or have we?

UNESCO (2012) expands the description of the learning environment beyond the learning space to include the structures and ethos of the course, the policies and principles of the organisation delivering it and any communities that may lend it support.

We often use the word 'curriculum' to encompass all of these things, particularly drawing on the praxis model described in our introduction.

Design in practice

So, how can all of this support our practice of creative teaching?

> ### TASK 1
>
> Compile a checklist of points to consider when designing bespoke teaching within your context. Rate your current practice against your list. What changes could you make that would benefit your students?

REFLECTIONS

Your list may include some or all of the following (note that 'design' here may mean design of a whole module, a course or a single taught session).

A. How will you enable students to learn actively? If you struggle to create a suitable physical environment because you haven't time to move furniture, ask learners to help. One teacher we know who has to move sites between sessions sends a message on ahead to his cohort to ask them to arrange the room in the way needed for the session (be aware, of course, of any health and safety issues that may arise here).

B. What are your own instincts about your design? Is it how you would like to learn if you were a student? Is it rooted in the principles of good practice?

C. How will you design in communication routes with and between students?

D. How does your design relate to other factors such as summative assessment requirements, course structure and staffing arrangements?
   You may find it useful here to use the concept of the situational analysis (Richards, 2001) as a design tool. In the situational analysis, you identify factors that impact on learning, look at what their impact is on learning and then make curriculum decisions that help to support learners in the context (or change the context). In a comprehensive situational analysis you would look at every aspect of the context – the learners, the room, the subject requirements, any external constraints, what you bring to the mix, etc.

E. Which aspects of your design allow for students to attend to their own emotional responses to the session?

F. What opportunities are available for flexible learning? Have you drawn on technology to avoid learners sitting passively for hours? How about planning tutorials to provide bespoke support (using video, email, messaging, etc.) to individuals or smaller groups?

G. How will you employ collaborative learning? Learners are not the only ones who need to work in groups. You may need to work with other departments and levels of management to facilitate your design needs.

H. What links will you make – or encourage the students to make – within the subject discipline, across other disciplines, in terms of future employment and in relation to the world at large?

(Continued)

(Continued)

I. How will you ensure that global perspectives are included in your design?

J. Does your design allow for you and your students to have fun when learning?

K. What orientation towards subject knowledge does your design embody? Pre-packaged or co-constructed? Does it align with your own epistemology?

L. How will you monitor and respond to your own teaching practices and your students' learning during and after the session?

M. To what extent does your design include opportunities for the students to consider their own approaches to learning?

N. In what ways have you taken account of the diversity of your students in your design and drawn on their knowledge and experiences as potential resources?
Consistency of 'delivery' is often a big concern for departments. However, it's impossible to teach exactly the same session twice. There is a tendency here to conflate 'consistency' with fairness and equity, but fairness and equity do not mean treating everyone the same. The 'consistency' lies in tailoring your teaching to the students who are in front of you.

O. Does your design allow the students to consider future goals and occupations?

P. If the design includes a presentation aspect, how will you encourage students to engage with this? In this book we've concentrated largely on small and large groups in classrooms, but you also need to design for learning in other contexts such as the working environment or the field trip.

Q. How will you 'hear' the quieter students?

R. How will you make use of the space and build in 'embodied' learning?

S. What approaches will you use to support skills development? The development of skills needs to be designed into the whole experience, not bolted on. If your course is designed to have cohorts from different disciplines in large groups, you may want to use these sessions for generic skills development, maybe allocating some of the time to small subject-specific groups working on an assessment that can be contextualised.

T. Are there any elements of narrative in your approach? Could there be?

U. How will you assess student progress and understanding during taught sessions? SMART learning outcomes are often a useful tool, even if you ditch these ten minutes into the session. You might liken this to the creative writer who knows the rules of grammar but then decides to subvert them. Design your feedback too, so that learners know when to expect comments on drafts, etc. Are the aims, outcomes, approaches and assessments aligned? Be careful of assessment backwash (Boud and Falchikov, 2007) where assessment dictates what and how you teach.

V. What resources are in your design? To what extent are they multisensory and multimodal?

W. Is your design sensitive to the wellbeing of students and of yourself?

X. Have you designed in a variety of opportunities for students to discuss their expectations? And to evaluate and provide feedback on your teaching?

Y. Is your teaching designed to elicit 'why' questions and promote critical thinking?

Z. What design choices have you made about variety, pacing and breaks in sessions? How about designing workshops that give learners more scope for taking breaks when they need them? In our definition of a workshop, students come together at a specified time to work on a specified task. A loose structure is advisable – for example, each participant states at the beginning what they hope to achieve in the workshop and the group comes together again at points to share reports on progress. The teacher circulates and provides support as needed.

If the list above seems daunting, we suggest that you consider each point as part of a longer process of improving your course/module/session design. And if in doubt about any of them, we direct you to the rest of this book.

is for
EMOTION

HOW FEELINGS HAVE A ROLE IN LEARNING

CHAPTER SUMMARY

This chapter is about the relationship between affect and education (where 'affect' refers to the experience of feeling emotions). We begin with a look at the history of mind–emotion dualism before considering startling findings from neuroscience on the role that emotion plays in decision-making. Moving on to the area of negative emotion and education, we examine fear and other related emotions, and the barriers to learning that these are associated with. Finally, we share a range of examples showing how teaching can be designed to use affect as a positive force for learning.

Introduction

The word 'emotion' has some interesting origins, including a mid-sixteenth-century term denoting a public disturbance and the Latin word *emovere* (*e* meaning 'out' and *movere* meaning 'move') (OUP, 2017). Such roots evoke notions of disruption and (com)motion. Is it any wonder that formal education in the Western world has sought to stifle its role in learning for the last few centuries?

The polarisation of emotion and reason – and its demise

For centuries in the Western world, philosophers and scientists have advocated a dualistic perspective regarding rational thought and the 'passions'. Plato's famous chariot analogy (written around 370 BCE and thought by some to have been drawn from earlier Hindu mythology), placed 'intellect' as a charioteer, with a white horse of 'reasoned impulses' pulling the right way, but a black horse of 'impulsive desires' (a 'massive jumble of a creature'), pulling the other and threatening to upturn the whole lot (Shiltz, 2006). Some centuries later (around 1640), Descartes sought to free the intellectual pursuit of Truth from the irrational havoc of emotion (Alsop, 2005: 6). This legacy has continued through the twentieth century and beyond, its effects still experienced by scholars today, particularly in higher education culture where the focus so often seems to be on reasoning at the expense of feeling.

It is worth noting, however, that the current usage of the term 'emotions' did not develop until the beginning of the nineteenth century. Before that, it was the 'passions' that were referred to instead. Solomon (1995) points out that different cultures across the world have dramatically different definitions of emotion, including the ways in which individual emotions are categorised, talked about and stigmatised. Others see emotion as *as a culturally situated discursive practice that shapes, conditions, preserves and sustains power relations* (Boler, 1999 in Benozzo and Colley, 2012: 308). So the concept of emotion, including its relationship to mind and body, varies considerably according to time and place.

Could it be, therefore, that the relationship between reason and emotion is not as clearly (and certainly not as universally) defined as we think it is?

TASK 1

Think of a decision you made recently. It doesn't have to be a life-changing one (although it could be). It could be standing in a supermarket aisle and deciding which sort of pasta or rice to buy. What role did emotion play in your decision-making? Could you have made the decision using logic alone?

REFLECTIONS

Towards the end of the last century, a Portuguese-American neuroscientist, Damasio, studied individuals with brain damage which affected their ability to experience emotions (1994). These people were high-functioning individuals, but they could not make decisions. Trying to choose a date for a meeting became a labyrinth of logical deductions. There was no 'gut feeling' to inform them. So even if you think you used pure logic to make your decision in the task above, emotion will have played a role. As Holloway (2013) says (writing in the arena of mathematics), the implications of Damasio's findings for learning and teaching are *stunning*. If reason requires emotion to function effectively, he argues, then all our efforts to keep teaching free of emotion must surely fail (2013: 259). We return to this idea later in the chapter when we consider the role of heuristics in problem-solving.

What other roles do emotions play in learning? Below we look at barriers to learning in higher education connected with negative emotion, after which we examine some approaches to teaching that harness emotion in order to deepen engagement and understanding. We do not, in this chapter, consider external factors that may contribute to student distress. For that, we direct you to W is for Wellbeing.

Emotions as a barrier to learning

> ... *anxiety is the most frequently reported emotion in education.*
>
> (Jackson, 2015: 356)

A common fear experienced by students in education is that of being *lost, either physically, cognitively or emotionally* (Hargreaves, 2015: 316). According to Foucault, this fear arises from an *authoritarian pedagogic system which focuses on difference*. Foucault also describes the ways in which individuals can be *judged, measured, compared with others* and *trained or corrected, classified, normalised, excluded etc.* (Foucault, 1979, in Hargreaves, 2015: 316).

Fear of not fitting in or not being able to find one's way can be accompanied by fear of being judged, not just by the teacher, but by one's peers also. Hargreaves (2015) explains that this fear can lead to risk-averse behaviour in students, not only in terms of not *answering* questions, but also not *asking* questions. She makes a link with the increasing dominance of a performativity culture in education, one where not just the students but the teachers themselves are fearful of judgement, their managers similarly so, and their managers, and so on. The ritualised performance of the traditional lecture (Goffman, 1956) reinforces the illusion that teacher and students all are achieving, when in fact emotions in the room may be ranging from indifference to turmoil. The alternative to 'authoritarian' teaching is what we tend to think of as 'messy' teaching, where getting it 'wrong' and being vulnerable are necessary parts of learning and teaching, and asking questions is normalised. Messy teaching is underpinned by sociocultural theories of learning and, while it may look less 'slick' than a teacher-centred approach, learning is authentic and knowledge is co-constructed.

If opportunities are not provided for students to be able to express their doubts and misconceptions, there is a danger of disengagement. Fear of failure can lead some to avoid situations where they can fail, a spectrum ranging from not speaking out in sessions to not attending sessions to dropping out altogether. The irony of this, of course, is that it guarantees the very failure that the student was trying to avoid (McGregor and Elliot, 2005, in Jackson, 2015: 358). It's important to understand this downward spiral. There is also the risk of being labelled by teachers as weak, lazy or unmotivated, if not explicitly then implicitly. Such labels are not only unhelpful, but they can be picked up by the student in question and internalised (Maughan, 2011).

Linked to this is Bandura's notion of *self-efficacy*, the *belief in one's agentic capabilities, that one can produce given levels of attainment* (Bandura, 1997: 382). Unlike self-confidence, which can be more general, self-efficacy is context dependent. Bandura's model is not without its critics. For example, Kardong-Edgren (2013) warns of the danger of giving students an inflated sense of what they can achieve and argues that simply measuring student progress can lead to *legitimate* self-efficacy in any case.

Harnessing emotion to support learning

> *Speaking is like conducting an orchestra; but instead of music, you are directing emotions.*
>
> (Joel Orr, 1993)

Are there ways in which we can rein in Plato's horses so that they pull in the same direction and work with 'intellect' (our charioteer) in the pursuit of Truth? This next section provides a kaleidoscope of ideas and examples.

One way to support students to engage and remember what they are learning is to tap into their *implicit* (unconscious) memories (Maughan, 2011).

These consist of emotional states, sensations, beliefs and principles, which in turn shape constructions of knowledge. The key point is that implicit memories are often stronger than explicit ones, which tend to be inaccurate and unreliable. An encouraging thought is the fact that as teachers we are already finding ways of engaging our students creatively on an emotional level in order to capture and hold their attention and fuel their motivation. The following are some examples from the literature and from practice.

Online presence

Sara, a Human Rights Education student, one day disclosed online to her peers not only her passion for her subject but the prejudices she had faced herself which had led her to study it.

> *Sara's disclosure unleashed a flood of empathy and other emotions from her classmates and simultaneously encouraged other students to open up about their experiences and observations. From that point forward, the online learning environment seemed to transform from a course to a true community of learners … Through Sara, we began to understand how the reflective qualities of online learning can create a powerful emotional experience for students; one that can, in fact, be greater than in a face-to-face course.*
>
> (Whiteside and Garret Dikkers, 2015: 225)

The authors discuss the essential role of the teacher in this process and the importance of retaining an online social – and 'human' – presence. Providing and holding a space for students to share what they care about applies to STEM subjects, too. Online environments can be constructed not simply to share solutions to problems, but also to express careers' interests or feelings about topics covered on the course.

Quiet time

Having rushed to a session and started teaching on auto-pilot, Joe began to feel that he had not properly 'arrived' in the room. Calling for a pause, he invited the group to attend to their breathing, their bodies, their feelings and the sounds and sensations around them before suggesting they each have a gentle stretch if they wanted to. After this, he sat quietly with the group and asked each of them in turn how they were feeling that day. The students all welcomed the opportunity for this 'quiet' time at the start and it became a regular feature of the module.

Heuristics

Game designers often use a heuristic ('rule-of-thumb' or 'intuitive') approach when assessing the playability of a prototype game. Some research has shown that, when compared with standard user testing, heuristic approaches in this context lead to similar results (Desurvire *et al.*, 2004). Heuristics can also be used to estimate answers to problem scenarios across a range of subject disciplines (do you have a 'feel' for the solution? What might it look like?), potentially enhancing engagement and encouraging creative approaches to problem-solving.

Comfort zones

Sometimes learning involves feeling disquieted. This approach was used by a Criminology tutor on our teaching and learning in HE course, Catrin, who showed students images of a range of members of society and asked them to decide who could be classed as 'deviant', before debating the legal definition of the term. The experience of discomfort in learning can help us to form stronger memories, as discussed earlier, but it is important also to provide a boundaried space for students to share their concerns and reflect on their discomfort, and on how this may have pushed them to learn.

Aesthetics

Aesthetics can be defined as a way of knowing, a process of learning or a mode of cognition, where *students engage in expressive experiences where sentiment interpretations and emotional responses are accessed* (Jacobs, 2011: 246). Jacobs goes on to justify its presence in the curriculum by suggesting that it is linked with intrinsic motivation in one's subject discipline. More than that, however, aesthetics is a skill, an alternative way of seeing the world and one's place in it. In a study she carried out on a group of university students, Jacobs found that the most common strategy for developing this skill was to pause. This might be, for example, to hear the rhythm and feel the fascination of the words in a literary text; to wonder at the images of cells under a microscope; to reflect on the complexity of an ecosystem or the potential for technology to enhance human communication; to marvel at the beauty of witnessing a child learning to read or the development of an individual's motor skills; to talk about the magnificence of sedimentary rocks; to share the elegant simplicity of a well-formed proof, or to empathise with the human spirit in the most difficult times in history. Higher education, the author argues, is the most challenging environment in which to make time for moments such as these. However, he also says that the joy of learning can still be experienced.

> *The path towards great aesthetic engagement in higher education can be found in collaborative partnerships that share knowledge between disciplines. This, along with a little imagination, will help to perpetuate the joy of learning about our world.*
>
> (Jacobs, 2011: 246)

Concluding feelings

Neuroscientists such as LeDoux (2000) believe that the relationship between emotion and cognition can never be fully defined because the concept of emotion is itself not easily defined. He questions whether these even exist as discrete functions of the brain. Buddhists refer to the 'subtle' (or ideal) body, mapped out as energy flows – an alternative conception of mind, body and emotion (Solomon, 1995). Perhaps one day in the West we will stop talking about emotion and reason as two separate things and recognise that learning encompasses both.

is for
FLEXIBLE

HOW TO ENABLE LEARNING ANY TIME, ANYWHERE

CHAPTER SUMMARY

Superhero and mother of three, 'Elastigirl' from Pixar's film *The Incredibles*, can flex her body into many different forms (including a parachute) when required to save the world. Director, Brad Bird, explained that it was because *Moms are always pulled in a million different directions, so I had her be elastic* (Barrier, 2005). The same could be said both of higher education teachers and of students, who are often juggling work, caring responsibilities and other issues on top of their studies. In this chapter, we look at the flexible opportunities for learning we need to create as alternatives to the traditional face-to-face 'lecture-seminar-tutorial' format in order to save ourselves and our students.

Introduction

The ability to be flexible as a teacher is vital in order to respond to the needs of the diverse learners that we meet. Teachers are sometimes referred to as the *bricoleurs* described by Lévi-Strauss (1966) – that is, people who put pre-existing things together in new ways and draw from everything available (for more recent discussions on bricolage, see Sharples *et al.*, 2014). A teacher needs use whatever methods work for the students. One of these ways is to support learners in studying outside 'contact time', partly to expand the time available and also to equip them as autonomous learners. The concept of the autonomous learner is an important theme across the curriculum.

> *Autonomous learning does not mean self-instruction or learning without a teacher. Rather it is a way of complementing face-to face tuition which makes learning more productive and develops independence.*
>
> (Gray and Klapper, 2009: 325)

Flipping

Using self-directed time *outside* the classroom for tasks that would usually be done *in* the classroom is known as 'flipped learning'. We're going to model some flipped learning now by setting you a task to do before you read the rest of this chapter.

TASK 1

Think about a time when you have set your students an activity to be done before the class. This can range from completing a short reading to a request for students to watch a video. Reflect on what went well and what didn't go so well. As you read on, compare the positive and negative aspects of the experience with those described below.

REFLECTIONS

We will address some of the pitfalls of flipped learning later in the chapter, but first let's look at some of its benefits.
   Why encourage your students to study outside the classroom?

- So that we don't have to spend the session *covering content* since not all the learning can or should be crammed between the start and finish of a single taught session (Ironside, 2004).
- So there's more space in sessions to discuss, critically analyse, explore and ask questions. Sitting in a session listening passively to endless content which is beyond your understanding can quickly become alienating. Having space in that session instead to ask questions and engage with the topic you've already struggled or interacted with not only provides the teacher with valuable formative assessment material but also builds both confidence and a sense of community. It also provides more opportunities for learning through social interaction (Vygotsky, 1978). *Ignorance is a lonely country. We need to allow students to talk about what it was like living there, but we also want to help them leave it* (Cousin, 2014 in Singh and Cowden, 2016: 94).
- So students have the space to process knowledge at their own pace (see Q is for Quiet for more on this).
- So that content is presented in a variety of modes and spaces (see V is for Visuals and R is for Room for more on the importance of this).

And flexing

With the flexibility afforded by the technological tools available now, there is no real reason why teaching and learning have to be compartmentalised into 'lectures', 'seminars', 'tutorials', 'lab sessions', 'field trips', 'workplace learning', and so on. When offsite, students can communicate via a variety of means; when in large group face-to-face context, they can take part in interactive tasks and quizzes via their phones. Presentations, tutorials, workshops and discussions can all happen at a distance if needed. Other practices can be disrupted, too – for example, S is for Skilful looks at reading activities that can be used during face-to-face sessions to support students in engaging with key texts. For this reason, we would like to talk in this chapter, not just about 'flipping' but also about 'flexing' – that is, creating or engaging with flexible learning approaches across a programme.

Seven ideas for flexible learning

Here are some examples of ways in which you can encourage students to work more autonomously, both outside and within 'contact time'.

Online presentations

Rather than present a set of slides to students in a face-to-face session, you can create a presentation that students can access themselves, in their own time. You could, for example, video yourself giving a presentation by using screen capture software. You can include your own 'talking head' where you talk directly into the camera or you can simply focus on what's on the screen, adding an audio commentary to supplement your slides. Another approach is not to use video at all, but to create a slide show that students can work through by themselves – for example, with hyperlinks, games, quizzes, audio and choices about which section to look at next. You can also include links to message boards for people to respond to the presentation content.

Discussion forums, blogs, online message boards

These platforms provide ways in which you and your students can engage in dialogue when you're not in each other's physical presence. Discussions can be asynchronous (individuals have time to ponder, find references and write more considered responses, but at the expense of spontaneity) or synchronous (communication is instantaneous but runs the risk of relatively shallow responses because of time pressure). Discussions can take place either in 'safe and controlled' spaces – for example, discussions in an institutional VLE – or 'organic and public' spaces on social media that have the benefit of being able to widen out the discussion to practising professionals and others. However, these also carry increased risks around professional identity, meaning that students can find themselves in potentially challenging situations.

Research such as that by Bassett (2011) in the context of a business studies course in Victoria University has shown positive reactions from diverse cohorts, indicating that

> *online discussion was perceived as a valuable learning strategy that resulted in increased confidence to interact in a collaborative online environment. Most students believed their knowledge, understanding, and critical ability were enhanced in this inclusive context.*

C is for Communicating explores this type of interaction in more depth.

Group work

This can be done outside class time and can be part of a summative assessment through, for example, a group blog which describes the work done by the group and each individual's contribution. Collaborative tools allow documents such as presentation slides, spreadsheets or word-based documents to be co-authored and edited, and then shared with a wider audience (Mills, 2013). For more on this, see G is for Groups.

Quizzes

These can be online (including via mobile phones) or on paper. They can be set as revision following a taught session, and you can sneak in a final question on metalearning asking for feedback on the way the session was delivered to see if students found it a useful way to learn.

C is for Communicating explores the use of quizzes in more detail.

A webinar

This is an online presentation where those watching can communicate in real time – for example, via instant messaging, file or screen sharing, or using an online whiteboard collaboratively. This needs careful planning and organisation, particularly given the challenges posed by the absence of face-to-face contact with the students (Guanci, 2010). An added benefit is that these can usually be recorded and so provide reference material for student revision and staff reflection.

Video or telephone tutorials

This is great for students who live at a distance, and can be one-to-one or group-based. Videoconferencing tools are also a useful way for academic tutors or mentors to stay in contact with students who are on placement – for example, O'Donovan and Maruthappu (2015) describe the positive effects of such an approach on peer-tutoring in clinical skills between UK and Malaysian medical students. Tutorials can also be recorded for later use by tutees.

Recording face-to-face sessions

Record yourself teaching a session and make it available afterwards. In our experience, students value the opportunity to revisit material with the luxury of pausing and replaying the bits they find difficult. Recording live teaching and learning will be far from perfect in terms of results. However, in our experience, students enjoy the authenticity of the experience. For example, Brandon Collier-Reed at Cape Town University talks of being aware of, not just your 'live' audience but your 'recorded' one – for example, using index markers for ease of content navigation. He also talks about the importance of considering intellectual property when making such recordings. Who has 'ownership' of the material? Is permission needed for recording? Can it be shared?

In the final section of this chapter, we look at some ideas for troubleshooting when things don't go according to plan.

What happens if ...

Your students aren't flipping or flexing – that is, engaging with flipped or flexible learning opportunities?

It's hard enough getting them to come in for the face-to-face teaching, but how do you get students to engage from a distance? Introducing the expectation right from the first time you meet your students that work needs to be done outside sessions in order to maximise opportunities for successful learning can help, as can 'normalising' this way of working right from the start. Building a strong sense of group identity during face-to-face sessions can also encourage participation in independent learning and promote the benefits of flipped or flexible learning (see, for example, Cronhjort *et al.*, 2017, who found that flipping calculus on a maths course improved engagement and achievement). Finally, treat the results of flipped tasks as an essential element of the curriculum, referring back to them in class, and talk to those who are not engaging to find out why this might be.

It's also difficult to manage a session that depends on students having done their share beforehand if some or all have not completed this. The following task explores this issue further.

TASK 2

Imagine that you arrive to teach a face-to-face session and you find that a number of students have not carried out the pre-session tasks. List a range of possible responses available to you.

REFLECTIONS

Here are some strategies to help with this.
    A Law teacher, Sarah, has developed the following strategy.

> *I teach in a big lecture theatre which is divided into different sections. I allocate one section (A) for the people who've watched the pre-session presentation – they get to ask me questions and I build on what they've learned. The other section (B) is for those who didn't watch it prior to the session. They settle down with their phones or tablets and their ear plugs and watch it there and then. So B get the basics but A get to develop their learning. Gradually over the module, the B group decreases and allows me to spend more time developing the understanding of those who have already done the preparation in the A group.*

Don't be afraid to do a quick 'test' at the beginning of a session to see how much people have done, retained and understood from their independent study. This will be a self-assessment, and students often value having the time and the tools to check their understanding. The more you can relate (align) these tasks to the summative assessment, the more comfortably this will sit within your curriculum and with your students (Biggs and Tang, 2011).

Hopefully, as a creative teacher in higher education, you will think of other ways that fit your context and allow your students to engage with your subject, particularly as the technology to do so continues to develop. At this point, therefore, we flip the challenge over to you ...

is for
GROUPS

HOW TO SUPPORT STUDENTS TO
LEARN TOGETHER

CHAPTER SUMMARY

Much of this chapter is written in the voice of a student, Yared, who joins a Social Work course. It tells his story in the form of a personal blog as he works on a project in a small group over three months. Threaded through the narrative is a description of the ways in which he is supported to work in this way and the impact this has on his learning. In between the diary extracts there are footnotes expanding on the ideas and giving references to related literature and research.

The focus here is on summative group assessment. We look at the use of groupwork as a more general teaching approach in other chapters.

TASK 1

Reflecting on group learning

a) Think about the last time you learned something as part of a group. In what ways did the group help or hinder you in the learning process?
b) What are the rationales for using group work in learning, teaching and assessment in education? Do you agree? Why? Why not?

REFLECTIONS

Yared's blog extracts below illustrate how group work can be both a supportive experience and an off-putting one, and how groups can be facilitated in order to maximise learning opportunities.

Social constructivist theorists hold that *knowledge is developed through contestations and struggles* (Scott and Hargreaves, 2015: 11) – that is, it is actively negotiated rather than received passively via transmission. Employing group work as a teaching and learning strategy is a way of creating an environment that better enables these processes to take place. It also changes the power dynamic within a classroom, where the students are increasingly seen as holders of knowledge, not just the teacher. And it is supported by other sociocultural learning theories such as communities of practice theory (Wenger *et al.*, 2002), where learning is seen as taking place through social participation.

This links to another compelling reason for paying attention to groups and group dynamics in learning, teaching and assessment – that is, the idea of 'belonging'. Masika and Jones, researching a group of first-year Business students, concluded that *Membership to a peer community of practice through face-to-face and online collaboration, communication and discussion increased student engagement, confidence and sense of belonging* (2016: 147). In this sense, peer groups within subject disciplines are an essential part of the forming of student identity. Careful facilitation of group work can therefore enhance individuals' feelings of being valued, accepted and included.

As you read Yared's blog, you may wish to make some notes on the steps that the teacher takes to ensure that the group work is supported.

> **YARED'S BLOG: EXTRACT 1**
>
> **August: first entry**
>
> I'm starting a social work course next month and I feel really nervous about it. It's supposed to be for newbies, but I already know one person on it and he's been working in the community for ages and really knows what he's doing. Apparently, one of the assessments is a piece of group work (1) so I'll get shown up as a fraud straight away when the others realise how little I know.

Notes

1. There are several useful definitions of 'group' in the literature. Jaques (2000) says that groups have seven attributes. He talks about members having a collective perception of themselves as a group, even when they are not together, and feeling that the group will meet some needs and that there are shared aims or ideals. He also says that members feel they are interdependent and interact for more than a few minutes with two or more people. Finally, in his definition of a group, he says that members wish to stay and to contribute. It could be argued that when we create successful groups in a classroom, they meet all the above criteria.

Research by Springer *et al.* (1999), shows that the impact of group work on retention and achievement can be considerable, demonstrating, for example, that small-group learning can lead to greater achievement and better motivation. In fact, this approach has been shown to be more effective than other educational innovations.

> **YARED'S BLOG: EXTRACT 2**
>
> **August: second entry**
>
> I've had several e-mails from the course tutor. She's already checked my application and seems to know a bit about my previous experience. She says there are some other people in the same position. She's also aware of my needs around anxiety and what the university is meant to have in place to support me (2). We're going to meet up to discuss the group work element and see what we can do to make it easier for me (3).

Notes

2. There may well be people in the class for whom group work is specially challenging and they may have specified statements of support in place which details ways to facilitate this for them. This is an example of making group work inclusive by differentiating.

3. Research indicates that building a positive relationship with teachers has a real impact on retention and achievement.

YARED'S BLOG: EXTRACT 3

September: first entry

I wasn't able to attend the first three days of the course because of illness. The tutor met with me and explained some tasks (4) she had used in the first few sessions to prepare people for working in smaller groups later on. I missed these but we've devised some ways together to 'catch me up'.

After that, in the next session, there was a slide asking for people to work in pre-selected groups. The tutor chose these to ensure a mix of experience. She's explained which one I am in and she's going to give me the e-mails of the other four so that I can contact them. They have done a small task together in the class and they have to write it up and submit it (5). The tutor says this is really to experiment with communication and cooperation rather than being task focused.

I was really worried about missing all this, but hopefully the four I'm working with will be OK with me e-mailing and joining in now. I was asked for a short description of myself and my work with a photo as I didn't attend so they do already know who I am and what I look like.

We've agreed that I won't be introduced to the whole group as this will draw attention to me, but the tutor will ask the cohort to sit in their groups again so it's easy for me to get to know my little group.

Notes

4. One such activity is called 'the name game'. The cohort sits in a circle. The first person gives their name and a positive adjective which begins with the same sound. The second person repeats the name of the first person and adds their own – for example, 'I am amazing Albert and this is fabulous Farzana'. This can take what feels a long time, but by the end, using repetition, even people who say they have a bad memory for

names can usually name everyone in the circle. There needs to be lots of scaffolding for those who find this challenging – maybe because they are not operating in their mother tongue or using a familiar naming system. The idea is to get everyone supporting each other rather than competing, and to begin building the idea of a community of practice. (It is worth noting that this type of activity needs to be handled sensitively, as it may cause anxiety in some participants.)

5.   The initial task will ideally involve possible different interpretations to encourage the group to work together to produce a collective piece in the face of different approaches or philosophies.

YARED'S BLOG: EXTRACT 4

September: entry two

The five of us in my group have talked a lot by e-mail and also Skyped because we live in different parts of the city. We also have a discussion board on the VLE which is useful. We're talking about using Google docs for the summative assessment (6) but for the quick task from the first session, we asked one person to collate our ideas. Problem is that she ran out of time and ended up submitting two versions as she couldn't reconcile the different ideas we sent her. Good job this was only a formative task or we would have failed.

October: first entry

I've just been to my first session and met the big group and my group of five. One of them was telling me how useful the name game was. She has got used to people mispronouncing her name but because she got the chance to say it clearly and the tutor stopped people rushing over it, she has got her identity back.

The tutor had copied the work we submitted as small groups and each group got to critique the work of another group. We then had half an hour to revisit the work and talk about how we'd gone about it. We can see in our group that we need to spend some time exploring the different ways we work and the different ways we view tasks. I just want to get it right and get it in on time, two others are really interested in the process and, if I'm honest, there is one person who isn't really taking part at all so far and another who just doesn't seem to understand what's going on (7). At least we know now and we can start working out how to tackle this before the summative task is set and we have to start working on that. The tutor circulated and sat in on our discussion so I think she'll be giving us some ideas on how to work together.

Notes

6. There are many ways to use TEL (technology-enhanced learning) to support group work. However, take-up of technological tools by student groups varies considerably. Witney and Smallbone (2011) question the efficacy of such tools if insufficient attention is paid to developing students' collaborative skills and steps are not taken to familiarise them with the technology available.

7. You may find it useful to critique the definitions given by Davies (2009) of roles adopted by group members

---

YARED'S BLOG: EXTRACT 5

October: entry two

In the session today we had a break from sitting in our groups and it was good to work with some different people. After the taught session, we had an hour this time to look at the summative group work task. There are lots of comments in the assignment briefing to ensure that we all contribute (8). The handbook suggests we might want to have a protocol for working together, and that the protocol for each group will be different. We've already decided we want to spend time looking at our basic beliefs about the topic before we even start to write it and to look at how we can all be represented without it looking incoherent. One person has an assignment for another module in the middle of the semester, so she's going to submit her work for this task to me and then come in again at the end to do some of the collating.

November: first entry

One of our group has just disappeared and we don't know how to manage this. Another is totally dominating the discussion and forcing his way of working on us. This is turning into a bit of a nightmare and all I want to do is pass. It isn't fair that the others are stopping me get a good grade. It reminds me of my team on my placement when we have meetings and we can't get anything done because we don't work well together (9). I'm beginning to have a lot more sympathy with people who say they don't like group work assessments ...

Notes

8. Guidance in the way the group task is set up can help members ensure that they make equal contributions. For example:

- in group presentations, each member should lead the material for x minutes;
- records such as e-mail chains or discussion boards should be kept as supporting evidence to substantiate the individual effectiveness of course members within the group.

9. The development of group work skills links to the employability agenda which is explored further in O is for Occupations.

YARED'S BLOG: EXTRACT 6

November: entry two

We've had several e-mails with the lecturer and last week we met after the taught session to talk about how the group is going. We've made a new schedule, worked out why someone wasn't taking part (workload issues) and the lecturer is working with one of the group who is from a different sector and was feeling lost with the terminology. She's also emphasised the fact that we need to show that we are all taking part and which aspects we have contributed.

December: final entry

Submitted! I'm really proud of the final submission and even more proud that I was able to work in the group. I'm sure we'll keep in touch now and I've got some new friends and colleagues as a result.

TASK 2

As a result of reading this chapter, what further steps might you take to support your students to engage in small-group work, either as part of a summative assessment or as part of an informal task?

REFLECTIONS

You may wish to exchange ideas with colleagues, perhaps even observe each other facilitating group work in teaching sessions, evaluating the extent to which this is rooted in good practice (see the Introduction). In doing this collaboratively, you will hopefully, together, create new knowledge about working with groups of students within your subject discipline and thus strengthen your own community of practice.

is for
WHOLE

HOW THE LEARNING PROCESS CAN BE MORE THAN THE SUM OF ITS PARTS

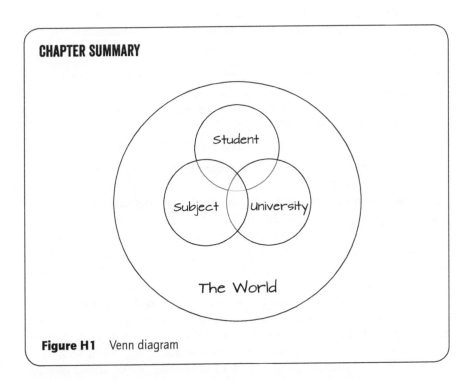

CHAPTER SUMMARY

Student

Subject   University

The World

Figure H1   Venn diagram

Blurring the boundaries

HE's been academised. Quality? It's 'measurable-ised' – part

Of the drive t' economise – the sector slowly casualised.

Higher Education is characterised by boundaries. Some are driven by political agendas: quantitative measures privileged over qualitative discourses as universities compete rather than collaborate, or human resources subdivided by the increasing use of short-term contracts.

Other boundaries are slower to evolve: lines drawn to demarcate subject disciplines or to show how they should be grouped; teachers boxed in roles denoting levels of power and students pigeonholed according to perceived characteristics. Knowledge is divided into subjects and levels. Outcomes are sought as ends in themselves and classroom windows remain opaque, the processes within them obscured from public discourse. Session content and pedagogical approaches become divorced from the way we manage problem-solving in the rest of our lives.

Students, too, start to narrow their focus so that success in assessment is all that is in view. Strauss and Howe describe 'Millennials' in the USA who

respond best to external motivators and are highly rationalistic, making long-range plans and thinking carefully about college financing, degrees, salaries, employment trends, and the like.

(2000: 182–3 in Wilson and Gerber, 2008)

As teachers, we find ourselves becoming co-conspirators in the game, teaching to the test and reacting to external targets and pressures.

Of course, some compartmentalising is required to ensure a fair, equitable and manageable system but when boundaries become normalised, we are left with an educational experience that is divided and broken into separate fragments. This fosters neither creativity nor learning.

How, then, can we encourage our students and ourselves to 'pan out' and to see higher education in a wider context and with a deeper purpose? Each of the sections below corresponds to one of the circles in our Venn diagram above. Through this chapter we've threaded in some lines from an anonymous poem found when researching for the chapter. We've added positive lines to this as our conclusion. If you put the headings and the final lines together you'll get a whole poem.

The whole subject discipline

Courses all are modularised and knowledge, compartmentalized

Teachers, students? Polarised. Theory, practice? Classified.

TASK 1

Pick a module that you lead/teach.

In what ways does the module enable you to situate the content in the wider context of your subject discipline?

REFLECTIONS

The exciting possibilities that can be created by a modular approach offer a radical and different way of tackling curriculum development that engenders new enthusiasm with the opportunities for diversity that it brings.

(Smith, 1992: 141)

This quotation, from *Nurse Education Today*, heralded the start of a brave new world of modular courses, with discrete units of study providing flexible learning opportunities in manageable chunks. We recognise the many advantages this approach brings – but there's a real danger of *students gaining knowledge from isolated packages rather than developing integrated knowledge* (Alonso, 1984 in Smith, 1992: 140).

So how can we encourage students to 'see the wood for the trees'? Here are a few suggestions:

- Compile questions that require an overview of how the different components of the course fit together;
- Ask students to explain cross-modular connections to each other, or to draw a diagram or a picture showing how the different elements link;
- Create an over-arching module or an assessment that pulls in elements from the others (the former is sometimes done via a 'Professional Practice' module on a vocational course and the latter is often done as a small-scale research project).

The whole university

Beyond the classroom, problems rarely confine themselves to a single subject area.

> *Societal, environmental, economic, and philosophical issues and challenges are often so complex that it is impossible to fully understand them from a single perspective or knowledge framework.*
>
> (Jacob, 2015: 2)

This is apparent in the increasing trend for problem-solving, interdisciplinary research approaches, compared to single disciplinary, hypothesis-based research (ASHE, 2005 in Jacob, 2015). For more on problem-based learning (PBL), see Barrett and Moore (2011).

So how can we promote cross-disciplinary approaches to learning in our own contexts? As well as preparation for future employment, experiencing a range of disciplinary responses to problem-solving can develop students' critical thinking skills (Kaur and Manan, 2013) and, as we have seen from our own interdisciplinary work with HE professionals, broaden perspectives and transform individuals. Kidron and Kali (2015) point to three main barriers in this process.

1. The compartmentalisation of subject disciplines by universities.
2. The dominance of traditional approaches to teaching.
3. The value given to hierarchies structured on the level of subject expertise.

In response, the authors developed a model, Boundary Breaking for Interdisciplinary Learning (BBIL), which suggested that the introduction of themes that cut across disciplines and the use of online learning communities leads to positive outcomes for students.

Here are some further steps you can take in your own context.

- Work with teachers from other disciplines to facilitate sessions with your own students. Make sure they align with your curriculum and are pitched at the right level.
- Design the analysis of perspectives from other disciplines into module assessments or even design a joint assessment across subject specialisms.

- Introduce students to multidisciplinary research literature right from the outset.
- Signpost extra-curricular community-based projects where students from a range of disciplines work together to address local problems.

The whole world

> *Learning's totally dualised – the head and brain prioritised.*
>
> *Real life's deprioritised, authentic meaning exorcised*

Wolfram, in an article referring to school children, makes an important point with global significance.

> *Instead of rote learning long-division procedures, let's get students applying the power of calculus, picking holes in government statistics, designing a traffic system or cracking secret codes.*
>
> (Wolfram, 2014)

We spend too long, he believes, teaching the algorithms of what he terms *hand-calculating* at the expense of analysing authentic problems and creating mathematical models. The computers can – and do – perform all the calculations. It's the innovators and the problem-solvers who we need.

How does this example link to the higher education context? There is often an emphasis on knowledge acquisition in the abstract at university. The trouble is that knowledge is not fixed, but socially situated and riddled with assumptions about the universe. To avoid the silo effect referred to earlier, try the following.

- Teach everything in a context, whether that be social, geographical, historical or cultural (see T is for Tales for an example of this).
- Make links to the students' own lives where possible, even if only through analogy.
- Use social media to share current subject-related news stories and invite students to comment.
- Make frequent links to research – your own or that of others in the field, including recent innovations and cutting-edge developments.
- Design in field trips, involvement with local communities, visiting speakers, conferences and external seminars.

- Bring yourself into your teaching (while retaining professional boundaries). Model yourself as an expert who is also human and who learns from mistakes.
- Give a rationale for all session content and assessment tasks.
- Where you mention famous scientists, historians, writers, mathematicians, poets, etc., give some background. Ensure a diversity of examples across time, spaces, cultures, social groups, and so on.
- Ensure your resources do actually reflect the 'real' world. Check for diversity in images and case studies, for assumptions and for language that excludes.
- Make links to employability and future possible careers, both directly and indirectly related to the subject discipline.
- Where appropriate, consider using a case study approach. Mark, one of our students on the LTHE course, has used case studies of service users with his computer science students to develop their social, communication and employability skills. Where managed effectively, case study approaches to learning and teaching help students to develop holistic perspectives of their subject discipline (Taneja, 2014).

The whole student

> *Students, they are categorised, their hopes (now 'targets') granularised.*
>
> *Achievements, ranked and quantified. If you don't fit, you're ostracised.*

It is a phenomenon increasingly acknowledged that an individual student who is at risk of non-continuation of studies or under-achievement needs to be supported to feel a sense of belonging at university, ideally long before they reach crisis point (see, for example, Soria and Stubblefield, 2015). Elsewhere in this book, we consider student wellbeing and skills support, expectations and induction, building group identities and responding to the diversity of the student body. We also look at emotion and the body in learning and teaching, since HE students are learners whose

> *practice should engage them in learning as whole persons, drawing on emotional and social intelligences as well as powers of reasoning, their tacit knowledge and intuition as well as public knowledge, their individuality as well as collaboration, their contextualised experiences as well as abstract, generalised thinking.*
>
> (Ovens *et al.*, 2011 in Dickerson *et al.*, 2016: 252)

We also need students to be able to place their learning in the broader context. Some science-based colleagues on our courses talk of how difficult it can be for students to move from a seminar on theory to a practical lab session and hold the bigger picture in their heads while following a step-by-step 'recipe' of instructions for an experiment. Table H1 illustrates a number of perspectives on the nature of this cognitive conflict.

Table H1   Perspectives in learning

Source	Seminar on theory	Practical lab experiment
Our work with science teachers in HE	Students are introduced to the big picture and how the topic connects with the subject as a whole	Students follow a series of step-by-step instructions with their heads down, willing the experiment to 'work' but forgetting why they are doing the experiment in the first place
Chinn, 2001	*intuitive and holistic*	*formulaic and sequential*
Chinn, 2001	Grasshopper (hops up high to get an overview)	Inchworm (crawls along and experiences learning one step at a time)

Before we stray too far into the miry slough of Learning Styles, allow us to explain the last two terms in the table. These approaches to learning were thus named by Chinn and colleagues when investigating *cognitive styles* in dyslexic pupils in a number of European countries around the turn of the twenty-first century (Chinn, 2001). The results were somewhat inconclusive as students' propensity to exhibit characteristics of one style or the other were, it seems, dependent not only on which country they were in, but also on the particular curriculum model used.

Our hypothesis here, however, is not that *students* have fixed approaches to learning, but that *teaching itself* can be characterised thus. In practice, it is our view (and, to be fair, that of Chinn and colleagues) that as teachers we need to be – and to encourage our students to be – both inchworm *and* grasshopper. This could mean planning to consider text-level analysis, not just word- or sentence-level; asking students to explore *how* history is recorded and reported according to context, not just *what* is reported; providing opportunities to compare a *range* of literary genres across modules, not just analysing one genre in depth, or encouraging students to apply the problem-solving skills gained from one module to another module. It also involves mixing the 'basics' with stories of research and contributions to knowledge in the subject field, cross-referencing to applications in industry or placing content in its historical context.

Just as students bring a range of skills and approaches to higher education, so they also have a range of needs. Adopting a holistic approach to addressing these needs and not compartmentalising student support can inform our teaching. There can be a tendency to signpost students to another part of the organisation and to then assume that whatever issue has arisen is quite apart from them as learners. Instead, we can look at working with our colleagues in, for example, wellbeing services or language support departments, and changing the way in which we work where possible to make a more inclusive classroom for everyone.

We've travelled round the elements of the Venn diagram one by one and hopefully highlighted the connections and made the argument that a holistic approach is not only part and parcel of teaching creatively in higher education but can help students to learn more effectively. Let's end on a positive note with the lines we wrote to make the poem 'whole'.

> *So … join the dots, embrace the whole, make connections, reach the soul.*
>
> *We need reminding, one and all, learning extends beyond these walls.*

is for INTERNATIONALISATION

HOW THIS CAN ENRICH YOUR CURRICULUM

CHAPTER SUMMARY

This chapter begins with an examination of the term 'internationalisation'. We reject the deficit model that focuses on adapting 'international' students to fit existing curriculum models. Such a model focuses on English language skills and cultural differences while assuming that students from other cultures have no knowledge to share. It's based on implicit notions central only to a specific, Western academic tradition. Here we use a 'multiliteracies' approach which equips all those involved to live and work in a global society. Two tasks are suggested to encourage effective intercultural engagement.

What do we mean by internationalisation and what does this mean for higher education?

> *At the very least we would expect graduates to be competent in intercultural communication and to behave ethically and with social responsibility in their professional practice. We should also prepare them for civic action and decision-making as the global managers of our future.*
>
> (Thom, 2014)

Drawing on the work of Crossley (2001) and Lunn (2008), a colleague (Viv Thom) began her talk on internationalisation to university staff with the statement above. So why did she think this expectation was so important? Here are some suggestions.

Many of our students have limited experience of the world. It could be seen as a moral imperative to support them to gain a wider perspective in order to further peaceful communication across the globe. More pragmatically, all of our students are going to be living and working in an increasingly interconnected world, so they need to be able to function in it. For employers, having the skills to operate in an international arena is increasingly important.

Theory, research and enactment across the globe

Multiliteracies

In 1996, ten academics formed the New London Group (NLG) with the aim of ensuring the quality of learning, teaching and assessment in higher education. It was felt that a response was required to the need for students to embrace *the centrality of diversity* (Cope and Kalantzis, 2009: 167). This diversity included an understanding of global issues.

The idea of 'multiliteracies', which developed from this work, suggested that academics use the communication channels and media already employed by young people to help them engage with difference, including cultural difference. To enhance this engagement, the NLG also promoted work across disciplines and the blending of formal and informal learning. Such work was seen as *a necessary, dangerous and a transformative business* (Rennie, 2010: 87).

Student responses to this agenda

Here's one example of an organisation exploring these ideas with students to *ensure graduates can negotiate their way successfully in a world where knowledge boundaries are constantly shifting and reforming to create new challenges* (Devlin, 2008: 5).

In research at Northumbria University funded by the HEA Engineering Subject Centre (Montgomery, 2011), engineering students were asked 'What do you need from your higher education experience to solve engineering issues?'. By the second year, in response to this question, the students started to move beyond the subject-specialist knowledge on which they had focused in their initial year and to mention multidisciplinary and global knowledge and skills. This reflects elements of the approach identified above by the NLG as appropriate in good quality higher education.

This is surely true across all subject areas since the challenges facing today's students are global and *an increasingly interconnected and globalised world has necessitated a parallel interconnectivity within the curriculum* (Razbully and Bamber, 2008).

A whole organisational response

In the Melbourne Project in 2008, a whole institutional approach was introduced that included internationalisation as a central principle (see Devlin, 2008, and Newman, 2015 for more information). General degrees were introduced with compulsory elements to ensure a broad education before specialisms were taken at postgraduate level. The 2010 audit report stated:

> *On internationalisation, the University's plans to position itself as a fully globally engaged institution are progressively shaping activities and approaches, as seen in its encouragement of increased student mobility and international experiences within curricula.*
>
> (TEQSA, 2010)

The report goes on to commend some of the initiatives taken, such as the attention paid to the development of English language for *all* students, but also requires more attention to be given to intercultural relationships in the institution. This model is a fascinating attempt to transform the curriculum and continues to develop and be critiqued by academics and students alike.

TASK 1

Assessing your curriculum from an international perspective

Hopefully, the section above has given you food for thought, but we're not expecting you to be in a position to revolutionise your entire institution overnight, so let's look now at what the work covered so far in this chapter might mean at course level.

(Continued)

(Continued)

Consider the following questions in relation to a course on which you are teaching.

- Is there a dominant culture reflected in the course in terms of language, references, images, etc.?
- Does the course encourage students to be curious beyond the dominant culture?
- Does the course seek to address intercultural relations and prepare students for a global world to enhance their personal development and employability?

REFLECTIONS

You may be looking at the questions above and thinking 'but I teach a subject where there is no scope or time for any of this'. If so, maybe consider again the opening comments to the chapter about the way in which the world is moving towards interdisciplinary and dynamic 'knowledge' and what students need as they prepare to live and work in a global setting.

The professional and academic context

You could begin with a course team audit of module content from an international perspective – for example, checking whether assessment tasks encourage students to make international comparisons or references. Creating a context in which both you and the students seek to *hunt the assumptions* (Brookfield, 2017: 21) underlying your work can really encourage a critical perspective and foster creativity and diversity.

When you are planning a course, you could use an understanding of how the subject area (and the professions associated with it) relate to the global context. For example, in an undergraduate degree course in Education and Learning Support, education systems from a number of different countries are compared and critiqued. Flagging up research from across the world, exploring what counts as knowledge, and how academic writing and assessment differ widely, and using wide-ranging case studies and examples to illustrate your materials is a good way to start.

For some subjects, a single national perspective is dictated – for example, in professionally accredited courses such as nursing or physiotherapy. Here, students could be encouraged to develop an understanding of what factors have influenced practice in that national context, to explore and engage with other approaches in order to appreciate how and why practice may differ elsewhere. One example of this can be seen in Hazel Horobin's description of physiotherapy in India conducted on the floor – not on a couch – and with different patient and professional expectations (Horobin, 2015).

It's impossible to know the details of how your discipline is researched, taught and conceptualised everywhere in the world, but being alert to the cultural particulars of our own practice and concepts, including where the (necessary) limitations of our knowledge and perspectives lie, is part of an intellectually rigorous approach (HEA, 2017).

Supporting intercultural relationships

Research by Harrison and Peacock (2010) suggests that forging relationships and having empathy towards others is actually more important than knowing about them, while Glass and Westmont (2014) talk about the way in which intercultural activities within and outside of the directed curriculum encourage a sense of belonging which has a strong positive effect on academic achievement.

Here are seven initiatives used in many institutions to support intercultural work:

1. exchanges and placements abroad;
2. online or video conferencing with students in another country;
3. internationalisation at home, such as student tutor or mentoring;
4. support for the enhancement of cross-cultural communication skills for all students; language, culture and cross-cultural capability development for those taking part in international visits;
5. volunteering programmes for staff and students and for international students to engage with the local community;
6. existing initiatives from international student support, clubs and societies to be used to develop intercultural understanding;
7. engagement with and promotion of cultural events and competitions, with support from the Students' Union.

Working with 'international students'

You may have noticed that in this chapter we have placed quotation marks around any use of the term 'international students' – this is because we are all ultimately international. In this chapter, we use the term to talk about students who are not from the UK since that is the context in which we are writing. How, then, do we as teachers make the most of our diverse classrooms by enabling our 'international' students to fully engage and our 'home' students to interact and value the international perspectives these students could share with us? It begins with seeing difference as diversity and as something that can enrich the lives and learning of others (Hockings, 2010).

Janette Ryan (2011) talks about the need to support international students and home students involved in international work with what has been referred to as three levels of shock, and these can be a useful structure with which to consider your work in this area. Of course, teachers can also experience these shocks as they work in different contexts across the globe.

The first shock is in encountering a different language. It's important that teachers do not conflate lack of language proficiency with lack of ability because they don't understand the complexities of language learning and learning in a second (third or fourth) language. Colleagues in Departments for Teaching of English for Speakers of Other Languages can often support both students and teachers in addressing this.

The second shock is in operating in a different culture, and some of the suggestions in the first task can hopefully help with this. Students need time and space to interact with 'home students' who are receptive and welcoming.

Finally, there may be a different style of academia and conversations to be had around academic practice – citations, academic writing, etc. (although it's easy to make generalisations about cohorts of international students which are built on stereotypes rather than research into educational background).

Concern is often centred on a cohort of students. The following is a quote from a situational analysis written by an accountancy teacher concerned with Chinese students in his class.

> *The module cohort comprises of [sic] 50% Chinese students. These students face a significant language barrier, and also often appear reticent to answer questions or to ask for help even when they are struggling. They are often slow to attempt practical exercises but will then decline assistance when offered! Any hints or tips for addressing these issues, and improving matters would be gratefully received.*

So – how can we address these concerns creatively?

This teacher attended a session run by Chinese students who talked about their previous educational experiences and were able to open a dialogue with him about ways to work together on reshaping sessions to include all students. One thing they identified was that all students and teachers had different perspectives on their academic journey (the third 'shock' referred to above). The task below was developed to foster a common understanding of university processes – for example, the role of the academic, the use of the VLE, academic values, etc.

TASK 2

Ensuring that everyone can access the curriculum

Ask all your students to make two lists:

1. ranking the importance of various sources of information (tutor, VLE, handbook, etc.); and
2. showing where they would look for various pieces of information (lecture times, assessment details, etc.).

Get them to compare their responses in groups and discuss any differences arising.

REFLECTIONS

This activity may highlight differing expectations of a tutor's availability – for example, expectations of being able to ask questions in class or expecting academics to be able to wait around after class; differing expectations of where information can be found, as well as different levels of comfort with a VLE as a source of information and a lack of clarity around the roles of people who can provide information – for example, department administrative staff, personal tutor, etc. Once these are overt, you can start to discuss these expectations and how they can be managed.

Perhaps the words of Gu Mingyuan are the best with which to leave you.

The internationalization of education can be expressed in the exchange of culture and values, mutual understanding and a respect for difference ... The internationalization of education does not simply mean the integration of different national cultures or the suppression of one national culture by another culture.

(Gu Mingyuan, 2001: 105)

is for
JOY

HOW TO FIND IT IN TEACHING AND LEARNING

CHAPTER SUMMARY

This chapter is written from the heart. It seeks to find the joy missing from so many experiences of education today, both for the learners and for ourselves. The justification for this exploration lies in the way that joy can enhance learning. We look at a definition of joy which clearly shows the links between enjoyment and effective and creative teaching. After two personal accounts of individuals describing joyous moments as learners or teachers, we look at ways to replicate these in our own classrooms and the joy we may find in our own subject areas. After a brief look at some pitfalls in the quest for joy, we turn to happiness and revisit the links between happiness, joy and learning.

Introduction

> *Joy – the emotion of great delight or happiness caused by something good or satisfying.*
>
> (Urdang *et al.*, 1967)

There are few references to joy in the literature on teaching and learning in higher education. There is certainly research on student happiness –for example, the 'Investigating Happiness and the Doctoral Student Experience' project by Carol Taylor, Gill Adams and Esther Ehiyazaryan-White. But of joy there is little spoken in this context and we doubt this will come as much of a surprise to the reader who is currently working in higher education. For this reason, and because joy is a very personal feeling, much of this chapter is in the form of first-person narrative.

What is joy and why is it important in learning?

When we use the word colloquially, we may place joy in the territory of childhood – an exuberant feeling that does not belong in the serious world of the adult learner. What a loss! Cottrell (2016) writes of joy and happiness in the context of nursing education and seeks to define both. She describes joy as bringing intense insight, leading to a connection with others which can in turn bring transformation of the self, of being outwardly focused and associated with laughter, dancing and clapping. She lists freedom, resilience and happiness as some of the products of joy. Since so many of these terms link with desirable attributes for the learner, who would not want such an emotion in their classroom? There are also echoes here of Maslow's (1964) peak experiences and of Csikszentmihalyi (1990) on 'flow' and 'post-traumatic growth' (PTG). And when learning is a source of pleasure, learners will have an intrinsic motivation to study, a willingness to take risks and a desire to tackle challenges. All of this will improve a student's ability to learn.

What makes us joyful as learners and teachers?

Here are some reflections by a higher education teacher about a personal joyous learning experience.

JOY AND HAPPINESS IN THE YOGA CLASSROOM

I currently attend a yoga class where the teacher always creates a truly joyous atmosphere. I've been trying to pinpoint the ways in which she does this and to work out how I could transfer some of these approaches to a higher education context. Some things I've spotted are:

1. *a constant affirmation of where we are up to as individuals with our practice at that time, on that week;*
2. *a lack of judgement together with the entreaty to lay aside our self judgements and an encouragement to speak using positive language – for example, instead of pointing out that I have my left arm round my right shoulder instead of my right leg in the air, the teacher will wait till I see what I need to do or help me then say quietly, 'nicely adjusted';*
3. *the way the teacher thanks us for coming and thanks us for sharing our practice when we leave, often saying how much she has enjoyed it;*
4. *an invitation to express curiosity about thoughts, feelings, sensations so that each student becomes more present and aware of themselves;*
5. *equal attention to everyone in the room and to their individual learning experience so that each student knows they matter and feels validated;*
6. *activities designed to reduce stress such as breathing techniques.*

Together these really make you feel good about what you are doing and give you a lift and a sense of achievement even if you are much less flexible than you were three weeks ago.

So – is there anything here of use to us in a higher education rather than in an adult education setting and in a regulated, accredited provision rather than one that operates without external validation for the students?

The first point – that of affirmation – is about the teacher celebrating the progress made by students or groups, regardless of whether it meets some external standard – for example, 'I think we did some really good work here today' (Of course, it's worth noting that to affirm learning, one should have planned teaching so that there are opportunities for the students to evidence that learning, whether in a 200-strong lecture or an individual tutorial). The idea that we as teachers – and students as learners – bring different things on different days is useful too. You can accept that some days your students (and you) are carrying different baggage and may be doing their best in the circumstances. Creating a culture where whatever students contribute is greeted with joy and interest goes a long way to fostering a positive atmosphere and to bolstering the self-confidence of all involved.

The idea that all contributions in a teaching and learning situation are of value is a tough one in a world of standardised assessment and performance indicators. This includes the way we and our students view mistakes. Perhaps we should take a lesson here from our childhoods. Holt (1964) makes this point as he talks about babies and toddlers playing and experimenting and not being afraid of *failing* (although the fear of failure is internalised later on, once they start school). Dr Samuel West, the psychologist behind the Museum of Failure points out that *Innovation requires failure. Learning is the only process that turns failure into success* (West, 2017). This echoes the *growth* versus *fixed* mindset model pioneered by Dweck (2017).

This suggests that formative ('interim') assessment can be viewed more as appraisal – as a way of checking what's working and what isn't, rather than as a chance to fail. Perhaps this is an opportunity to 'forget your perfect offering', to see the cracks in our practice as a way of letting in the light (a nod to Leonard Cohen here) and the errors of our students as an opportunity to try another way. For more on this, see U is for Understanding.

On the next point – how many times have you thanked students for their contributions to and attendance at a session, and shared with them how much you enjoyed their input? On the occasions when we see this happening in our observations, there is a real feeling of welcome and an acknowledgment that this is a shared adventure and a voluntary one, which sets a positive note and builds the possibility of a joyous experience. This helps to build the community of practice of students and staff. And there are other ways to provide a welcoming atmosphere – chat to students a little before the start, greet them by name if possible, be happy that they are there, not frustrated about the ones who aren't.

The final observation from the yoga class is about the reduction of stress. Obviously, yoga classes are designed partly for this very purpose, but in any subject discipline, creating a calm, quiet atmosphere can be conducive to more effective learning (Postholm, 2013), although there may be times when you want to generate more of a buzz as well.

The following is another account of a joyous educational encounter.

JOY AND PRIDE IN THE MATHS CLASSROOM

When I was an adult education teacher, I often worked with people who felt that they were complete failures when it came to maths. One time I taught this student, Jenny, to add fractions. In spite of saying that she

(Continued)

(Continued)

hated fractions and had never understood them, she was determined not to give up. As she worked through some questions, I grinned at her and said 'Hey, Jenny, guess what? You're "doing" fractions!' We looked at each other, laughed and exchanged a high five, Jenny bursting with pride and pleased as punch.

Perhaps the lesson for higher education here is simply to notice more when learners 'get it' and to celebrate more overtly rather than rushing to the next thing. It's also about acknowledging personal goals within a subject area. In large group teaching, or when teaching small groups where you don't know the students very well, the teacher can still create a celebratory atmosphere – for example, when going through the answers of a quiz that the students have completed. 'Anyone improve on their score from last week? Well done!', or in asking students to share in small groups examples of recent study-related successes. In this way, effort and 'distance travelled' are valued and praised rather than the achievement of a set standard or 'natural' abilities, and the teacher and student alike can rejoice in progress made (Stan, 2012).

TASK 1

Think of a joyous learning or teaching situation that you have experienced. Identify anything you think contributed to this and see if there is a way you could transfer this to your practice.

REFLECTIONS

Steven Walk (2008) lists ways in which to create a joyous atmosphere. He's writing about schools but everything on his list could be transferred to higher education. He talks of:

- encouraging students to immerse themselves in a creative task;
- showing off student work so that the environment is full of inspiring research posters and other displays;
- going outside so that we allow opportunities to connect with the external environment (these could range from field trips to outdoor tutorials);

- allowing some time for learners to innovate and dream rather than having a prescribed curriculum for every minute;
- building in choice when possible – for example, learners researching topics that they have selected (Hoskins and Mitchell, 2015).

Joy in one's subject

As observers, we have often seen teachers light up with passion when they talk in class about their own research. Sharing this with students can bring the subject alive and engender a lifelong enthusiasm. As experts in our own subject disciplines, we are often filled with joy and excitement about a particular discovery or an interesting aspect. Indeed, writing this book together has given us real moments of joy as we craft our writing.

A note of caution: be careful that as you go into depth about something you love, make a note of whether you are taking your students with you. Are they as enraptured as you are, or are they still worrying about how to convert your lecture into the answers to their next exam?

Some pitfalls in the quest for joy

As you seek to be affirming, remember that this has to be genuine – students can spot insincerity a mile off. And there's a danger that too much praise can backfire. Students get complacent, or strive to obtain more praise, which means playing 'guess what's in the teacher's head' or other forms of 'gaming' – that is, surface learning – or a deficit model is inadvertently created in that an absence of praise is construed as criticism (Stan, 2012; Holt, 1964).

Not all learning can be joyous – different students will like different aspects of the subject. Pehaps this fact can be utilised by, for example, getting students to talk about which bits they love and why, and which not. We need to be honest about the hard graft and even, at times, the tedium of learning, especially when it's for uninspiring standardised assessments.

Joy is not the same as fun – though you may have fun when you are experiencing joy. The increasing focus on students as consumers (SAC) can mean that teachers rely too heavily on trying to make every session a bundle of laughs so that they get good evaluations, rather than so that the students are enabled to learn. Conversely, there is a danger that, in an increasingly marketised system, teachers *give the students what they need to pass* rather than rejoicing in knowledge for its own sake (Williams, 2003).

A colleague recently referred to be 'all tefloned up' as she taught. What she meant was that, because she had had a bruising experience recently with some students, she felt she needed a protective covering. Sadly, she explained, this led to an atmosphere of wariness rather than joy. It's really hard to function after a difficult teaching experience and we need to consider ways in which to reappraise situations of conflict, ideally with collegial support (Clara, 2017).

Further barriers to teacher joy include stress, limited time, unreasonable curriculum demands, and so on. Joylessness in teachers is not conducive to creating joyful learners (Noddings, 2003), and W is for Wellbeing looks at how we can better take care of ourselves and our students.

We've seen some great uses of humour in our observations over the years and these can at first glance create a positive, happy and relaxed classroom, but beware the humour that excludes. We have also seen jokes made which at best are culturally exclusive and at worst are used strategically to show solidarity and power by dominant groups (Rogerson-Revell, 2007).

And so to happiness ...

Cottrell (2016) makes some interesting comparisons between joy and happiness. The latter she sees as more long-lasting, something that we have more control over and as something more related to the growth of the self rather than connection with others. Could it be, then, that in creating the possibility of joy in our classrooms, we create an environment for happiness to grow? As noted above, so many of the characteristics that Cottrell describes as products of joy and happiness are exactly those we want to develop in our learners.

is for
KNOWLEDGE

HOW TO TRANSFORM, NOT TRANSMIT

CHAPTER SUMMARY

The writing of this chapter, and indeed of many of the chapters in this book, looked something like the following (only non-linear).

- Having discussed and decided the topic of 'Knowledge', we each went away and wrote something, accessing various notes, experiences, conversations, books and journal articles.
- Sharing and comparing our work, we diverged on some points and converged on others but eventually, realising we were headed in the same direction, we put together the chapter.
- At different times, we each of us experienced joy, frustration, despair, rage and excitement.
- We drafted, redrafted and redrafted again, batting the chapter from one to the other. Eventually, the final version emerged.

The point of the chapter, however, is that it is never really the final version. The learning, the making of connections, the development of knowledge (in this case, knowledge about knowledge) simply goes on, spreading and subdividing, forging new links, changing and transforming.

Introduction

This chapter is hooked on just three questions.

1. What do we mean by knowledge?
2. How do we think we access knowledge?
3. What does this have to do with creativity in our teaching?

If you want definitive answers, you won't get them, but if you trust us to explore these issues in a meaningful and thought-provoking way, read on.

TASK 1

Complete the following sentence:
    Teaching is {...}

REFLECTIONS

Try this with some colleagues – from your own subject discipline and from others if possible – and compare your answers.

Sometimes we begin our courses on learning and teaching in higher education by asking participants to complete this sentence, writing their responses on post-its or uploading them to an online pin board. Occasionally we put them into a word cloud, like the one in Figure K1.

Figure K1   Word cloud

Looking at the resulting wall of responses, the words 'transmit', 'transfer', 'deliver', 'knowledge' and 'subject' tend to pop up a lot, as well as the occasional appearances of 'share', 'enthusiasm' and 'passion'. This fits with the 'traditional' view of universities as being places of knowledge and of scholarship, where academics *pass on* their expertise (Akerlind, 2004).

Another conception of universities is as creators of highly employable graduates. This is not merely a recent concept. In 1554, Roger Ascham stated: *I know universities be instituted only that the realm may be served with preachers, lawyers and physicians* (O'Day, 2009: 79). While this might feel different from teaching an academic subject, many new teachers in vocational areas draw confidence from their knowledge of industry.

It's not surprising, then, that it's unsettling when we challenge people to define what they actually mean by 'knowledge', or to define 'how we come to know'. The question is whether, and to what extent, our views on knowledge and knowing shape our definitions of teaching and learning.

TASK 2

Here are two more questions for you to ponder. This time they relate to your own discipline. Is there a canon of knowledge that belongs to your subject? What's in it? You may wish to consult the Quality Assurance Agency (QAA) benchmark statements, which *describe what gives a discipline its coherence and identity* (QAA, 2017), but there may be things you also wish to add or remove.

REFLECTIONS

Revisit your answers to the above and consider the following additional questions.

- What did the canon look like 20 – or 200 – years ago? Will your subject discipline even exist in 20 – or 200 – years' time?
- Is knowledge in your subject disputed or set in stone?
- Is it discovered or invented? Ernest, for example, argues that *not only is mathematics fallible, but it is created by groups of persons who must*

(Continued)

(Continued)

> *both formulate and critique new knowledge in a formal 'conversation' before it counts as accepted mathematics* (1999), implying, therefore, that mathematical knowledge is, to a degree at least, invented.

- Is knowledge in your subject geographically, socially, culturally, politically and/or historically situated? Should it be?

And finally:

- How do your answers affect the way you teach your subject? For example, do you suggest to your students that there are other perspectives? Do you prepare them for possible challenges to the 'canon'? Or do you teach your discipline as if the canon of knowledge therein is sacred, engraved in tablets of rock?

REFLECTIONS

Here's a precis of the position of the authors of this book. No matter what the subject discipline is, we see knowledge as mutable and learning as a creative process, a joint enterprise with our students in which we negotiate shared meanings and look at ways to understand our values and beliefs, and how they shape the way we interpret the world.

There are many theorists on whom we can draw here. Bereiter and Scardamalia (2014: 35) took the concept of knowledge construction from the world of Business and applied it to Education.

> *Knowledge is the product of purposeful acts of creation and comes about through building up a structure of ideas (for instance, a design, a theory, or the solution of a thorny problem) out of simpler ideas.*

In addition to creativity, they see collaboration as key to the building of knowledge. Mezirow talks of transformative learning – that is, learning that

> *involves transforming frames of reference through critical reflection of assumptions, validating contesting beliefs through discourse, taking action on one's reflective insight, and critically assessing it.*

(Mezirow, 1997: 11)

What do these paradigms of knowledge and of learning look like in practice? The answer is messy, unpredictable, spontaneous, collaborative, creative, challenging, at times uncomfortable and at times joyful. In fact, however, in our roles as teacher educators in higher education, what we see again and again is the playing out of a tension between a prescribed, time-constrained content-heavy curriculum on one hand, and the development of opportunities for critical thinking and innovative problem-solving on the other (see Y is for Why). All too often, it seems, the latter loses out at the expense of the former.

'Two and two make four and there's an end to it'

At this point you may be thinking, 'but sometimes I simply need to teach facts'. How one arrives at the 'facts' may vary between students, arriving at the 'wrong fact' may be a really useful learning process. Even if you believe that we are here simply to lift the curtain on a world which is fixed and immune to value judgements, you can perhaps relate to a model of the curriculum that focuses not on delivering a product made of facts but also looks at the process of getting to them, since *In such a model, the community is not the path to understanding or accessing the curriculum; rather, the community is the curriculum* (Cormier, 2008).

To get practical – this may mean fewer slides with facts on and more slides with questions on. It means less of your voice and more of your students' voices in the room as they struggle with ways to understand the material and become a community of, for example, physicists. It means facilitating, nurturing and challenging – much more skilful tasks than simply 'delivering'.

Connections and nodes

Know-how and know-what is being supplemented with know-where (the understanding of where to find knowledge needed).

(Siemens, 2004)

This quotation, by George Siemens, forms part of a response to a fourth, somewhat unsettling, question: 'Has technology revolutionised the whole concept of knowledge?' Various metaphors and models have sprung up to explain how knowledge is created and shared via networks. One such example is Siemens's own theory of Connectivism (2004), where personal knowledge consists of a network, and learning is the process of making, nurturing and maintaining the connections between information sources.

TASK 3

Read the following quotation and answer the questions below.

The pipe is more important than the content within the pipe. Our ability to learn what we need for tomorrow is more important than what we know today. A real challenge for any learning theory is to actuate known knowledge at the point of application. When knowledge, however, is needed, but not known, the ability to plug into sources to meet the requirements becomes a vital skill. As knowledge continues to grow and evolve, access to what is needed is more important than what the learner currently possesses.

(Siemens, 2004)

To what extent might this be true within your own subject discipline? How is this reflected in the way it is learned and taught?

REFLECTIONS

For some of the teachers on our higher education course, subject content knowledge is at the centre of their curricula, often specified by external professional awarding bodies. It is worth considering, however, in what ways this knowledge might be accessed by students. Rather than operate in the belief that all course content must be 'transmitted' by the teacher, try to think of other ways for students to access what they need, thereby developing research, investigation and communication skills in the process.

New roots

Connectivism focuses on how the individual accesses learning through networks. As with its sister theory, social constructivism, learning is dynamic and knowledge is negotiated. And yet, in this age of information, some feel that an even more flexible model is needed. Drawing on the work of Deleuze and Guattari (1987), Cormier (2008) uses the metaphor of a rhizome – that is, a plant type that has no one root and can spread and multiply. Cormier points out that while it's easy to test some knowledge against 'the canon', newer online issues have overtaken existing truths and cannot be reviewed in this way.

The increasingly transitory nature of what is lauded as current or accurate in new and developing fields, as well as the pace of change in Western culture more broadly, has made it difficult for society in general and education in particular to define what counts as knowledge (Cormier, 2008). He goes on to argue that while social constructivist and connectivist pedagogies refer to learning by negotiation and as an organic process these approaches still assume a defined end to the learning, whereas in the future, learning may need to be viewed as more of an open-ended investigation. This really shakes up the notion of the 'expert academic'.

In less traditional curricular domains, then, knowledge creators are not accurately epitomised as traditional, formal, verified experts; rather, knowledge in these areas is created by a broad collection of knowers sharing in the construction and ongoing evolution of a given field. Knowledge becomes a negotiation (Farrell, 2001).

Sources of primary data are now available to all instantly for interpretation and analysis. A good example is that provided by the Europeana website. Traditional research methods mean that new ideas developed by 'experts' may be percolating for years before they are released. Wikis can offer a new way to peer review quickly and within a dynamic community, although further skills are required for this, such as the ability to critically appraise the work of others.

Burnett's work on virtual learning environments (VLEs) makes an interesting point about the way in which the internet allows for a more democratic 'ownership' of knowledge.

> *Reflecting work that has explored the diverse and potentially egalitarian learning communities that have evolved around everyday virtual spaces (Lankshear and Knobel, 2006), educational researchers and developers have seen possibilities for encouraging new kinds of relationships between learners and knowledge.*
>
> (Burnett, 2011: 246).

Burnett's research on identity and VLEs, however, reveals a rather passive relationship between her interviewees and the VLE rather than one of creativity and empowerment. Students exchange well-researched 'facts' in a professional and guarded manner as an obligation rather than using the space to explore new ideas and experiment. In contrast, different relationships formed on informal online networks, where learning can be, perhaps, more spontaneous, but is also less moderated. As teachers, we need to be aware of the identities our learners are constructing and encourage them to see themselves as knowledge participants and creators.

On a practical level, what does this narrative suggest? Perhaps more use of online research, collaboration, problem-defining and problem-solving, debate and sharing in sessions and much more openness to challenge from our students as co-creators of the material. More ideas are suggested by Jenkins *et al.* (2007) in different disciplines, when they refer to a research-oriented curriculum that emphasises the teaching of the processes of knowledge construction in the subject. Collaborative approaches to learning – for example, group work, learning sets, consultancy projects – are perceived as being crucial to a high-quality learning experience as they allow knowledge and understanding to be co-constructed and contested.

There is much talk in higher education about 'research-informed' teaching. What does this mean and what view of knowledge is implicit in research-based approaches? Nicholson (2015) in a review of some of the literature on this topic offers several definitions – for example, learning about research findings within the subject discipline; learning about how to carry out research, perhaps as part of a project or dissertation module, and learning through the process of research, perhaps through a process of enquiry or a problem-based learning approach. It is in the last example that students have the opportunity to construct – and be transformed by – knowledge in their field. Furthermore,

> *By also teaching students to become researchers, universities can equip students with the skills they need to acquire additional knowledge for themselves, even after their course has ended.*
>
> (Nicholson, 2015: 45)

This links with Siemens's idea, as described earlier, of the pipe, where knowing how to access and construct (and here we would add, critically evaluate) knowledge in the future is more important than the current content. The 'students as researchers' approach also supports communication skills and can be seen as a process of *legitimate peripheral participation* in the research community (Lave and Wenger, 1991: 27).

Objections

'But students don't want all this negotiating the truth and enquiry-based learning – they just want what they need to know for the exam. That's what they see themselves having paid for us to give them.'

Tipping away the idea that we as teachers can pour knowledge into the empty vessels of our students may be a creative act based on exciting current research into learning, but it is completely at odds with the 'students as consumers' (SAC) concept of higher education (see X is for Expectations for more on this).

> *the SAC approach is concerning for universities, who do not traditionally regard education as a product or service, as it is said to create a 'conservative status quo' mentality; for what is there left to learn, when you already know it in order to demand it?*
>
> (Lesnik-Oberstein, 2015 in Bunce *et al.*, 2016: 1959)

So our job becomes again to bridge the chasm between the idea of *buying* higher educational knowledge as opposed to *engaging* with it.

Conclusions

In this chapter, we hope to have disrupted traditional notions of knowledge and of knowing, and considered the implications for the ways in which learning and teaching take place. Perhaps the job of both teacher and learner is to negotiate what knowledge in higher education really means, and to accept that it is being created all the time, and not only in the universities.

is for
LISTENING

HOW TO ATTEND TO YOUR STUDENTS AND INFORM YOUR PRACTICE

CHAPTER SUMMARY

In this chapter, we use 'listening' in its broadest sense – that is, cultivating a consciousness of what's going on in a taught session. We explore the idea of teaching reflectively, developing an awareness not just of your students but also your own behaviour, feelings and thoughts, and developing a repertoire of possible responses from which to choose. We also consider the significance of being sensitive to the sociopolitical forces at play in any teaching situation.

Introduction

Are you really 'present' in your teaching? Do you ever get so caught up in your subject or the assessment requirements that you forget to check whether the students are learning?

Being attentive

In his book *Researching Your Own Practice: The Discipline of Noticing* (2002), Professor John Mason of the Open University asserts that all acts of teaching involve 'noticing'. This could be, for example, observing your students' progress and what they need at that point to achieve their learning objectives, or it could be becoming aware of some aspect of your own behaviour that is having an unintended consequence, such as speaking too fast and then finding out that no one has understood your instructions. Working to improve one's 'noticing' skills as a teacher is an essential part of becoming more expert, where noticing involves being sensitive and 'present' or 'awake'. If this notion suggests to you some of the philosophies of Buddhism and of 'mindfulness', this is no coincidence. Mason himself identifies connections between his work and such perspectives, referring to texts on mindfulness such as those by Langer (see, for example, Langer and Moldoveanu, 2000). Later in this chapter we critique and then build on his model. First, however, let's examine some aspects of it more closely in a higher education context.

The expert teacher is attentive to the teaching and learning situation, able to assess what the students need and can draw on a repertoire of possible appropriate actions. The novice teacher, by comparison, struggles not only to notice, but to act accordingly (Mason, 2002: 2). We discuss some possible barriers to noticing (or 'listening') and our responses below. Some are described in *Researching Your Own Practice: The Discipline of Noticing*, and others have come from our own observations.

I can't change what I don't notice.

We need to become more alert to what is going on when we think we're teaching. As Mason says, this takes time and discipline. To this we would add that what you don't notice, others will. An obvious source of feedback is your students. Find ways to collaborate with them to improve teaching (and learning), but draw on your own professional expertise as well, and that of others.

But there's too much going on. How can I keep track of what's happening?

You change what you can. It's work in progress and will always be so – your whole career. The authors of this book have over fifty years of teaching experience between them, and we're still learning to listen and to respond. One way to improve practice in this respect is to have trusted colleagues come and observe you, with a predetermined focus such as 'Can you check if student A is joining in? I'm worried that the pace is too fast for her.' You can't listen to everything while you're teaching, but a critical friend who is observing has the luxury to 'hear' more.

Another option is to video or record yourself (request permission from the students to do this, explain why it's helpful for you and what will happen to the recording) and play it back afterwards. There is even hardware available that can track you and swivel the camera to you as you move around the room. However, being filmed, recorded or observed may affect the students and the dynamics in the room, so be aware of this.

I'm anxious about changing what I do. What if it goes wrong?

We tend to develop habits and rituals as a way of managing the often-overwhelming demands of the role, slipping into auto-pilot, staying in our comfort zones (Mason, 2002: 8). It can be intimidating to break out of this, so start with something small.

Even if I notice something, how do I know what to do about it?

Once something has been noticed, the teacher needs to be able to have at their fingertips an array of choices that might better facilitate learning (2002: 9). You can develop your own personal library of strategies by talking to or observing peers; listening to your students and trying things out, reading (papers, books, tweets, blogs) and hearing others speak on similar topics.

I've been told that I can't deviate from the slides and the script because the other seminar groups need to have the same experience.

Teaching equitably does not mean teaching everyone in the same way. Teachers need to use their professional judgement to adapt teaching in ways that will facilitate learning. This will be different for different groups and individuals. You are also unique and will bring different benefits to your students from your colleague in the next room even if you have identical material to 'deliver'.

The scope of reflection

You listen. You reflect. You decide on a course of action. You try it out. You listen. You reflect. You decide on a course of action. You try it out ...

This cycle of experiential learning was popularised by theorists such as Kolb and Fry (1975), and inspired by Dewey (1933). Although Dewey's theories have, like Mason's, been compared with some of the teachings of

Buddhism (Stroud, 2007), others have criticised the 'Western-centric' focus evident in the work of both Dewey and that of Kolb and Fry, along with the isolation of the individual practitioner, the idea that the process involves discrete 'stages' and what one does with knowledge thus gained (Smith, 2001, 2010).

The fictional tale that follows is an illustration of how the *scope of reflection* (a phrase adopted by Valli, 1993 in Mason, 2002: 15) can be broadened out to encompass a broader, more holistic perspective. The paragraphs are given letters for ease of discussion afterwards. You may recognise parts of yourself in the main character at the beginning of the story (we certainly did).

SIMON AND THE LEARNING OUTCOMES

a) There was once a university teacher called Dr Simon Harker, who always started his sessions by reading the students his intended learning outcomes. 'By the end of the session today, you will be able to critique a research paper', he would announce. Some days it might be 'analyse a case study', on others, perhaps 'find a solution to the problem of ...' and so on. You get the idea.

b) At the end of each session, Simon would revisit his list of learning outcomes, since this, he believed, was standard good practice. True, his students were often busy packing up their belongings and getting ready to leave by this point, but if he rattled off the outcomes quickly, he could usually finish the list by the time they were out of the door.

c) One day, as he raced through the list of objectives at the close of the session, he faltered slightly. He listened to what the students were doing. They aren't paying attention, he thought in frustration. What can I do?

d) 'Wait a minute!' he called out to them. 'Please sit down, we still have a couple of minutes left.' Once they were seated again, he carried on. 'Who thinks they've achieved outcome number one on the list?' he asked them. 'Thumbs up if you're confident, down if you're not!' There was a moment of silence, and then, glancing at each other self-consciously, the students began to give their verdicts. From this, it seemed, at least half the room did not understand the basics of the topic being taught.

e) Afterwards, Simon thought about how he might ascertain the level of understanding of the students at an earlier point in the session. He built in more opportunities for the students to contribute, so that he – and they – could assess their progress towards the outcomes. Having tried his new plan, he reflected on the impact of his interventions.

(Continued)

(Continued)

f)   Using formative assessment is obviously the way forward, he surmised. But do the students understand *why* they are learning this stuff? Who decides the session outcomes anyway? Why can't they be student-negotiated? Who exactly are the stakeholders in relation to what these students are supposed to be learning? What is it that we are preparing them for?

g)   The following session, instead of learning outcomes, Simon began with a question, a problem to solve. 'Where might you see this problem? What information might we need to solve it?' he asked the students. 'And what skills?' He set up a shared document online and gave the students access to record their suggestions. These were collated and negotiated, until the students had arrived at a set of possible learning outcomes: 'To solve this problem we need to be able to ...'. At the end of the session, Simon returned to the original question. Could the students now solve it? If so, then clearly their collaborative and negotiated outcomes had been achieved.

What types of 'listening' and reflection were taking place here? Paragraphs (c) and (d) would be what Schön (1983) describes as 'reflection-in-action' – noticing, deciding and acting in the moment. As Mason points out, a supply of fresh alternatives is needed for this, something that can be gained from experience.

Paragraph (e) matches Schön's 'reflection-on-action' (1983), where events are reviewed and approaches revised once the event has taken place. For some theorists, no further input is needed here, but we would advocate connecting with a community of practice, with people who understand and care about the integrity and 'rootedness' of the strategies attempted with students, and who value the range of experiences they bring with them.

Paragraph (f) widens the scope of the reflection somewhat further. This is what Brookfield (2017) describes as *hunting assumptions*, questioning the very premises of phenomena that we take for granted. Mason, who calls this *reflecting outwards*, suggests focusing more on *inwards* reflection, as our own actions are things that we *can* change. However, the personal and the socio-political contexts are interlinked. The one affects the other, and while teachers in higher education may be constrained in their actions, that does not mean they cannot critique the status quo. For example, as Mason himself observes,

trying to be more efficient and effective in 'covering' a curriculum has a much more narrow scope than considering how the curriculum comes to be specified and what economic and political interests it serves.

(2002: 15)

From this it can be seen that personal professional practice cannot be separated from the wider sociopolitical context. Challenging assumptions may not have an immediate or obvious effect on teaching and learning, but the process of doing so keeps us rooted in pedagogical integrity. It reminds us of how things *could* be, and it has the potential to bring about change beyond the immediate context (see, for example, Argyris and Schön (1974) on *double-loop learning*).

TASK 1

Table L1 Observations/reflections on students in a group

What's been noticed	Immediate response	Later thoughts
Three students sitting at the back are all looking at their phones. I feel my temper rise.	Check in with how I'm feeling, then consider my options: • let it go; • challenge them in a friendly, non-confrontational way (they may be looking something up that's relevant to the session); • suggest we all have a 5-minute 'check your phone' break, or • introduce a task that involves everyone in the room.	Did I set ground rules with this group? Where are they? What did we agree about the use of phones in sessions? What were the power dynamics in that session? Did I treat the students like children? How did they perceive me? How can I negotiate and manage the students' expectations regarding phone use? Can I find a way to actively use phones in the session – e.g. setting up a Twitter wall or doing an online quiz? I need to look at some of the literature around young people and phones, and the benefits/pitfalls of using phones in learning and teaching. This includes asynchronous and off-site learning too. Are we really exploiting this resource as much as we could?
The students who have joined the course in the second year, from the 'feeder' college, are having difficulty keeping up.	Slow down pace, ask more questions, get students to explain the session so far to each other. Set some questions/tasks for everyone to be getting on with, and invite those	Flip the learning so that students access the session materials (including online ones such as video presentations) beforehand. Then the session can be used to troubleshoot. Discuss the issue with colleagues. Should extra support be offered? Is it viable to run a summer school/bridging course?

(Continued)

(Continued)

What's been noticed	Immediate response	Later thoughts
	who are still confused to come and talk to you at the front.	Read some of the literature on foundation courses and college–university partnerships.
		Look at other models of undergraduate education that are less didactic – e.g. students as 'producers' (Neary and Winn, 2009).

Table L1 shows some example scenarios and related reflections.

Think of something you have noticed in your own teaching practice. How did you respond and what were your reflections afterwards? Did you question any assumptions? What did you learn? What might you do differently? Are your choices potentially rooted in good practice and pedagogical integrity?

What happens when you are successful in noticing the impact of an aspect of your practice and you manage to disrupt your usual routines and try something different, and it 'works'? Mason describes these as *creative moments*:

in those few brief moments when we feel we have participated in an informed choice, when we have acted freshly and appropriately, there is a sense of freedom, of meaning, of worthwhileness and self-esteem. It is these moments of personal freedom which keep us going.

(2002: 8)

You may just find that such moments awaken and refresh your students, too.

is for
METALEARNING

HOW YOUR STUDENTS CAN LEARN TO LEARN

CHAPTER SUMMARY

Knowing how to learn is seen by many as a key skill for the twenty-first century (Dumont *et al.*, 2012). In this chapter, we introduce the concept of metalearning – taking the opportunity to deconstruct the myth of 'learning styles' along the way. We then look at the value of metalearning and describe some approaches and principles about how to enable students to engage with this process.

Most of the chapter is written in the form of a dialogue between a practitioner and a theorist (P and T respectively). We hope that by the end of the chapter they find that they can assimilate each other's perspective.

TASK 1

As you read, keep your own context and discipline in mind. How does the content of this chapter relate to your students and your subject? What can you do to encourage reflection on metalearning in your curriculum?

Dialogue 1: The meaning of metalearning and the vanquishing of learning styles

P: *So, what exactly is metalearning all about then?*

T: The prefix 'meta' from the Greek, means 'after', 'beyond' or 'behind'. Examples include metaphysics, meta-analysis, metafiction ...

P: *Metamorphosis, metacentre, metabolism, metatarsal ...*

T: Yes, that's right. If you were to investigate these terms, you'd find a common theme in their meanings – that of the metalevel.

P: *Which is ... ?*

T: A metalevel is defined as *a level which is above or beyond other levels* (OUP, 2017).

P: *So ... metalearning is kind of like ... super-learning?*

T: Yes! Before we go further, though, I'd like to ask you a question. How would you define 'learning'? What images or words come into your head?

P: *Well, learning can happen on all sorts of levels. You can be transformed by it, empowered by it, even. Learning allows you to see things differently. It enables you to do things you couldn't do before. Learning with others is a way of building knowledge ...*

T: Exactly. I couldn't agree more. Sadly, not everyone has the same idea, and instead they see 'learning' as something that is done 'to' you. But what if you could step back from the process of learning and take a good look at it? This is where the term 'metacognition' comes in – that is, an awareness of, and regulation of, your own cognitive activities (Flavell, 1976 in Butler, 2015: 294). A decade later, Biggs (1985 in Watkins, 2015: 323) defined metalearning as *being aware of and taking control of one's learning.*

P: *Oh, so is it about learning styles then? You know, where you take some sort of test or quiz to find out what your 'style' is. There's VAKT, Honey and Mumford ...*

T: Aaaargh!

P: *Are you OK?*

T: Yes, it's just the phrase 'learning styles'. Don't be led down this path! Many of these learning style models have largely been discredited (see, for example, Coffield *et al.*, 2004). More recently, a large group of neuroscientists also spoke out against the use of learning styles approaches in Education (see Weale, 2017). And another objection to learning styles is that this whole genre is dominated by a psychologised view of learners and learning.

P: *Meaning what?*

T: Learning styles models and questionnaires are based on the assumption that learning happens in a vacuum, and that how you learn can be divorced from what and where you're learning (Coffield, 2012). What's more, the tests themselves lack validity, are over-simplistic and, ironically, don't even allow you to complete them in your 'preferred mode', being predominantly textual–visual in nature. And, even if it was true that students had one preferred and most effective way of learning, failing to expose a group to many approaches would eclipse any opportunities for them to learn in other ways.

P: *OK, I get it! You don't like learning styles! But you know, for some students, finding out their 'learning style' is really liberating. It's like someone telling them, 'It's not your fault you failed your GCSE Maths exam three times – you were just taught in the wrong way!'*

T: Yes, and that empowerment is important. Bekkering (2017) says that the danger of debunking learning styles is that teachers *neglect individual differences* instead of using them as an opportunity to improve learning – what we call 'differentiation'. 'Learning styles' approaches may lead us down the wrong path, but a 'one-size-fits-all' philosophy doesn't help either, as illustrated by your GCSE Maths example.

P: *What does help, then, according to the theorists?*

T: I suspect you already know from your own practice. You can read about some alternative approaches elsewhere in this book – for example, in V is for Visuals or H is for Whole. But metalearning can help too, and especially in terms of empowering learners.

P: *Hey, I just had a thought – is there such a thing as 'meta-teaching'? Being aware of and taking control of one's teaching?*

T: That's an interesting idea! I think you'd better read L is for Listening, about teachers 'noticing' and acting on their practice (Mason, 2002).

P: *OK, will do. But in the meantime, back to metalearning ...*

Dialogue 2: Why metalearning is a good thing and what it might look like

P: *So why encourage metalearning and how do you do it?*

T: Chris Watkins makes a good case for metalearning when he says, *One of the most curious things about classrooms is how little they focus on learning*, meaning that, in many education systems across the globe, *learners' experiences as learners are hidden*, since most of the activity that takes place tends to be teacher-driven (Watkins, 2015: 321).

P: *I know what you mean. A lot of the learning is reduced to 'guess what's in the teacher's head?'...*

T: ... which of course is a lot easier if you understand the culture that the teacher is coming from. Meanwhile, a related problem is that students' own conceptions about the nature of learning vary hugely, and this in itself can lead to ineffective learning (Ning and Downing, 2012; Watkins, 2015).

P: *Students with completely different ideas about what learning is and no space to discuss this in formal educational settings? Bad combination.*

T: Yes, indeed. Ning and Downing (2012), among others, found that if you design metalearning activities into your curriculum, this can improve students' approaches to learning and thus, potentially, their academic performance. This this is particularly true for those with previous negative experiences and limited conceptions of learning (e.g. memorisation, surface learning, fixed mindsets, and so on).

P: *I can see the benefits, especially for the ones that struggle when they get to higher education. So how do you design 'metalearning' into your curriculum?*

T: In spite of a proliferation of *learning inventory questionnaires* (e.g. Meyer and Norton, 2004), there's no single, universal approach. I can, however, give you a few general principles.

THE THEORIST'S PRINCIPLES FOR EXPLORING AWARENESS AND CONTROL OF LEARNING WITH STUDENTS

You can't 'teach' metalearning in a didactic way. It's a contradiction in terms. What you can do, however, is build in opportunities for students to develop their awareness. It's not simply acquiring study skills. It's about transformation.

To develop their metacognitive skills, students need agency – that is, they need to be able to exercise choice over their learning (Butler, 2015). This includes finding and defining problems as well as deciding how to respond to pre-set problems or questions (Dumont *et al.*, 2012). It's important, therefore, to include a focus on experiential learning.

To exercise agency, students need not only to have the appropriate language, but to own that language. This can be achieved by *remembering, discussing and reflecting on stories of yourself as a learner* (Watkins, 2015: 325).

Metalearning is a process, not a product. It's ongoing – observing yourself, describing, reflecting, planning, evaluating. It's non-linear.

P: *You know what? I think I already do a lot of this. Last time my lot completed a formative assessment, I got them to share how they approached it. I used questions to probe a bit deeper, and we discussed any issues people had experienced. Then, they all shared their reflections on a virtual message board, commenting on each other's posts.*

T: Yes, I can imagine the sort of thing ... (T visualises examples from different subjects, along the lines of Figure M1). Go on!

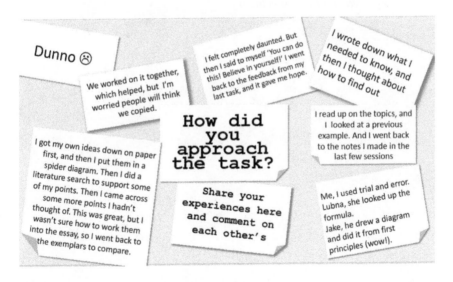

Figure M1 Message board

P: *So when they get the next task, they can each use this as a basis to plan, monitor and review their progress (Watkins, 2015: 327), as a blog, say. I'm thinking of getting their input into the design of the next task as well ...*

T: I'd love to know how that goes. You know, it's like being on a journey, and every so often you turn around and look back at the way you've come, and you think about how you overcame obstacles and what you did to help yourself, and look ahead, and you plan for the next stage of the journey (including deciding which way to go, or whether to go back and revisit any points you passed on the way). And the cycle repeats.

P: *You know, it's like being on a journey, and every so often you turn around and ... Hang on, didn't you just say that?*

T: I did.

P: *We sound like we're one and the same person!*

T: Perhaps we are, and this is an internal dialogue.

P: *No way! But you see what this means? If you and I are part of the same person, that means it's possible to be a theorist and a practitioner at the same time!*

T: Which means it's also possible for the readers of this chapter!

P: *Phew, d'you think that's our bit done?*

T: I expect so. They're bound to have closed the book by now.

P: *Cuppa tea? I'll put the kettle on ...*

is for
NO ONE EXCLUDED

HOW TO CREATE ENVIRONMENTS THAT ENABLE EVERYONE

CHAPTER SUMMARY

In this chapter we begin by questioning our everyday practices and problematising some of the discourses around who is 'included' and who is 'excluded' in higher education. Going on to examine some of the processes of labelling and potentially stigmatising specific groups of students, we focus on the term 'Black and Minority Ethnic' (BME) students as an example. Finally, following our argument that 'inclusion' is not an afterthought or an 'add-on', we end by visualising an environment where 'difference' is normalised (Baglieri and Knopf, 2004) and higher education pedagogy is about teaching students and co-constructing knowledge with them, not just about teaching subject knowledge in ways that may also homogenise students.

Introduction

In our original outline for this book, we had a different title and topic for Chapter N. However, then people asked us where the 'chapter on inclusion' was. 'The whole book is the chapter on inclusion!' we replied. For us, 'inclusive' practice is synonymous with 'creative' practice. We feel that the whole point of 'good' teaching is to find new ways to reach all our students and support them to learn, and an ever-changing, non-linear, messy, discursive and dynamic process it is, too. But somehow, at some point, this chapter emerged. It has fewer direct, practical teaching ideas than some of the other parts of the book. Instead, the focus is more on overarching policies and themes, and on personal and professional principles of practice.

First, however, we're going on an *assumption* hunt (Brookfield, 2017).

TASK 1

What you see and hear depends a good deal on where you are standing (Lewis, 1955).

Think of a session that you have taught recently. What assumptions were implicit in your choice of approach? Were these reasonable assumptions or not?

REFLECTIONS

We believe that everyone has expectations and assumptions about how people should 'behave' or 'perform' at university: administrators, researchers, teachers and students alike, as well as those outside the sector. Anecdotal examples of possible assumptions may include:

- students can sit and listen for long periods;
- teachers are called 'lecturers';
- students get drunk and have lots of parties.

To an extent, everyone performs to their assigned roles, behaving as they think they're expected to, following well-worn rituals and procedures (a process well documented by theorists such as Bourdieu, Butler and Goffman). But what if, as a student, you don't fit your assigned role? What if you're not even sure what the role entails? What if you can't make a 9.30 am tutorial because of caring responsibilities or you don't join in social events because drinking culture is alien to you?

The danger is that the student starts to think it's they who are the problem, not the institution or the culture (Miller, 2016). Thus, if a student struggles to engage with the content of a session and becomes a non-attender, the teacher can go unchallenged ('If you never came for 3 months no one would know,' says a Law student in Maughan, 2011). Individuals who don't fit the mould of the 'traditional' student are some-times assigned new, stereotypical roles such as 'weak' or 'lazy' (Maughan, 2011). In this way, discourses about what constitutes a 'good' student and what constitutes a 'poor' one can serve to exclude some students from educational success (for an example of this from a different educational phase, see Bradbury, 2014). This in turn links with the idea of 'othering' in terms of the abuse of power and knowledge, which can happen as groups form identities and, by definition, exclude others (Foucault, 1977).

The excluded and the excluding

So who is being 'othered', or excluded, and who is doing the excluding? There is a yawning trap that lies before anyone seeking to answer this question because the premise suggests a deficit model within which we can list the 'others' as those who fail to fit the mainstream community of the classroom. If 'inclusion' means welcoming those who have been historically excluded, then

Who has the authority or right to 'invite' others in? And how did the 'inviters' get in? Finally, who is doing the excluding? It is time we both recognize and accept that we are all born 'in'!

(Asante, 1996)

It's important to recognise that, while the contexts in which we teach are defined by power relationships in the wider world, we also play a part in defining 'the normal student' and 'the normal teacher' – that is, those on the inside. After all, *the idea of a norm is less a condition of human nature than it is a feature of a certain kind of society* (Davis, 2006: 3). There is always the danger of thinking that if we just had 'good, normal' students, our lives as teachers would be so much easier. But this translates into an assumption that our students need to change who they are even if they are comfortable in that identity. As Mrs Winterson, mother of Jeanette so aptly put it, *Why be happy, when you could be normal?* (Winterson, 2012). The 'normal' higher education student is the one in front of you right now.

Similar considerations apply to the concept of the 'non-traditional' student, where Widening Participation policy determines who can be assigned such a label (Burke, 2012: 53). Legislation also plays a role. The UK Equality Act (2010), for example, lists nine defining 'characteristics' of groups that come under its protection: age, disability, gender reassignment, marriage and civil partnership, pregnancy and maternity, race, religion or belief, sex and sexual orientation. But there are other disadvantaged groups who do not fall under the Act – for example, 'working-class' white boys (see, for example, Baars *et al.*, 2016 and Rubin *et al.*, 2014 for a deconstruction of this particular label).

The bad news, however, is that if as a student you find yourself falling into one or more of the categories such as those listed above, you're likely to be disadvantaged during your spell in higher education and beyond. But rather than rushing headlong into UK university entry, achievement and employment statistics (which you can access yourself – along with global comparisons – through organisations such as the Equality Challenge Unit, the National Union of Students, Universities UK and the National Audit Office), let's pause and reflect on some of the ways in which students (or prospective students) are categorised in the data.

Classifying and ordering

TASK 2

1. Write down a list of the ways in which you and/or others categorise your students. What kinds of labels are they assigned?
2. How would you categorise yourself?

The trouble with assigning labels is that it often assumes a binary classification ('white' versus 'non-white', 'male' versus female', and so on). Various writers and activists have challenged such binary analyses, and this has given rise to a number of related academic disciplines such as Critical Race Theory, Queer Theory, Gender Studies, Feminist Theory, Women's Studies and Disability Studies (also Fat Studies, Indigenous Studies, Mad Studies, Crip Theory and other emerging disciplines). In Critical Social Theory in general, critical thinking can be defined as

being able to identify, and then to challenge and change, the process by which a grossly iniquitous society uses dominant ideology to convince people this is a normal state of affairs.

(Brookfield, 2005: viii)

For introductions to some of these debates, we suggest the following: Mallet and Runswick-Cole (2014) on notions of ability and disability, and Somekh and Lewin (2011) on Feminist Theory, Critical Race Theory and Queer Theory.

A key point arising from many of these debates is that labels such as those in the Equality Act and beyond have been imposed on to individuals and groups by others – they are not necessarily categories that people have chosen themselves to identify with. And a related point is that, when discrimination occurs, it is on the grounds of *the perceptions by others* of these categories.

A final comment to make here is that we all inhabit multiple identity positions, which suggests that the analysis of data based on single (or even dual) assigned categories does not adequately account for *the interconnections between different social identities, especially between collective groups of minorities and the systems of oppression and discrimination with which they live* (Mallet and Runswick-Cole, 2014: 99).

This is not to say that we should ignore statistics based on single social identities – far from it. These are warnings that inequality in HE is alive and well, and must be tackled. The risk, however, is that we then focus on these categories at the expense of everything (and everyone) else, and this carries its own dangers. In the next section we illustrate this by focusing on a particular group and a specific issue currently being debated in HE in the UK.

'White students and the attainment advantage'

Here we'd like to consider the assigned group identity of BME students (and thus, by default, their white counterparts – hence the heading of this section), including the homogenising effect of the 'BME' label and the disaggregation of this data. First, however, some headline statisitics. The basis for the current debate about BME students can be illustrated by the 2015 Equality Challenge Unit national student equality data report for HE (Equality Challenge Unit, 2015), which found that, in England in 2013/14, 76.3 per cent of white students achieved a first or 2.1 in their degree, compared with 60.4 per cent of BME students. Although the gap has narrowed marginally compared to the previous year, this is still a highly disturbing statistic, and universities have, rightly, galvanised themselves in terms of readiness to address it (see, for example, McDuff and Barefoot (2016) who describe the work being done at Hertfordshire University and Kingston University). What concerns us, however, is (a) labels such as 'BME' and (b) the dangers of the deficit model which we perceive to be implicit in some of the discourses about this topic. Regarding the BME label, disaggregation of the data (Equality Challenge Unit, 2015) shows some considerable differences according to ethnic group as well as in relation to subjects studied, suggesting a far more complex picture than assumed. Meanwhile, in relation to discourse, the constant use of the term 'attainment gap' suggests to us an athletes' sprint, where the students in the 'white' category are crossing the finishing line, while the so-called 'BME' ones come up behind, hopelessly trying to catch up (also dotted around at various points on the track are other 'disadvantaged' students such as the disabled, mature, part-time and poor). All of this suggests that it is the students who are the 'problem', not the universities – in other words, the very 'yawning trap' that we referred to earlier in this chapter. These fears of over-generalisation and a deficit model of certain groups of students are documented in Miller (2016), along with the danger of students internalising attainment gap issues, leading to low self-efficacy and poor performance. It is this that we consider in the next section.

Attaching labels to under-represented groups in higher education in association with discourses of attainment gaps poses the potential danger of 'stereotype threat' – that is, *being at risk of confirming, as a self-characteristic, a negative stereotype about one's social group* (Steele and Aronson, 1995 : 797). However, all is not lost.

> *What is exciting about these stereotype threat experiments is the revelation that the impact of stereotypes can be weakened or eliminated by material presented immediately before performance is measured. So combating the effect of stereotypes in the classroom does not require decades of social change, only that teachers, resources and learning environments tell learners that they can succeed.*
>
> (Holloway, 2013: 263)

This is not just true of 'BME' learners, but all learners. In her interview with students from BME groups, Stevenson (2012) found that:

> *In relation to receiving targeted support for BME students, however, the students interviewed were almost wholeheartedly against it. They felt that singling them out for support smacked of inadvertent racism, even where students recognised that they needed extra help. Rather they wanted support mechanisms to be available to all students, but for those mechanisms to be more diverse and varied, with staff reaching out to help those students reluctant to access mainstream support.*
>
> (2012: 15)

This is why we don't have a chapter in this book entitled 'BME students', or one entitled 'Disabled students', or one entitled 'Poor students', and why we resisted initially having a chapter on 'inclusion', as if all the other chapters were for the apparently white, heterosexual, cis male, middle-class, able-bodied 'mainstream' students and the 'inclusion' chapter for all the rest.

Inclusion is about everyone, but the question remains as to how universities repay their 'educational debt', not just to those students who are labelled 'BME', but to all those who are failing to reach their full potential or to thrive in the HE environment. Examples of good practice in this respect from a number of different UK universities can be found in Hooper (2016). Below, we consider the possibility of developing a learning culture where 'difference', rather than 'sameness', is the cultural norm.

Normalising difference

When observing teaching and learning in sessions where the students are predominantly from groups that are under-represented in the wider academy – for example, mature students or those on foundation degrees – we have witnessed some rich and creative activities. Traditional lecture-style approaches are put to one side for the simple reason that there is no such thing as a traditional student. Difference is normalised, a phrase used by Baglieri and Knopf (2004). Although writing in the context of school pupils with learning disabilities, their recommendations have relevance for the HE sector too. Employing a Vygotskian framework and influenced by the critical pedagogy of Freire, the authors describe an English lesson where students are asked to read and respond to a text.

> *They may choose to read aloud to each other, for example, or listen to a recording so that even students who do not read proficiently can gain access to the text and engage in discussion and reflective activities. Student responses may also be enacted in various ways, such as illustration, discussion, performance and writing ... the use of this model allows and encourages multiple ways to participate and also reinforces the value of difference in the classroom and society. In this way, difference is reconstructed as 'normal' in the classroom community.*
>
> (2004: 529)

It is not too much of a stretch of the imagination to envisage such practices in higher education, too. A description of a similar approach for a mathematics lesson can be found in Spurr *et al.* (2013). As discussed in A is for Action, the role of the teacher is paramount, teaching responsively and flexibly, with grace, creativity and respect. Further, evidence-based approaches that embrace and celebrate 'difference' can be found elsewhere in this book.

One of the recommendations in Stevenson's report (2012: 17) on BME students' experiences is *a greater diversity of approaches to LTA (learning, teaching and assessment) practices*. For us, diversity in 'LTA' approaches and creative teaching go hand in hand. Creative teaching is good teaching, is inclusive teaching. If you don't believe us, read the rest of these chapters, try out some of the ideas and find out for yourself.

is for
OCCUPATIONS

HOW TO NAVIGATE THE RELATIONSHIP
BETWEEN HE AND EMPLOYMENT

CHAPTER SUMMARY

This chapter begins with a look at the relationship between higher education and the 'employability' agenda. We then present some ideas from the perspective of various stakeholders. The chapter also focuses on the ways in which supporting students' learning can support the development of a graduate confident in their identity and ready to enter the world of work.

Current perceptions of the link between higher education and future occupations

> *Graduates in creative arts and mass communications might find that their three years at uni is not worth the cash.*
>
> (Rodionova, 2016)

How do you measure the value of a university degree? Increasingly, journalists and students now assess them against the size of the salary to which they give access. Such thinking is, of course, fuelled by the fact that there is now a need (in England in particular) to earn well to pay off student debt (Kentish, 2017). This links with X is for Expectations where we look at the commodification of higher education.

What is our role in this as higher education teachers?

TASK 1

List the ways in which you relate the course on which you teach to the world of work.

REFLECTIONS

Here are some examples of ways in which this is done:

- a student-run law clinic with a focus on reflective practice;
- accountancy students using real-life case studies to develop their skills;
- arts students sourcing and carrying out a work placement and completing a portfolio and reflective account of the experience.

Here are some thoughts from the perspective of each of the following: the Idealist, the Career Adviser, the Higher Education Teacher, the Student, the Employer and the Quality Assurance Departments. Some of these characters are based on real people, some are imagined. The perspectives we describe are not necessarily representative of all idealists, all career advisers, all teachers, etc., but we hope that their voices raise some interesting points. Let's meet the stakeholders.

THE IDEALIST

It is my belief that this chapter shouldn't exist.

First, I feel very strongly that higher education should not be seen as merely an expensive product that is a passport to a well-paid job. It's a time to follow your interests and develop yourself, not be groomed for the world of work. And it's a chance to change society, not replicate it.

Take my subject, Engineering. Some people teach it like it's a 'product' (Tyler, 1949), with prescribed content, the main aim being to pass the exams and get the qualification as a ticket into a job. At its worst, it's about jumping through hoops by following instructions. It's basic stimulus-response training like the old behaviourists (Skinner, 1974).

What about problem-solving for its own sake? What about students exploring their own areas of interest within the subject discipline? This becomes more of a process (Knight, 2001). Or, instead of 'Here's a worked example with all the necessary information included, now try one yourself', you take them outside their comfort zone and set a *real* problem scenario, where they have to formulate the questions themselves, and then retrieve what they need to solve it. You get them talking like engineers, because they *are* engineers (Lave and Wenger, 1991).

Even more radical, instead of re-creating the status quo, can we disrupt it, create some cognitive (and affective) conflict for the students so that they have to think beyond the formulae and the sums and consider the global picture? We can ask questions of the sector itself, use a diverse range of role models (see, for example, the Magnificent Women and their Flying Machines website) and bring in other critical perspectives such as the sourcing of materials and environmental impact. This is transformative (Mezirow, 1997), not just for the students themselves, but potentially for the industry, too (Grundy, 1987).

TASK 2

The Idealist describes three types of curriculum. The first is the 'product' model, the second, a problem-solving or 'process' model, and the third, which they refer to as 'radical', is about empowerment and transformation (a 'praxis' model).

Revisit Task 1 and see if you can spot any similarities in the models above to the elements you identified in your delivery. Describe how you feel about delivering in this way. Do you resent the focus on work? Do you feel there needs to be more emphasis on developing certain skills?

REFLECTIONS

In some subject areas, professional bodies have a considerable influence on the content of higher education courses and there can be tension between the requirements of the employer and the philosophy of learning, teaching and assessment in the provider. In other, non-vocational courses, it can feel as though employability is 'bolted on' to the content in a way that does not feel integrated or appropriate. The challenge for any practitioner is how to respond to the drive for 'employable' graduates while remaining rooted in the principles of higher education as empowering students through the development of critical enquiry.

In the next few 'dialogues' we see emerging a way in which we can address the employability agenda without compromising our pedagogical integrity. There emerges the notion of a graduate identity which is all about being reflective and critical, being able to embrace diversity and able to work in a global context. Such ideals fit well with our other chapters and it is in this spirit that we continue our chapter O is for Occupations.

THE CAREERS ADVISER

If I could ask lecturers to do just one thing, here's what it would be: for HE teachers to situate their teaching in the 'real' world and contextualise their material. An example is a maths teacher I once worked with who explained the application of the mathematical concepts that she was introducing – for example, the use of complex numbers in electrical engineering and in quantum mechanics. Raising awareness of these connections can help students to think about possible areas they would like to work in after they graduate, and it can be motivating to learn that the content of their courses does have relevance beyond the classroom.

There is a link here with the theory of situated learning (Lave and Wenger, 1991). In this case, learning about the application of knowledge to the wider world (we prefer this term to 'the real world', since higher education is real too) needs to be authentic – that is, examples are properly researched and up to date. For more discussion on the nature of 'authenticity' in learning, see Herrington and Herrington (2005).

THE SUBJECT-SPECIALIST TEACHER: 1

It's really important that we help our students to identify employability skills, and that, where appropriate, we help students explore possible work routes in addition to the one for which their course qualifies them. My subject is History. As part of the course we get the students to analyse authentic historical artefacts and to search archives – in other words, to be historians. But these tasks have other, more general skills embedded in them, too – using initiative, being creative, developing a systematic approach, communicating, researching and so on – all of which are of interest to employers in a wider range of vocations.

THE SUBJECT-SPECIALIST TEACHER: 2

I'm quite new to teaching, having been a Quantity Surveyor. Coming from industry means that I bring valuable experience to courses, but I'm struggling to get my head around the fact that the students have quite diverse reasons for choosing this course. For example, not all of them want a career in this area, so it seems I'm preparing them for a bigger range of future jobs than I thought. It's not just about the subject, there are other skills to develop too, including academic skills, as well as 'soft' skills such as team-working.

While the History teacher above aligns herself with the 'process' model alluded to by the Idealist, the Quantity Surveying teacher is finding that a 'product' model is too simplistic for the context of learning and teaching that she now finds herself in. This illustrates the difference in the context and purpose of the workplace and the classroom.

Working with careers advisers

Reflecting on our work with higher education careers advisers, we have learned that some of their skills lie in questioning assumptions about work and seeking to understand the motivation behind certain career goals or choices. This is something we as HE teachers can also do, rather than assuming that careers work means knowing, for example, the entry requirements for every profession.

Where careers staff can be involved in working with cohorts of students, it's vital that their sessions are embedded into courses rather than seen as bolt-on events. This can be achieved by meeting with the teaching staff prior to and after the session and perhaps team-teaching such sessions. Learning outcomes for careers sessions can be devised together and assessed in an ongoing process by the subject-specialist teacher. These learning outcomes may be around, for example, looking at integrity (Barnett, 2009) or awareness of diversity (Hinchcliffe and Jolly, 2011). Such an exploration of personal values could also underpin learning outcomes within subject sessions. Making employability skills explicit can also help students to gain *a shared vocabulary with which to present their graduate identity to employers* (Weller, 2016: 120).

Graduate narrative identity

What we have found is that there are creative ideas coming from careers services such as using narrative with students to explore employment ideas. This links very much with the idea of a graduate narrative identity where the student, in moving from university to work, learns to *act in ways that lead others to ascribe to them the identity of being a person worthy of being employed* (Holms, 2013: 549). Try the next activity for yourself as a way of exploring how you might use it with your students (the actual use of a real-time travelling machine is optional).

TASK 3

This is an activity that a colleague has used with students. Imagine you are a time-traveller – get in your time machine and travel to a place where you are really happy in the perfect job, for which you are tailor made.

Now travel back a few years to a time before you were working in this role.

Your task is to describe the assistance (or assistants) you received when you travelled from one place to the other. You also need to describe the monsters that tried to stop you and the terrain in which you travelled. Do it as a piece of writing, a drawing, a comic – any way you like.

REFLECTIONS

Doing this for yourself will hopefully give you ideas about ways in which you could do this with your students – perhaps even sharing your own creation with them first.

Developing employability skills

TASK 4

Imagine you have some students who consistently turn up late for sessions and some who find group work very difficult. These are two issues that could prove difficult when transferred to the workplace (as well as perhaps causing barriers to learning).

What do you do, as their teacher?

REFLECTIONS

Ban them from entering the classroom if they are more than five minutes late?

Fail them on their group work?

After all, if they consistently behaved like this at work they could be sacked. Here it's important to remember that the classroom is not the workplace and there needs to be a different ethos. Latecomers (and non-attenders) will have a variety of reasons for their behaviour, which could range from caring responsibilities to a lack of understanding about the impact this could have on their learning. There's a role here for the higher education teacher in identifying the causes of the lateness and in working with individuals to address these causes. There's also a place for critiquing employer responses so that our students, as the potential managers of the future, act in a way that is informed by research and integrity. Just one example of this might be to look at interpretations of equalities legislation within a profession.

There's an argument to be made that work is where you learn about work (Smith and Comyn, 2003 in Tran, 2015: 211). Similarly, with group-work, there are skills to be learned and this learning requires support (see G is for Groups for more on this).

THE STUDENT

I did a degree in the UK, followed by a Master's in Holland, both in Ancient History. Throughout the degrees I worked in a bar and I didn't really know what I would do for a job when I finished. I just loved the subject but I didn't want to stay in academia. Working in the bar was really public facing so I learnt how to deal with customers and I took lots of responsibility. I ended up being in charge of staff on some shifts. At Master's level my work was really personal and based on my own values, so talking to adults who rated what I said really boosted my confidence. I feel both degrees taught me 'life admin'. I had to organise meetings and do presentations in a tight time-scale. At Master's level, the small class size meant you were really visible. At the moment, I'm lucky enough to be an archaeologist. It's not my subject, but with the confidence I gained and my interest and knowledge in what we find, I am learning fast and earning a living. (Oisin, Sheffield).

What do students think?

Results from Universities UK (2016), the HEA's undergraduate engagement survey of UK students, show that while overall 88 per cent of undergraduates say they find their course challenging, just 51 per cent reported that they have strongly developed the skills that prepared them for the world of work and will help them get a job. There is clearly an issue here, although the survey does not ask students if they feel that employability should be a priority in higher education.

What helps students gain employability skills?

Research suggests that student involvement in course planning and in extra-curricula activity supports their graduate identity:

there is more to be done to increase engagement between students and institutions in those aspects of higher education that directly improve employability, such as staff/student partnerships and student interaction with staff on activities other than course work ... Employability improves where institutions provide a complete and rounded experience for students that builds their social capital.

(Jones, HEA, 2016)

THE EMPLOYER

Weller (2016) notes that there is a range of views among employers on whether graduates are well prepared for work. She quotes from a number

(Continued)

(Continued)

of surveys, some of which consider graduates to be highly employable and some of which bemoan a lack of work experience. The 2016 CBI/Pearson education and skills survey of employers indicated that there was a high level of satisfaction with graduates' skills in literacy, numeracy, teamworking, problem solving and communication. There is a clear shift in the literature, which suggests that lists of job-specific skills are just one tool with which to foster the growth of a graduate identity (Hinchcliffe and Jolly, 2011).

QUALITY ASSURANCE DEPARTMENTS

The metrics used to measure the success of an institution in terms of its employability rates are highly contested. The debate around these is worth considering when higher education teachers are deciding what exactly it is they are helping their students to aim for. One article on the gathering of 'destination data' in the USA suggests that a successful outcome could be measured in several ways (Kovacs, 2016). Some occupations offer more job security, some offer higher earnings.

We would expand on this to include job satisfaction and ask our students what they see as the most important aspect of work for them – then, of course, challenge them to research this so that their transition to employment is well informed and based on their values.

P is for PRESENTATIONS

HOW TO PRESENT SO THAT YOUR STUDENTS LEARN

CHAPTER SUMMARY

What's the difference between a lecture and a seminar? Are all presentations supposed to be interactive? What counts as a large-group-learning-and-teaching-session? Dr Mira Maravilla, Professor Emerita of Excellence in Exposition and our fictional presenter for this chapter, begins with some definitions before challenging the reader to question whether learning by listening is as passive as it appears. Focusing on presentation skills rather than learner–teacher interactions (which are addressed elsewhere in this book), she then goes on to explore some of the characteristics of a good presentation, including when and where it's most appropriate to use one.

Hello, Dr Mira Maravilla here, Professor Emerita of Excellence in Exposition at the A–Z University, giving you a presentation about presentations. First, we must work out what we mean by a 'presentation'. I will begin, somewhat controversially, by consigning the words 'lecture' and 'seminar' to the dustbin. Yes, that's right – we are throwing them in the trash! Instead I propose to talk about 'large group teaching' and 'small group teaching' (see Figure P1).

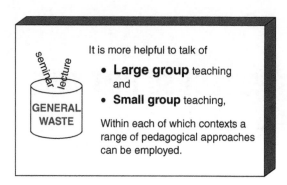

Figure P1   Presentation slide 1: binning the words 'seminar' and 'lecture'

The reason for this is that just because you have 150 people in a room, it doesn't mean that you must give a didactic lecture. And what people think of as 'seminars' are all too often, as the authors of this most excellent book have found from their many observations of teaching, merely 'lectures' with a smaller audience. Other equally vague interpretations depend less on the size of the group and more on the perceived nature of the session or the way it is timetabled. Indeed, at times it is not uncommon to observe a two-hour 'lecture' followed by a one-hour 'seminar' with the same cohort of students in each and no discernible difference between the two sessions.

To avoid such murky and ambiguous distinctions, I offer an alternative discourse, with use of 'presentations' as opposed to 'lectures', bearing in mind that presentations can take place with a small or large group of students, and as part of a session or outside of a session, by video or webinar – and that presentations form but one teaching and learning approach among many.

By 'presentation' in this context I mean a teacher-led approach, where the teacher 'imparts' knowledge to the students (see Figure P2). Of course, presentations can be student-led too, but that is outside the remit of this chapter, while more direct, 'active' approaches to teaching and learning are discussed, I believe, in Chapter A of this volume. Here, my role is to critique the 'pure' presentation as a teaching and learning approach and to look at ways to enhance its effectiveness.

Now, I imagine that you're wondering, in the age of 'active learning', why bother with presentations at all? There is indeed plenty of evidence

> **To present**
> Has origins in the Latin word
> *praesentare*, meaning
> 'to place before, show,
> exhibit'

Figure P2   Presentation slide 2: what is 'presenting'?

to suggest that sitting and listening passively is *not* always how people learn best (see Figure P3 for an example).

> **Research Example**
>
> Freeman *et al.* (2014) meta analysed 225 studies of student performance on Science, Technology, Engineering and Maths courses in the USA according to teaching approaches used.
>
> Their findings supported calls to **abandon 'traditional' lecturing and support active learning.**

Figure P3   Presentation slide 3: passive vs. active learning

Constructivist learning theories tell us that people learn by interacting with their environment and creating knowledge for themselves (Pritchard *et al.*, 2010). Learning by osmosis or absorption or, as Laurillard (2012) calls it, 'acquisition' just isn't going to cut it, is it?

But are you *really* 'inactive' while you're watching, for example, this presentation? I do hope not, otherwise my 'excellence' at this role may be called into question.

So here I'll show you how to get an audience actively thinking.

TASK 1

Please think of a lecture or presentation, either face-to-face or on screen, that you've experienced recently and that has made an impression on you. This might be an academic lecture, a 'TED' talk (www.TED.com), a video presentation or even a student-led presentation (for example, you

(Continued)

(Continued)

can find some short, sharp deliveries by doing a video search on 'Three-minute thesis' competitions).

Consider the following questions and make some notes while you are sitting here.

- Why did the experience of watching/listening to this presentation make an impression on you?
- What did you learn?
- What was it about the presentation that enabled you to learn from it?

REFLECTIONS

I will now discuss an example – a presentation by Herine Otieno, a Ph.D. student, explaining the subject of her thesis in three minutes as part of a national competition (after my presentation you should be able to find her via a simple search on the Web). Table P1 shows an extract from my own notes on observing her.

Table P1   Observing Herine

What Herine did	How this helped me to learn
Non-threatening body language – e.g. eye contact with everyone, outspread hands for emphasis.	This removed defensive barriers, so I trusted her.
Good pacing – even though she only had three minutes.	I had enough time to reflect on what she was saying, but not enough time to get bored.
She told a story.	This engaged me. I wanted to see what happened next.
She drew on her own personal experience.	I respected the fact that Herine had lived through the stories she told. It made me try to imagine myself in that context.

How does this compare to your own notes for the presentation you've selected? I have no problem with you choosing this very talk to critique – we can all benefit from constructive feedback. You may have come up with other strategies that helped you to learn, such as those shown in Table P2.

Table P2   Other strategies to help you learn

Using a metaphor.	I enjoyed the demonstration of the free market as a balloon. It made me think about it from a different perspective.
Providing opportunities for the audience members to assess their own understanding and knowledge.	The short tasks that were set at various points enabled me to test my own understanding. Obviously, the lecturer couldn't 'mark' my responses, but listening to her go through the answers from the front really clarified some things for me.
Having a clear structure.	The presenter told us how the presentation would unfold, posed questions, worked towards answers. This helped me to organise the content and anticipate the next step.

Let's return to our earlier debate. 'But Mira,' you asked, 'how can you learn as a student when there is no direct interaction with the presenter?' (OK, let's assume you would have asked had I given you the opportunity.) Well, it depends on what you mean by 'interacting'. In the examples above, the participants were not in *active dialogue* with the presenters. They were not raising their hands, tweeting the presenter or answering multiple-choice questions via a hand-held device. So what *were* they doing in order for learning to take place?

TASK 2

Now I want you to go back to Tables P1 and P2 and your own notes from the first task, and underline or write down all the *active verbs* or *verb phrases* in the right-hand column of each table. For example, 'trusted', 'wanted', 'try to imagine'. What do these words tell you about what the audience members in these presentations did to learn?

REFLECTIONS

Here are some more verbs and verb phrases from the examples given:

enjoyed, paid close attention, decide if I agreed, apply theory, test out my own understanding, listening, organise the content, anticipate.

So perhaps in a presentation where the audience appears to be *passive*, there is more activity going on than you think.

In my experience as a Professor of Exposition, I often find that people talk about constructivism as if it's a learning or even a teaching *style*. But it isn't. It's a *theory* about how we *learn*. This means, if you 'believe' in constructivism, then what you're saying is that people learn by constructing meaning and knowledge and accommodating or assimilating information *all the time*. It's the only way we can learn.

What does this have to do with lecturing and with the examples discussed above?

Well, when you're listening to a lecture on the causes of the First World War or how to interpret X-rays or the properties of different materials, even if you think you're doing nothing, if you are learning, then according to the constructivists, you are, in your head, deconstructing and/or reconstructing your existing framework to accommodate or assimilate new knowledge (Boeree, 2001). You are interacting – not directly with the lecturer, but at least indirectly with the lecturer via the content of the lecture. It is this interaction, even though it may to you seem quite passive, that is enabling learning to take place. Again, the converse holds. So, if you're thinking about what you're going to have for tea or checking your phone messages or whispering to the person next to you, then you're not interacting with the content and therefore you're highly unlikely to be learning (unless of course, like me, you are very good at multi-tasking).

This means, if constructivist theory is true, then the best way to support learning is to give students lots of opportunities to try things out, get it wrong, negotiate and renegotiate meaning. In this way, strategies that support direct interaction are best. But that doesn't mean that you can't facilitate active engagement in a recorded lecture or in a context where audience–presenter dialogue is limited. Look at all the work you've been doing during this excellent lecture.

How to present so that your students learn

Figure P4 illustrates a list of ideas for supporting students to interact with subject content, even when they're unable to engage with you directly. I call it Presenting for Learning (PfL) (as opposed to 'Presenting because I love the sound of my own voice' or 'Presenting because I want you to see how wonderful I am', or 'Presenting because I'm so excited about my subject that I forget to go at the pace of the people following it').

I will now provide an explanation of each of the ideas listed in turn. Since this is an asynchronous presentation, please feel free to pause and reflect on each point, particularly in terms of how it might apply in your own subject discipline. I won't be offended if you choose to close this book and let your mind wander for a little bit.

Presenting for Learning (PfL)

1. Body language and movement
2. Personal experience and goals – yours and theirs
3. Continuous formative self-assessment
4. Acknowledge and accommodate prior knowledge
5. Clear and logical structure
6. Visual imagery
7. Challenge and critique taken-for-granted assumptions

Figure P4   Presentation slide 4: Presenting for Learning

1. If you are visible to the students (note that if you are recording yourself using screen capture software you may not be), use body language actively and positively. This makes your content more memorable and you more personable (Mehrabian in Kuhnke, 2012), just like me.

2. Share personal experiences of the subject matter – e.g. industry experience or life history. Acknowledge the motivations of the audience too, where these are known. In this way you humanise the subject and begin to develop an interpersonal relationship with the learners (Rogers and Freiberg, 1994). I hope very much that you are beginning to feel you know me.

3. Set brief tasks or problems to solve, then provide hints, tips and suggested solutions. Use prediction – e.g. posing a question and giving pause for thought, before showing the answer on the next slide. Individual development can thus be supported through 'scaffolding' by a more learned 'other' (Vygotsky and Cole, 1978).

4. Assume that everyone has prior knowledge but that each person's prior knowledge will be different. Start with a recap, or a short quiz, use an analogy with an everyday experience, and/or situate the presentation content in its appropriate context. Spending time on this will enrich your students' subsequent understanding (Jeanne, 1990).

5. Use a clear and logical structure. Pause regularly to recap or to explain what's coming next. This provides opportunities for the audience to reflect on new information and the extent to which it is consistent – or not – with their existing mental structures or 'schemata' (Smith, 1999).

6. Employ visual imagery – e.g. graphics, charts, diagrams, narratives or metaphors to support explanations of content (Sadoski and Paivio, 2001). There is more on this in Chapters T and V of this book.

7. Challenge the audience to question their own values and assumptions, to make links to wider society, situating the subject content in time and place. This kind of critical reflection goes beyond the usual linear ritual of the *teaching, learning and assessment* game (Sambell *et al.*, 2013) and authenticates learning as messy, risky and transformative (Mezirow, 1991).

To these I would add one more: whether recorded or 'live', keep it short, one approach of several (both online or face to face). No one wants to listen to you waffling on for more than 15–20 minutes or so maximum, not even when it's me. So if you're stuck in a lecture theatre for a two-hour session, mix it up. Have breaks, have extended individual tasks, have paired discussions, try out more active approaches, elicit some feedback, show a film, play a song, engage in some electronic audience interaction, do a role-play. And, now and again, present some content.

Conclusion

There are many ways in which presentations can be enhanced to maximise opportunities for students to interact with the content and construct knowledge and meaning for themselves. I have listed only a few here. To improve your own presentation skills further, I suggest the following:

- Watch others present, online and in person, and note the techniques that they use to engage the students. For example, what techniques have I used here to engage you? How effective have they been?
- Have trusted colleagues watch you and give you supportive and constructive feedback on your presentation skills.
- Remember that context counts. What might work for one person in one environment may not be as effective for you and your own students, and vice versa.
- Consider alternatives to the traditional lecture as described elsewhere in this book. There are many ways in which to disrupt the ritual of the lecture, but you must always evaluate the degree to which such initiatives enhance learning, thus remaining rooted in pedagogical integrity.

The key message of this chapter can perhaps be summarised thus, that

> *the constructivist notion that learners have to make their own sense, or be enculturated into the practices (mostly linguistic ones) of the community applies equally well to learners sitting in rows in lectures …*
>
> (Mason and Johnston-Wilder, 2004: 230)

Thank you for your time.

is for
QUIET

HOW TO CREATE A SPACE WHERE ALL STUDENTS CAN BE HEARD

CHAPTER SUMMARY

How do we ensure that our quieter learners have sufficient space to engage with learning in sessions? In this chapter we look at the possible reasons behind the silence and at how we can ensure that we all feel like part of the same community of practice. We seek to celebrate the virtues of a quieter approach to teaching and learning.

Why this chapter?

We have included a chapter on quiet learners because we realised that in many of our feedback sessions following observations of teaching, we find ourselves in discussion with our colleagues about students who have said little or nothing during a participative session.

As teachers, should we be worried about quiet learners?

Table Q1 shows some arguments for and against teacher intervention with quiet students, presented here as a dialogue between two university teachers.

Table Q1   For and against teacher intervention with quiet students

Learning occurs through social interaction (Vygotsky, 1978). If we don't encourage quiet students to contribute, are we denying them the opportunity to learn in this way? And what about employability skills? How will they survive even the interview stage?'

Social interaction doesn't have to mean speaking out in class. You can interact internally with your teacher or your peers, by listening and making notes. You can interact with artefacts such as textbooks or journal articles. And you can interact with peers outside formal teaching contexts ...

Yes but how do you know if learners are doing these things? If they're not speaking, how can you assess what they're learning? Black and Wiliam (1998) describe *assessment for learning* as using information to adapt your teaching. How can you do this if you can't assess them because they never say anything?

There are other ways to assess learning and to get students to speak or to contribute to sessions. You can talk on a one-to-one basis when you're circulating the room during a task. You could pair people up. If you like, the pairs can then become quartets etc. so that students gradually work in larger groups. Targeting students in front of the whole group could be very off-putting.

I'm worried that they might not feel part of
the group. Students like this can end up
dropping out.

*I agree. That's a very valid concern. Maybe we
should find out from the quiet learners
themselves what they think?*

Good idea!

Let's pipe down ourselves for a moment and listen to some quiet students

TASK 1

- Think about the quiet learners in your groups. Describe their interaction with you and with other learners.
- If you already know why they are quiet, describe the reasons (careful not to make assumptions or rely on stereotypes – imagine this was a research project and that you would be asked to provide evidence for anything you have just said).

REFLECTIONS

Here are some examples of responses from quieter learners across different disciplines and levels. These are based on real examples of students we have known.

On a good day I love the course and feel like I get a lot from it. On a bad day, when my meds are making me sleepy, or it's been a major battle getting my daughter to nursery, I really struggle to concentrate.

Mostly I don't speak up because I know that the loud ones are going take over, so what's the point?

In the sessions, I'm listening and thinking, listening and thinking. I work out the answers in my head, but I don't like drawing attention to myself, so I usually let someone else answer. It's OK. I still feel like I'm part of the dialogue, even if I'm not contributing out loud.

(Continued)

(Continued)

The responses here suggest a variety of reasons why some students remain quiet during taught sessions. You may have added further examples.

Student activist Marsha Pinto who founded softestvoices.org warns against making judgments about reticent class participants, reminding us that *still waters run deep* (Pinto, 2014). The key thing, she suggests, is not to make assumptions in terms of level or motivation.

What quietness can bring to learning

Before we look at the positive aspects of quietness, it's worth remembering that people can occupy different roles at different times and that thinking of our students as having fixed introverted or extroverted personalities can be unhelpful for our practice.

Scott (2007: 9) contends that *shyness* is socially constructed and the introvert is a role that *we learn to inhabit, and one that involves socially-shaped processes of identity work*. This suggests that as teachers we could develop confidence in quieter learners by providing safe communities of practice. Collins and Ting (2010: 902) assert that everyone *may exhibit a variety of both 'introverted' and 'extraverted' behaviours, at times simultaneously*. This is in keeping with the spirit of this book, which argues that blunt characterisations and generalisations about ourselves and our students are rarely useful when designing teaching environments. Rather than indulge in constructing these, we should learn as much as possible about our learners, embrace and build on their diversity and work to make our classes accessible.

Akinbode (2015) gives a fascinating discussion of the way in which different societies value the qualities associated with the introvert and the extrovert, and includes a list of the positive qualities the quieter teacher and student can bring to the classroom which include:

- thoughtfulness (before speaking);
- thinking through issues thoroughly before taking action;
- good active listening;
- good at noticing what others miss;
- engaging in quiet leadership.

More strategies to support the quiet learner

Some need space for reflection – perhaps needing us to pause when we ask questions and giving them time with no distractions to consider their answers. As Pinto (2014) points out, *we may not raise our hands as quickly as you want us to or say as much as you wanted us to, but honestly we just like to take our time to process our ideas.*

TASK 2

What strategies do you use, or have you experienced, for giving students thinking time and alternative ways to respond in taught sessions? You may wish to share and compare responses with a colleague.

REFLECTIONS

There are many ways to create thinking time. Some are suggested below.

- Ask for a show of hands instead of people calling out. This can take some perseverance and is a practice that is best established early on in a course or module. Explain that you may not necessarily ask the first person to put their hand up each time. For example, you can ask a question and say 'Take a moment to think about the answer. Don't call out. When you have something to contribute, please raise your hand.'
- Use paired and small group discussion as an alternative to whole group question and answer sessions. Circulate and interact with students individually.
- Find alternative ways for students to present answers or ask questions: post-its, writing on a flip-chart sheet or whiteboard, mini-whiteboards, online message boards, voting technology, survey tools. Jamie, a computing teacher, would pause in his delivery at regular intervals to check student questions via his phone. He would sometimes read out the 'silly' comments for fun, but would then take time to respond to the more serious queries before moving on. Online tools can also be used prior to or following a session, for questions or tasks.

Research has shown in some cases that creating an interactive environment in this way can lead to meaningful learning as in this survey of students in a large chemistry class:

Silent students report that, despite their silence, the active environment enhances their engagement in the class and understanding of the content ... This active learning environment encourages

(Continued)

(Continued)

> *participation and benefits both vocal and silent students even within a large class.*
>
> (Obenland *et al.*, 2012: 90)

- Use turn-taking techniques where discussion is structured, perhaps with the use of counters. Each learner has a number of counters and forfeits, one each time they speak. Used sensitively, the exercise can serve to highlight any imbalance in speakers and generate reflection about ways in which everyone could be given space and time to contribute. Deborah Richmond offers several ideas for this in her blog post (2013).
- Other ways to encourage a wider number of responses include the invitation to a row or section of the room to answer rather than allowing a free-for-all of raised hands. Even a simple request for someone to speak 'who's not spoken so far this session' can have an effect.
- Pose a question but don't ask for a response directly. Simply allow some thinking time, and then present the solution (or possible answers). You will be able to tell which students are engaging simply by observing them, and you can always ask for a show of hands to see whose responses matched yours.

Cultural expectations around being quiet

Others refer to their experience of education so far, where respect for teachers and a non-adversarial approach are required. In a discussion of East Asian students, Swee-Hoon Chuah (2010) says that, without wanting to generalise, some students

> *learn by listening; they want to fully absorb and understand what is being taught. They don't feel that they have the 'right' to question what is being taught until they have completely understood all aspects of it. Moreover, they avoid being critical out of respect for the teacher, so that the teacher will not lose 'face' in front of other students, and to preserve harmony in the classroom, so that everything runs smoothly.*

She goes on to say that as students' confidence grows, they are able to take a more active role and that small groups can really help to foster such a journey. Leaving space at the end of a session – where practical – for individuals to come and talk one to one can also build relationships and allow for differentiation.

As with many chapters in this book, the focus here has been on changing the environment, not necessarily changing the student. We have also sought to focus on the strengths that quietness can bring to a group. Active learning need not mean that we sacrifice stillness when it benefits us all.

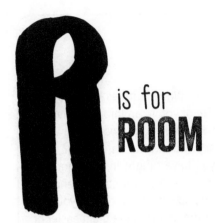

is for
ROOM

HOW TO FACILITATE SPACES FOR
LEARNING

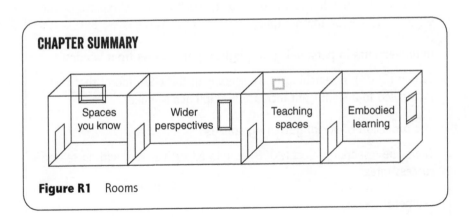

CHAPTER SUMMARY

| Spaces you know | Wider perspectives | Teaching spaces | Embodied learning |

Figure R1   Rooms

TASK 1

Spaces you know

1. Where are you now, as you read this? What features of the space help or hinder your reading? For those of you in an informal environment (in the bath, on the loo, in bed) could you (or would you want to) replicate any aspects of this space within a formal setting?
2. Think of two different rooms that you have taught in, one that you have positive memories of, and one that you found challenging. Alternatively, try to recall some of the spaces in which you yourself learnt as a student. What features of the rooms made them easier or harder to learn or teach in?

REFLECTIONS

What features of formal learnings environment are helpful for learning? Some examples of research are given below. Note that here we restrict our discussion to formal seminar rooms, lecture theatres and classrooms. The dynamics of other learning contexts, such as the workplace or the science lab, are for another time.

Improvements in personal space, lighting and views from windows

Tanner (2008), researching in 24 schools in the USA, found that these factors led to a significant increase in pupil achievement.

The provision of social gathering spaces

The same research project (2008) correlated such spaces with increased success rates.

Temperature

Mendell and Heath (2005), in a review of over 500 texts on environmental factors and learning/performance, looked at lower achievement and increased reported concentration difficulties among students, and office workers, when in rooms at higher temperatures.

Flexible use of space and free movement within that space

Jindal-Snape et al. (2013), in an international literature review on the impact of 'creative' learning environments in schools, found that these factors had a positive impact.

Seating locations of students

Regarding more traditional classroom layouts, in their paper 'Does where a student sits really matter?' Fernandes *et al.* (2011) review a wide range of research that suggests seating locations of students are related to academic achievement and classroom participation (although they question whether, for example, high-achieving students are more likely to sit at the front, or whether the front row of seats creates high-achieving students, and they warn against making assumptions about students based on their seating choices).

To what extent do these research findings correlate with your reflections from the task above?

Theoretical, political and sociocultural perspectives

Is this all about Maslow's hierarchy?

The research evidence examined thus far follows Maslow's model (1970), by focusing on physiological needs in a hierarchy of conditions necessary for motivation and thus learning (see Figure R2).

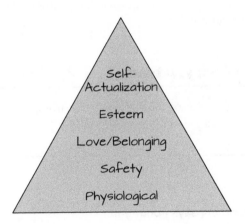

Figure R2 Maslow's hierarchy

In practice, teachers can help students to overcome physical barriers to learning by enabling them to pole-vault the bottom layer of the pyramid and aim straight for the 'love', 'belonging' and 'esteem' strata nearer the top. In this way, a humanist-oriented teacher who puts the learners at the heart of the learning can mitigate the effects of a poor physical learning environment to a certain extent (as evidenced in Heron and Heward, 1982). However, the fact remains that a low-quality learning environment can not only restrict the range of possible teaching and learning approaches, it can also impact on student–teacher and student–student interaction, prevent individual needs from being met and be inefficient and costly (McGregor, 2007).

Relations of power

> *The box-like structure of many classrooms, with the 'teacher zone' of the desk or dais (in laboratories) at the front, sends immediate messages about control, supporting a didactic approach and mindset, yet the pattern is so familiar, we often fail to question it.*
>
> (McGregor, 2007: 16)

Looking at physical features solely in relation to student achievement tells only a part of the story. The design and layout of learning spaces can affect social relations, dynamics of power, culture and identity, and embody particular ideologies in relation to education. In this way, control over others is possible without physical restraints or implications (Foucault, 1972 in Fernandes *et al.*, 2011). As McGregor (2007) observes, the design and layout of rooms for teaching and learning convey messages of socialisation that we are often not even aware of. For example, she suggests, a poor learning environment can carry the message that the learners within it, and their learning, are given little value.

The space in which *you* teach

What are the implications of all this for the learning and teaching spaces within which you work?

TASK 2

What your classroom says about you

Consider the following quotation from Fernandes *et al.* (2011: 4): *Commonly, the instructor's teaching style dictates the classroom's seating arrangement.*

Having ascertained in the previous task what you consider to be the optimal physical features for an effective learning environment, what does this say about your own approach to teaching (and thus learning)?

REFLECTIONS

Do you tend towards a teacher-centred approach, your preferred class-room arrangement a matrix or U-shaped formation, where you can observe every member of the group and maintain control over the session? If so, you are far from alone, for this is still the dominant form of teaching and learning in many universities. Such a layout has been likened to Foucault's Panopticon (Foucault, 1977), where every member is placed where they can be under surveillance by those in authority. This approach is not only well within the comfort zone of many teachers; it can also be popular with some students – in fact, I have seen students, on their own initiative, rearrange a room from tables in 'islands' to tables in rows at the start of a session, before the arrival of the teacher. There are several disadvantages to such an arrangement, however. These are listed below.

- We have stated throughout this book our enthusiasm for active learning strategies that support students to construct, deconstruct and reconstruct knowledge as they negotiate and attempt to solve problems collaboratively. In 1950, the psychologist Bernard Hunt Steinzor (1950) found that conversation is easier across a table than between people seated side by side. For this reason, tables in 'islands' can encourage more peer-to-peer interaction than rows.
- Having students in rows limits the ability of the teacher to circulate and assess and support individuals as they complete tasks. It also limits the ability of the students themselves to move around, effectively pinning them to their seats for the duration of the session. As we shall see later in this chapter, this can have an adverse effect on learning.
- As mentioned earlier, the 'traditional' classroom set-up reinforces notions of the teacher as the holder of power, knowledge and authority, and the students as passive recipients of that knowledge. To truly enable, empower and provide a meaningful identity for students, an environment needs to be created that disrupts these notions (Lippman, 2015). This view is supported by many employers, who frequently ask educational settings for students who can solve problems and use their initiative rather ones who have been 'filled up' solely with subject content (see, for example, Burns, 2017).

So, having read thus far, are you ready to abandon the *lecture theatres of tradition and knowledge* in favour of *the carpets and beanbags of innovation*

(Savin-Baden, 2008: 9)? If not, the next section sets out some less drastic ways of organising your teaching and learning spaces within the constraints within which you work.

Practical implications

If we, as teachers, need to optimise the features and layout of the rooms in which we teach in order to maximise opportunities for learning, how might this be done?

This room is too ...

What do you do if you are in a room that feels inadequate for the active learning approaches that you wish to employ? Figure R3 shows some suggestions.

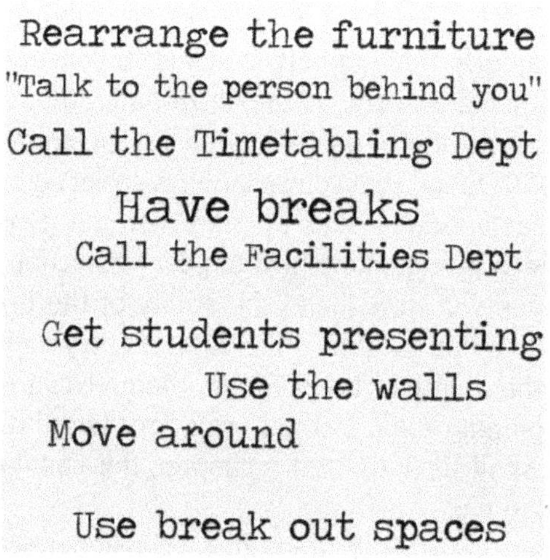

Rearrange the furniture
"Talk to the person behind you"
Call the Timetabling Dept
Have breaks
Call the Facilities Dept

Get students presenting
Use the walls
Move around

Use break out spaces

Figure R3 Suggestions for an inadequate room

In short, use your imagination – and that of the students – and know the right people to contact. But how important *is* it to create a learning space where students can move around?

Embodied learning

For the most part, formal learning spaces in higher education settings are designed on *the assumption that the body has no role to play in cognition* (O'Loughlin 1998, 2006, in Stolz, 2015: 475). However, there is a significant and growing body of neurological research that suggests otherwise (see, for example, Blakemore, 2003).

Kontra *et al.* (2012) describe an experiment (later published in a paper by Kontra *et al.* (2015)) in which a group of students of physics studying angular momentum and torque were asked to manipulate bicycle wheels on an axle in given conditions. Another group simply watched someone else manipulating the wheels. The physically active group performed better in subsequent testing than the passive group. Subsequently, the same experiment was repeated under controlled conditions and included brain imaging of the students involved. The improved quiz scores were explained by activation in the 'sensorimotor' regions of the brain as the 'active' group members tried to recall what they had learned.

This finding links to theories of experiential learning such as those of Dewey (1933), who asserted that experiencing or 'doing' an action or phenomenon directly leads to more effective learning than simply seeing or hearing about someone else's experience of it. However, not all knowledge translates so directly into physical action. Goldin-Meadow *et al.* (2009) in Kontra *et al.* (2012) looked at school pupils using given, appropriate gestures to explain their answers to maths calculations compared with those that did not, and found the 'gesture' group to perform better. So, actions that *represent* knowledge in an appropriate way can also enhance learning.

Another reason for introducing more movement into teaching and learning across the disciplines includes a more general connection between physical movement and academic achievement (JOPERD, 2010; Berg, 2010). Recognition of this relationship is reflected in the increasing popularity of 'walking meetings', originally in the business sector and now in universities (Robeznieks, 2015). The trouble is that the cultural norm in academia is that students in seminar rooms and lecture theatres sit still – all day.

How can we create opportunities for movement within the limited spaces in which we teach? The following section looks at some possible strategies.

Room to move and space to learn

UP AND ABOUT

How can you get your students moving in a traditional taught session, and how can you use space creatively? Here are some suggestions (you are invited to add more of your own). Do make sure that you design such activities in a way that your students can all participate in.

- Go for a walk. Devise a treasure hunt; send students off to different locations to complete a task; have a small group discussion standing up.

(Continued)

(Continued)

- Ask a question and get students to move to different parts of the room depending on their answer.
- Devise a mini-survey. Get students moving in order to gather data from each other.
- Hold a 'market' with student-run stalls or posters trading in 'knowledge'.
- Create an 'art gallery' – for example, give each table a different task and then get the students to wander around and see what the others have done.
- Employ a 'carousel' approach with specific activity zones or stations in different parts of the room.
- Use a human scatter graph or bar chart.
- Engage students in role-play, including acting as non-human objects such as submolecular particles in given conditions, or being an item in an algebraic expression (half of a pair of brackets, a multiplication sign, an 'x' or 'y'), being rearranged or substituted in order to produce a certain value.
- Stage a debate in which the opposing sides sit on opposite sides of the room, facing each other. People are allowed to switch sides during the discussion if they so wish, but no one is allowed to stay in the middle. Also, the chair reserves the right to request someone to switch sides and argue from the other perspective, particularly if they are getting quite heated.

Note that each of these approaches needs to be carefully planned. While some students may find it challenging to sit still for a prolonged period, others may have difficulty in moving around. Creativity and preparation are essential in addressing the needs of your learners. Be clear also about the intended purpose of the way in which you plan to use the space available. Will your approach enhance learning? Is it rooted in the principles of good practice?

In this chapter, we have looked at the physical spaces in which teaching and learning take place and how teachers can utilize them in creative ways to maximise opportunities for learning. Other parts of this book explore 'space' in a different way – for example, D is for Design, E is for Emotion, L is for Listening, V is for Visuals and Z is for Zzzzzzz. All too often, in formal education, we deny ourselves and our students space to learn and room to move. We cram learners into classrooms and lecture theatres; we talk at them endlessly. We structure learning so tightly that it's hard to catch a breath. By paying attention to learning spaces, both literal and figurative, we can allow both our students and ourselves to grow and flourish in unexpected ways.

is for
SKILFUL

HOW TO DESIGN SKILLS DEVELOPMENT INTO YOUR CURRICULUM

CHAPTER SUMMARY

'Skill is better than strength', says the Polish proverb. But what skills are we trying to equip our students with? Furthermore, which ones do we assume they already have? This chapter focuses mainly on the skills of academic writing and mathematics, but has resonance for the development of a whole range of competencies within your subject discipline. The first part of this chapter considers some ways in which you can teach your students to write well, while the second part examines how to support them to become confident mathematicians. We recommend that you read both parts no matter what your subject discipline, as you may find strategies that can help in other areas too.

TASK 1

What skills do your students need by the time they graduate? Which of these are addressed in your curriculum?

REFLECTIONS

You may have identified some or all of the following:

- academic writing skills, reading skills, oral skills;
- mathematics skills, statistical skills, IT skills;
- team-working skills, general communication skills, problem-solving skills;
- learning skills, study skills, organisational skills;
- research and enquiry skills, analytical skills, rhetorical skills;
- social or 'people' skills, management skills, leadership skills.

There could be others related to your subject discipline, such as lab skills, archaeological skills, measuring skills. A Universities UK report (2016) lists 49 transferable skills, from active listening to using IT effectively. How many of these are addressed explicitly on the courses you teach, and for how many is it assumed that students will either arrive with them or pick them up naturally as the course progresses? To what extent is it reasonable to make these assumptions?

Some skill-sets are considered in other chapters in this book – for example, graduate employability attributes; student awareness of learning skills; team-working ability and language skills. Here, we look at language and maths.

Mind the gap

The 'massification of HE' is a global phenomenon (see the British Council report 2014 for evidence of this) and means that we now teach students who bring diverse qualifications, a wide range of life experiences and differing skill-sets. The danger is that we see this as a deficit model of students, as indicated in Figure S1.

Instead of bemoaning the poor spelling of our students, let's look again at the skills they need to flourish in higher education and beyond.

Figure S1   Newspaper headlines

Expanding the definition of language and maths

> *Rather than regarding numeracy as a set of 'stand-alone' mathematical skills, we can think of it as a social practice, embedded in people's purposes as they interact with the social world.*
>
> (Oughton, 2013: 16)

In today's world, we use language and maths in a myriad different ways. A standard confidence-building task for adult literacy students is to ask them what they have read in the past twenty-four hours – in the past their answers would have included items such as 'the cereal packet, the clock, the front of the bus, the street sign, the toilet door', etc. Today, this list would include much more varied media – perhaps social media or on the phone, a scrolling screen at the bus stop, a bill online, a text. For many, this might also have involved more than one language and script, and communicating across more than one continent. The need for our higher education students to engage with this plurality of skills and to be able to analyse the use of these skills in the social context in which they are operating has never been greater. You may wish to encourage your students to do a similar exercise where they recall the critique, the blog, the web page, the slides, the spreadsheets they have been involved in creating over their last semester. Academics have responded to this agenda – see, for example, work on multiliteracies by Cope and Kalantzis (2009). The chapter I is for Internationalism has more on this.

Drawing on existing skills

Oughton (2013) writes of a *funds of knowledge* approach as described by Moll *et al.* (1992) who proposed that informal knowledge and skill should be celebrated and drawn upon in the classroom. Students are not empty vessels waiting to be filled up with skills. In fact, what they may need to learn is to switch from one social literacy or numeracy (or IT) practice to another – for example, creating a blog post vs. writing a literature review, solving a complex problem through heuristics (how much stock to order given anticipated sales figures) to modelling the solution through a computer algorithm. Older students who bring experience of applying skills are sometimes predicted to be 'weaker', but in fact may have a better approach to study than younger ones, although both may need help with specific academic skills (McCarey *et al.*, 2007). In Chapter K, we look at experiential and problem-based learning. Using these approaches will make the transfer of skills from other contexts to the higher education more likely to occur naturally as learners recognise familiar scenarios.

So how do we support students to develop their language skills and draw on their experience?

Explain how your subject interacts with language skills

TASK 2

Think about the way you require students to use language in your subject area. Are there specific conventions for writing reports? Are students required to debate, talk to service users, describe their artistic process?

REFLECTIONS

As suggested above, it's sometimes the way in which we need students to use their generic skills within the context of a specialist subject which is the stumbling block – being able to write, for example, may not mean being able to write an academic essay on law or a laboratory report. So part of our job in addition to teaching our subject is about teaching how our discipline uses language (Chanock, 2000). It's easy when you've been immersed in a subject for years, and are used to the conventions used, to forget that these need to be made overt for newcomers to your community of practice. This could be, among other ways, through providing examples of assessments, writing frames or through feedback. Wingate (2015) refers to the idea of a *literacy window* – the point in a session when you can refer not only to what you're teaching but how it is communicated.

Explain the use of academic writing

No one speaks (or writes) academic English as a first language (Bourdieu and Passeron, 1994: 8), so all learners will need support with using this new medium of communication. Whenever we communicate, we need to think about who we are writing for and who we are 'being' – that is, our identity as we write. So, when a student uses informal language in an essay, you may want to compare this to the papers they have read and to encourage them to begin to think of themselves as potential authors of new research rather than as outsiders looking in (McGrath and Nichols, 2017). In a section above, we introduced the idea of literacy as a social practice in which power relations influence the way in which certain types of literacy are privileged above others. While it is only fair to prepare our learners to operate in the current academic climate, we may also want to discuss with them the times when using certain conventions are really about 'playing the game' rather than really communicating – more of this below.

Ensure that your curriculum delivers the intended skills

Biggs and Tang (2011) talk about aligning the elements of the curriculum so that, for example, learning outcomes, delivery and assessment fit to make a coherent course. While auditing your teaching along these lines, you may also wish to check that the skills demanded of your learners are actually those demanded of graduates or postgraduates by your subject area and by the wider context. Flexible assessment tasks can often be devised so that students can offer the evidence needed to meet course requirements without, for example, writing a 3,000-word essay. You can also encourage them to join you in transformational practice by using innovative ways to engage with subjects that have hitherto relied on formal written communication. As Lillis and Scott (2007) point out, if students are socialised into a dominant discourse, this will limit their ability to innovate and transform their discipline.

See writing as a craft and support it accordingly

We talk in other chapters of the book about the importance of seeing learners as a whole, of considering multisensory and emotional aspects of learning. There is also an argument for seeing writing as a more 'embodied' task rather than an intellectual activity that can be taught separately from all other higher education as a disembodied skills experience. This may encourage, for example, the fine art student to transfer some of the skills they bring to 'making' to the art of writing. Lisa Clughen (2014) makes a case for this, saying:

> *As you write, you build something, add bits here and there. You might make a complete mess as you write with ideas and quotations all over the place, have to screw your writing up and throw bits away, or sometimes you even have to go back to the drawing board. Similarly, the thinking you produce for writing can be conceived as an active craft, as ideas are often produced as you write or move.*

She goes on to make some interesting suggestions for more holistic ways in which we can support students with their writing – for example, talking more about assignments before they are written, taking the focus off *high-stakes writing* in order to give time to address any emotional issues clouding creativity, suggesting that students *sleep on* their ideas to allow them to percolate or encouraging learners to walk and think before they commit to writing.

How do we support students to develop their maths skills and draw on their experience?

In the 2016 report (Universities UK, 2016), graduates were asked about a range of transferable skills and to what degree they felt these had been developed during their courses. 'Working with numbers' was the skill that scored consistently lowest.

How does your subject interact with maths skills?

> **TASK 3**
>
> Think about the way you require students to use maths in your subject area.

> **REFLECTIONS**
>
> Many courses require mathematical knowledge and skills – engineering, business, science, nursing and other health and wellbeing courses, sports science, biomedicine, accountancy, computing, any subject involving the collection or analysis of quantitative data – and lots more. Look back at the comments on Task 2 – most of these apply equally to this task.

Issues and suggestions

- As with language skills, there's often an expectations mismatch between new students and university teaching staff about levels of formal mathematical skills and knowledge required. You could be explicit about what's needed and promote engagement with study support services, not just at induction but also at regular intervals throughout the course. Make sure students know what is happening when and where to go. 'Normalise' study support.

- Entry criteria are sometimes 'low', but without the infrastructure in place to respond to resulting student skills needs. For home students in the UK, emphasis on numbers passing GCSE Maths has led to a 'gaming' of the system, resulting in surface-level learning and leading to gaps in basic level understanding. For example, students may know how to substitute numbers into a formula, but then get stuck when it comes to rearranging the formula.

  One way of addressing this is to put on a summer school or send out a pre-course self-study pack (online or on paper) to help new students get up to the required level.

Ways in which maths support can be delivered

Just as with language support, maths does not need necessarily to be 'disembodied' from the subject area and taught separately – and sometimes disjointed support just doesn't work.

SACHA'S STORY

I did OK in my Maths A-level, but at university studying for an Engineering degree, Electronics and Mathematical Modelling completely floored me. The lecturers went too fast – no space for trying to understand it. I went to some workshops but the postgraduate students running them couldn't grasp my lack of understanding. In the end, I was embarrassed to ask for help and I stayed away from lectures – what was the point? I thought I might learn it all from books or online, but I struggled to motivate myself. I felt like everyone else was achieving except for me. My deepest moment of shame came when I failed my Electronics exam – 6%! A term into my second year, I'd had enough, and I dropped out. (For more on maths and engineering, see Bamforth et al., 2007.)

In the case study above, we see that lack of confidence and opportunities for collaboration were key in the student's failure and subsequent with-drawal. Warwick (2016), in his paper on student expectations, hones in on the need to take into account the emotional component in maths support which must complement the cognitive aspect. As a result of his research, he says:

> *I try to promote mathematics learning as a collaborative process: a collabora-tion between the student and the teacher and between the students themselves. I try not to put students into situations of working individually on problems unless there is support available as the positive feedback process can easily become negative feedback if frustration grows and confidence weakens.*

In a similar vein, universities such as Loughborough in central England have adopted more holistic approaches to support (Croft *et al.*, 2009). In fact, there is a wide variation from HE provider to HE provider – there are often different models of funding and different levels of priority. SIGMA, the Network for Excellence in Mathematics and Statistics support, suggests many ideas – well-publicised and evaluated workshops, tutorials, paper-based and online resources, drop-in sessions, maths cafés, all-day drop in centres, and so on.

In addition to 'bolt-on' initiatives, there are ways in which you yourself can design maths support into your curriculum. The following are some ideas.

- Include a 'maths portfolio' as part of the summative assessment for a module. This could include a diagnostic maths assessment, target setting, written reflections, progress reviews and examples of work completed and problems attempted.
- Set up small study groups that can meet up to work through practice questions together and promote a culture of 'It's OK if you don't know', of learning from mistakes, of learning from each other.
- Create screencasts of online tutorials, or signpost students to existing ones on the Web.
- Discuss with students the extent to which surface-level or deep-level learning is appropriate according to context (this is sometimes referred to as 'relational' and 'instrumental' understanding (Skemp, 1989). Is con-ceptual understanding the best way forward or is simply knowing how to find the answer sufficient?
- Set projects or problem-based learning tasks that involve the use of mathematics. Don't 'pre-teach' the maths, simply flag that it is there and that students may need to go and research some of the skills needed.

Then observe what happens when students reach the 'mathematical' part of the problem – they may surprise you. Have some support materials ready in case they are needed.

- Acknowledge with students the varying levels of mathematical confidence within the group. Avoid assumptions that everyone will be able to tackle the mathematical elements of the course with ease, but be careful about a culture developing where everyone panics about these.

If we do nothing else, let's say, 'You can do this ...'

As teachers, we need to know what skills our subject requires and our students need to develop. Skills development can build on experience, but students need to be confident in their ability to learn and be clear about what's needed. Collaboration between teachers and students is key, so that no one feels like Sacha – unable to access support and feeling alone in their confusion.

is for
TALES

HOW TO TEACH THROUGH STORYTELLING

CHAPTER SUMMARY

This chapter is presented as a tale, to illustrate teaching through the medium of stories. The overarching narrative is a dialogue between a book writer and Lena, a higher education teacher of maths and science (if you are from a different discipline, don't worry – the content is transferable). As they travel through the chapter, Lena and the author encounter a number of narrative teaching approaches in different contexts. Along the way, they debate the features of good stories and how they can be harnessed to enhance learning.

Lena and the Book Writer

O nce there was a book writer who wished to write a chapter on the benefits of telling stories when teaching students in higher education. They were inspired by the idea that ...

> *The venerability and universality of the storytelling instinct suggests that there is something innate in the human mind that makes the narrative form an especially attractive medium in which to contain, transmit and remember important information.*
>
> (Kennedy, 1998: 465 in Sanchez, 2014: 18)

The Book Writer's colleagues, most of whom taught in the Arts, were inclined to agree with this. The same was true for the Sociologists, Lawyers, Sports Scientists and Business Studies experts, many of whom used case studies, reflective blogs or journals, and 'real-life' problem scenarios in their sessions. Not so for Lena, who worked across the science, technology, engineering and maths disciplines.

'This is all very well for social scientists, but what have stories got to do with pure scientific fact or logic?' Lena grumbled to herself.

'Aha!' said the Book Writer (who could read the thoughts of all of the protagonists in their chapters), 'But what if the scientific argument is *itself* the outcome of a particular "story" about the world as we believe it to be – merely one more "form" of narrative, albeit a very compelling one?' (Mergler and Schlafer, 1986: 1282)?

'So you're saying science is a story as much as everything else is?' queried Lena. 'That's ridiculous! Prove it!'

'Very well,' said the Book Writer. 'I shall prove it via the medium of a story itself. Are you seated comfortably? Then I shall begin.'

A STORY TO LOCATE US

Once, many centuries ago, there lived in Gujarat a mathematician named Brahmagupta. He was fascinated by the concept of zero, which he defined as the result of subtracting a number from itself. This new way of looking at 'nothing' made it easier not only to write down large numbers, but also to perform complex calculations. Later, in the Middle Ages, Arab traders brought Brahmagupta's 'zero' to Europe, along with the other Hindu-Arabic numerals. Here, however, the new numbers were met with resistance. Using the old Roman numerals meant that calculations must be performed on a counting board, and with this came power, which some were reluctant to

(Continued)

(Continued)

relinquish. Eventually, however, after another 500 years, the 'new' number system took hold, and the so-called 'Hindu-Arabic' numerals revolutionised the way in which we do mathematics (O'Connor and Robertson, 2000).

Upon finishing this story, the Book Writer waited in silence. Eventually Lena spoke.

'OK, that was interesting. We grow up believing that the maths we know now has always been there, but your story shows that it's a product of time, place and culture. I get that. And don't even get me started on the history of the irrational numbers. But why would I use up valuable lecture time telling tales like these to my students?'

The author responded, not with answers, but with a question. See the box below and try to answer it for yourself.

TASK 1

Consider the following question:

What effect did the story have on the way you perceive the subject of mathematics? Why should such stories matter?

Lena went away for a while to reflect, but found herself coming back to the author with more questions. Here follows an extract of their discussion.

Lena: So, OK ... Maths (and to a certain extent science) are traditionally presented in education as 'true', 'absolute', 'incontestable', 'apolitical' and 'universal' (Ernest, 1994). Stories can disrupt such notions and thus remove some of the stigma associated with these subject areas. But maths and science *are* true, aren't they?

Book Writer: Hmm. Your question reminds me of the radical constructivist Von Glasersfeld (2001), who said that scientists must suppose that the world they study exists independently of the observer. But just because they *assume* the world to be 'real' in some object sense doesn't actually mean that it *is*. Hadzigeorgiou (2006: 42) puts it another way:

humanising the teaching and learning of science means helping [students] appreciate science as a human activity, and hence scientific knowledge as something that cannot be isolated from the people who created it.

Lena: So whatever we learn, we're learning it through someone else's story and through their eyes.

Book Writer: Yes, that's it! And stories of people innovating and making 'mistakes' about subject knowledge link with constructivist theories of learning. In this paradigm, 'truths' (in this case, scientific ones) are considered to be constructed and negotiated, rather than 'absolute' in any sense.

Lena: So stories like this could be quite challenging – and also empowering or liberating – for students who see mathematical or scientific knowledge as being uncontestable ...

Book Writer: And, for that matter, as Eurocentric. A global, historical perspective can disrupt all of that (Joseph, 2010).

Lena is lost in thought, until gently interrupted.

Book Writer: So, are you a convert? Do you agree that stories can enliven the teaching and learning of traditionally 'dry' subjects by adding depth, colour and 'romance' (Hadzigeorgiou, 2006)?

Lena: I'm coming round to the idea. But I still think that some students will see them as a waste of time.

Book Writer: In that case, may I present my quality checklist for using stories in teaching and learning?

Hadzigeorgiou (2006), in using narrative to teach about the discovery of current electricity, focuses on the following elements.

- What are the central ideas of the story? Can they incite wonder?
- What human values are being presented and why might they be important?
- What are the narrative features (e.g. protagonists, plot, mental images)?
- What are the ideas to be learned, and what is the 'moral' or central message?

To this I would also add the following.

- How does the story enrich or enhance the aims of the session, module or course? What purpose does it serve?
- What are the underlying epistemological assumptions (principles about the nature of subject knowledge) being made here?

Lena: Phew! Telling tales is a whole profession in itself. Exactly how much time are you suggesting we need to spend on stories when we're teaching?

Book Writer: Oh, stories can take up as much or as little time as you wish. A 'starter' task while students are still coming in, an aside during a lecture ...

Lena: A self-directed activity on a virtual learning environment – a tweet!

Book Writer: And they can be multimedia – for example: spoken word, images (including comic-book style), video or audio files or even role-play. The point is that stories can be used to provide a historical, sociocultural 'frame' for your subject in a way that entertains and engages your students.

Lena: Multimedia? I'm on it! Are historical stories the only kind of stories you can use?

Book Writer: No indeed! Come with me into the realms of fantasy and science fiction ...

A story to ignite the imagination

The room dims and spins, until it slows to a standstill. When the lights come up, Lena is sitting with the Book Writer in a lecture theatre in a USA University.

Lena: Where are we?

Book Writer: We're in Maryland University, in a Physiology Class. They're going to use a visualisation exercise in which the students become red blood cells. It's to study changes in fetal circulation (Nguyen and Carvalho, 2014).

Lena: What do you mean, *become?*

Book Writer: Shh! It's starting!

Lecturer: Today, we are going to imagine fetal circulation from the point of view of a red blood cell (RBC) using a *visualisation* exercise. In this exercise, I want each of you to imagine you are an RBC, travelling the intrauterine circulation system. You will be given instructions and questions to consider along the way ...

Soft music plays, the lights are dimmed and some of the students close their eyes. Some time later, Lena and the Book Writer re-emerge in their own world.

Lena: That was brilliant! Now I know how oxygen is transferred from mother to infant via the placenta! And who knew there were all these bypasses for us to travel through as red blood cells? When the baby was born and the pathways shut down I was really worried that we weren't going to find a way through ...

Book Writer: The question is, would you have learned as much about changes in fetal circulation postpartum had that simply been a traditional lecture? Or did the visualisation and the storyline help?

Lena: Oh, I'm sure I'd remember it better as a story and a visualisation. Somehow the fact that it's so far-fetched to imagine yourself as a red blood cell makes it even more memorable. It was so much fun. Do you have any more like that?

Book Writer: Well, I can give you some further examples that have been used in practice, but I'd like you to answer some questions about them please, if you would be so kind ...

TASK 2

There follow some authentic examples of the use of aspects of narrative by HE teachers with students, as observed by the authors of this book. Can you match the techniques below to the examples? In what ways might the approaches used here enhance learning?

Techniques: (a) personification; (b) role-play; (c) autobiography/personal anecdote; (d) analogy; (e) prediction; (f) turning a routine task into a quest; (g) simile.

1. *Drew (Economics)*: 'OK, so you stand here in the "factory" and transfer all the tennis balls from this bucket here into that one over there. Great! Another volunteer please? Welcome! I'd like you to stand next to this person and help. OK, now we'll add another couple of people, and hey why not, a couple more again ... that's it ... pass the balls along. So what's happening with the productivity now we've got extra resource?'

2. *Graham (Maths Education)*: 'These researchers worked with street children in Brazil who were selling fruit to passers-by and doing quite complex financial computing in their heads. What do you think happened when they asked the children to sit in a classroom

(Continued)

(Continued)

and do the same calculations using pencil and paper?' (Nunes *et al.*, 1993).

3. *Jamie (Computing)*: 'What happens if we instruct the program to do that?' 'Oh, see, it doesn't like it!'

4. *Somporn (Maths):* 'A representative from each group needs to ask me for the instructions for the first task. These will be given to you in a sealed envelope.'

5. *Yasmin (Social Anthropology):* 'I was utterly miserable, more an "outsider" than ever. I'd made all the wrong assumptions about the best way to carry out this research. I contacted my supervisors and told them I wanted to come back and start again, but they told me to stay where I was.'

6. *And finally, Danny (Chemistry)*: 'Aldehydes? In this reaction, I like to think of the aldehyde groups as the wildebeest adrift at the back of the pack. The reducing agent picks them off first!'

REFLECTIONS

(Answers: 1 – d; 2 – e; 3 – a; 4 – f; 5 – c; 6 – g)

You can see from the examples listed that sometimes a mere flavour or a whiff of tale-telling is sufficient to add a little spice and bite to your subject knowledge.

Here are a few more reasons why stories can support learning.

- Gottschall (2012) suggests that stories help us to navigate life and to locate ourselves in future or alternate realities. They also provide a sense of security.
- Storytelling is a way of developing your relationship with your audience. The brain of an engaged listener will 'synchronise' with that of the speaker and even anticipate content (Stephens *et al.*, 2010). This process can be supported by the use of story.
- Narratives elicit emotional and sometimes physical responses, which are important dimensions of learning. They can prevent a subject from becoming too 'technicised'.
- The poet Ben Okri describes stories as 'secret reservoirs of values', with the power to transform individuals and even nations (Parekh and Runnymede Trust, 2000: 103). However, we would add that

being a storyteller carries responsibility – for example, identifying political agendas and avoiding propaganda.

- We relate to stories and identify with the protagonist(s), even in an unfamiliar context. This encourages real, reflective learning, whether or not the experience itself is imaginary. The Turkish writer Elif Shafak (2010) talks of stories 'punching holes' through our mental walls, and giving us glimpses of 'the other'.

'Hang on a minute. Are *we* in a story, then?', mused Lena, looking shrewdly at the Book Writer.

'What on earth do you mean?', the author blustered for a moment and then gave up. 'Well, it seemed silly not to use a story as a frame for a chapter about stories.'

'So what happens when the story ends?', she demanded, incredulous.

'I hope the reader will take some of the story with them and enact it in their own professional practice.'

'And us? What about us?'

'Us?', the Book Writer asked, a little sadly. 'I think, Lena, our work here is done. Once this chapter has been read, you and I will, I believe, simply disappear.

The End

U is for UNDERSTANDING

HOW TO TELL IF AND WHAT YOUR STUDENTS ARE LEARNING

CHAPTER SUMMARY

Sometimes as teachers we become so obsessed with 'covering content' that we forget to check what learning has actually taken place. In this chapter we focus on the concept of using informal, continuous assessment strategies as a part of the processes of teaching and of learning – sometimes referred to as 'assessment for learning', or, if possible, 'assessment as learning'. The chapter is interspersed with examples from teaching sessions that we have observed on our Pg Cert Learning and Teaching in HE course (included with kind permission of the observees), exemplifying a range of approaches that allow the teacher not only to *appraise* learning but also to promote autonomous enquiry and deeper understanding within the subject discipline.

Introduction

> *Like musk oxen we hunkered*
>
> *while his lecture drifted against us like snow.*
>
> *If we could, we would have turned our backs into the wind.*
>
> (From *Transcendentalism* by Lucia Perillo, 2009)

What happens to the material that you introduce as you teach? Does it drift like snow against the sides of your students, only to melt or be blown away? Or do you provide opportunities for them to take it, work with it and make something meaningful of it?

In higher education, Assessment for Learning (AfL) focuses on how to design assessments and to give or use feedback constructively to check and to promote understanding. We draw on the definition of McDowell *et al.* (2010: 751), where an assessment environment that promotes AfL:

- is rich in formal and informal feedback;
- creates authentic opportunities to rehearse knowledge and skills; and
- supports students to take responsibility for directing their own learning.

Formative feedback is examined in C is for Communicating and self-directed learning in M is for Metalearning. This chapter is about the creation and use of assessment by teacher (and students) to develop understanding of a subject discipline in a formal learning and teaching environment. It's presented as a series of steps.

Step 1: Be clear about what you want learners to take and understand from a session and how this will happen

> *If you're not sure where you're going, you're liable to end up some place else – and not even know it.*
>
> (Mager, 1962: vii)

Although there may be times when you want to facilitate an open-ended exploration with students, a more typical session will have learning outcomes that are closely aligned with those of the overall module. An example of learning outcomes is given below, courtesy of Joe, who teaches on a Sport and Exercise Science course. This is a true story of what Joe did.

Joe's session

TASK 1

Joe was teaching 22 students on a Level 6 module called Advanced Motor Skills. His session was about the principles of feedback to practical applications in sport and exercise. As two of the outcomes of his session, he wanted learners to be able to:

- explain the meaning of key terms in the area of feedback research;
- apply knowledge of key terms to locate examples of 'feedback manipulations' in a range of texts.

How would you go about assessing whether students could explain and use key terms in your subject area?

REFLECTIONS

At this point, the Traditional Lecturer might step in and say, 'Well, you just *tell* them the definitions, surely? You'll soon find out if they know their terminology when it comes to their summative assessment.'

Joe, however, analysed the situation and explained the following about his context:

- There was a diverse range of background knowledge within the group.
- Some were less confident than others.
- Different individuals had different ways of learning.
- Some students had learning contracts related to reading text.

So how did Joe assess the students' understanding and application of the key terms?

- He flipped the learning by setting the students a 'key terms' quiz to complete before the session.
- When they arrived, he asked them to compare answers if appropriate, or, if they hadn't done the quiz, to try it there and then.
- Having introduced the session, Joe then went through the answers with the students, addressing misconceptions, elaborating where needed and eliciting responses and further questions from the group, until they had constructed a comprehensive list of key terms and definitions.

This could be described as 'assessment *as* learning' (Earl, 2003), where opportunities are provided for students to self-assess and thus actively direct their own learning, identifying and addressing misconceptions and gaps in their knowledge.

This, however, was not the end of the story. Later in the session, Joe divided the students into set groups and gave each group a section of a research paper along with the task of identifying different types of 'feedback manipulations'. While this was going on, he walked around the room and listened to the discussions, further assessing the students' understanding and use of the target vocabulary. When the groups fed back to each other, he facilitated, adding in what had been missed and modelling the use of some of the key terms studied earlier.

Another approach would be to have the key terms embedded in specific texts, and to ask the students to identify and define their meaning from the texts. What is of note in Joe's approach, however, is that

- Joe used the students' self-assessment following the quiz as a tool and a motivator for further learning and deeper understanding:

  > *Self-assessment tasks are an effective way of achieving self-regulation ... Indeed, teachers' feedback responses need to be interpreted, constructed and internalised in the student if they are to have a significant influence on subsequent learning.*
  > (Nicol and McFarlane-Dick, 2006, in Ibabe and Jauregiza, 2010: 255)

- He continued to monitor the students' use (and lack of use) of the target language throughout the rest of the session.
- He didn't just monitor the students – he responded to them directly ('Yes, you're right, but can someone else give me the correct term for this?').

Joe's role may be described thus:

> *During a discussion, a teacher must listen to student answers, watch other students for signs of comprehension or confusion, formulate the next question, and scan the class ...*
> (Doyle, 1986, in Lefstein and Snell, 2014: 5)

In this sense, assessment – both 'for' and 'as' learning – is indistinguishable from teaching.

Step 2: Use the results of any assessment activity to promote learning

You've facilitated a group task; you've listened to or observed the results and you've made an internal, informal assessment of the group's understanding. What next? In their definition of 'assessment for learning', Black *et al.* (2004: 10) state that

> *Assessment for learning is any assessment for which the first priority in its design and practice is to serve the purpose of promoting students' learning. It thus differs from assessment designed primarily to serve the purposes of accountability, or of ranking, or of certifying competence.*

They go on to talk about using the information provided by such assessments to inform future teaching and learning.

Sukey's session

Here are some further ways in which assessment information can be used to promote learning. These are framed as extracts from an observer's report on one of our Pg Cert Learning and Teaching in Higher Education students, Sukey (teaching on a Foundation Award in Working with Children, Young People and Families, in a session entitled 'Appraising the Research Literature').

- I liked the way you asked each person to contribute and valued their answers ... you took their responses as a starting point for creating a definition. By doing this you used community of practice theory – by 'translating' the students' answers into professional and academic discourse and thereby enculturating them into both the Academy and the professional/vocational community (Lave and Wenger, 1991).
- Your small group support was effective in using assessment as learning, as you used questions and prompts to develop their thinking ('What do you think?' 'Be a bit more controversial'!). Here you drew on social constructivist theory, where you were co-creating something with the learners and helping them develop their own knowledge and understanding by supporting them to bridge their individual 'zones of proximal development' (Vygotsky, 1978).
- During feedback from students, you checked whether you were recording answers accurately with the person speaking.

There is a close link here with A is for Action. In fact, active learning and assessment for/as learning could be said to be based on similar principles, where the teacher's role is to facilitate rather than transmit, and to build on students' existing knowledge rather than treating them as blank slates.

How can we assess learning in a subject area that is not so negotiable?

Thus far, we have used examples from subject disciplines where knowledge could be said to be somewhat more fluid and contested than other disciplines. The next section considers this issue via the framework of 'convergent' and 'divergent' teacher assessment.

TASK 2

Pryor and Torrance (1997) describe two forms of classroom assessment by teachers (these apply to schools and children, but their model arguably applies to higher education too).

Convergent teacher assessment determines *if* the student knows/understands/is able to do a defined thing. It is characterised by a focus on the curriculum, and *It is routinely accomplished by closed or pseudo-open questioning and tasks and results in judgmental or quantitative feedback* (1997: 153).

Divergent teacher assessment, on the other hand, is about discovering *what* the student knows/understands/is able to do. The focus is on the student and the methods employed tend to be open questions or tasks, with qualitative feedback.

While convergent teacher assessment is associated with behaviourist theories of learning, divergent teacher assessment is associated with constructivist theories.

Which of the following examples of assessment for learning are convergent and which are divergent?

1. Accountancy: students fill in a task sheet with fixed answers part-way through a lecture, then compare it against the one the teacher completed.
2. Maths: students rearrange expressions involving complex numbers according to set conventions and rules. These gradually increase in difficulty.
3. Biochemistry: students are asked to predict the result of combining two substances. They then observe the outcome, which has been filmed in a lab and converted to a gif file.

REFLECTIONS

At first glance, it would seem that all these examples are convergent. But STEM (Science, Tenchnology, Engineering and Mathematics) and finance-related subjects don't have to be about closed answers. In example 1, for instance, the students could compare answers with each other first and then talk about any differences. Or in example 2, students could make up their own expressions using complex numbers and try them out on each other.

There are a number of benefits to this. One is that getting students to talk to each other about what they're learning helps to develop their communication and thus employability skills. It can also focus them on self-assessment and the metacognitive aspects of learning, helping them to become more self-aware and regulatory in their approaches to learning. Finally, it can encourage deeper learning.

Step 3: Use assessment as a positive and caring part of your teaching

This chapter concludes with another perspective on assessment, that of 'assessment-as-caring'.

What if, instead, we cared about our students, and not their products. The essay is no longer the simulacrum for learning, for the student, but instead what if we make the student the thing we care most about ... Grading and assessment become conversations, instead of two competing monologues.

(Skallerup Bessette, 2016)

Assessment as a conversation sounds like a worthy goal and one in which everyone can come up with the answers and the understanding.

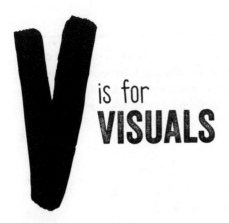

is for
VISUALS

HOW TO USE DIFFERENT MEDIA TO SUPPORT LEARNING

CHAPTER SUMMARY

Introduction	Why and What	Guidance
• Multi-*what* now? • Modes • Senses (not styles)	• Rationale • Examples	• Accessibility • Design tips for creating visual resources

Figure V1   Bullet list

Introduction

This chapter explores alternative ways of presenting information. The ultimate focus is on visual representations, but first we examine the theory and practice of harnessing other senses as well when designing and facilitating learning opportunities. To begin with, however, we need to clarify some terminology.

Multi-*what* now?

Table V1 provides a glossary of key terms used in this chapter. The meanings given are in the context of teaching and learning.

Table V1 A glossary of key terms

Mode	A meaning-making system. Modes can include written or spoken language but also layout, shading, image, gesture, action, etc.	Kress *et al.*, 2001
Multimodal	Learning via a range of modes (in fact, since all human communication is multimodal, so is all learning).	
Sense	'A faculty by which the body perceives an external stimulus; one of the faculties of sight, smell, hearing, taste and touch.'	OUP, 2017
Multisensory	'any learning activity that combines two or more sensory strategies to take in or express information'. Note that multisensory learning encompasses multimodal learning.	QIA, 2008
Medium	'A means by which something is communicated or expressed' – for example, music, video, text in print or in digital form, images, games, augmented reality, blogs etc.	OUP, 2017
Multimedia	Learning via a range of media. Mayer (2001) defines this as learning via words and pictures, while others interpret it more broadly or technologically.	Mayer, 2001

Modes

The purpose of the following task is to provide an illustration of the ways in which different modes of communication can combine to produce meaning.

TASK 1

Look back at the chapter summary for this chapter. How does your experience of the diagram compare with the use of block text (for example, in other chapters in this book)?

REFLECTIONS

The visual representation of the chapter summary uses three modes of communication: the *image* shows how the chapter is structured; the *writing* names the chapter sections, and the *shading* highlights the main section headings. This is what Kress (2010: 3) calls a *division of semiotic labour*, with each mode performing a different kind of semiotic work ('semiotic' referring to signs, symbols and meanings). In the case of the chapter summary, writing alone could perform the same role, but has its own advantages and disadvantages. In his book *Multimodality*, Kress describes a street sign in a similar way to illustrate the multimodality of the way in which humans communicate. It is the exploitation of this to enhance learning that is the focus of this chapter.

Senses (not styles)

What about if you looked at the diagram while someone talked through the different sections of the chapter? Combining visual and auditory input (as well as verbal and spatial) can, if used well, help us to absorb and engage with new information more deeply. And adding speaking to the mix of modes above means that we are now harnessing the faculty of hearing as well as that of sight (we consider accessible learning for those with sensory impairments later).

The process of focusing on more than one of the senses when facilitating learning was pioneered by Dr Maria Montessori in the first half of the twentieth century (1912 in Montessori, Gutek and Gerald, 2004). Her idea was that experiencing a range of sensory inputs supports learning more effectively than simply listening to a teacher. More recently, advances in the fields of neuroscience and cognitive psychology have indicated *the extraordinary capacity of our brain to capture and process information from [all of] our senses* (Staley, 2006, in Katai et al., 2014: 227).

Multisensory learning is associated with visual, auditory and kinaesthetic or tactile media, but any resemblance to models of 'learning styles' stops right there. In the words of learning theorist, Howard Gardner:

Sometimes people speak about a 'visual' learner or an 'auditory' learner. The implication is that some people learn through their eyes, others through their ears. This notion is incoherent ... these labels may be unhelpful, at best, and ill-conceived at worst.

(Gardner, in Strauss, 2013)

We refute the idea of learning styles more thoroughly in M is for Metalearning. A multisensory approach, on the other hand, engages several senses to support learning.

Why use multisensory learning and what does it look, sound or feel like?

In this section, we provide a rationale for multisensory learning and some examples of its use in practice in a range of contexts. You may also wish to search for evidence of good practice in this area within your own subject discipline.

Rationale

There is a close alignment between the UK government 'Early Years and Foundation Stage' (EYFS) curriculum and the principles of the Montessori approach (Montessori Schools Association, 2008). A number of studies also exist that suggest that the use of structured multimedia learning environments at different educational phases can deepen understanding and support engagement. We consider three such examples here.

1. Reeve (2014) gave Art and Design students the opportunity to create visual representations of their research interests and related questions, and found that not only did this help students overcome their fear of writing, but it helped them to engage more deeply with research.
2. In Computer Science, Katai and Toth (2010) developed an interactive e-learning environment using European folk dancing to illustrate sorting algorithms (to see the dancers in action, try searching for 'AlgoRithmics' online). This creative combination of a multisensory approach, a novel stimulus and an intercultural experience was found to help students to engage with and understand various algorithms in informatics.
3. The discipline of writing was the focus of a study by Hatfield *et al.* (2014), who worked with neurodiverse students who had difficulty with working memory. For example, they colour-coded paragraphs of text to distinguish between 'points', 'evidence' and 'comments' (the authors do this in the actual article itself, too). Strategies such as this can help all learners, they believe.

So, if multisensory learning works, how does it do so? Research by Katja Mayer and colleagues at the Max Planck Institute on the memorisation of foreign language terms has shown that this is easier when the brain can make a link between a word and another sensory perception

(Neuroscience News, 2015). It is important, however, that the different sensory stimuli are closely aligned – bombarding students with visual and auditory inputs that do not support each other in meaning can lead to 'cognitive overload' and hinder learning (Sweller, 1999 in QIA, 2008). This means that opportunities for multisensory learning must be carefully and thoughtfully designed.

Examples from practice

Multisensory learning opportunities can be created in many different ways. Some examples – from the literature and from practice – are listed in Table V2.

Table V2 Examples of multisensory learning

Subject discipline	Approach	Media/modes	Source
Chemistry	Constructing and explaining 3-D models of molecules	3-D models of molecules, speech	Alex (former Pg Cert LTHE student)
Architecture and Building Engineering	Students use hand-held augmented reality (AR) tools to superimpose virtual models on to real scenes	AR technology, images, 'real' landscapes	Redondo et al., 2013
Music	Apps that allow students to compose without needing to understand notation	Tablets, apps, 'touch feedback', sounds (music)	Criswell, 2011 in Riley, 2013

Guidance on using multisensory learning

Multisensory learning can involve all the senses, including smell and taste. Here, however, we focus on combining different modes of *visual* communication or *visual and auditory* or *tactile/kinaesthetic* communication. 'Embodied' learning is further examined in R is for Room.

Mayer (2001) offers some tips on good design for resources involving images and words. These are summarised in Figure V2.

The general message is that images should support words and vice versa. Anything else is a distraction. Remember also that you can explain visuals through speech. Other options to consider when designing or selecting images are:

- Computer-generated or hand-drawn? There are a number of websites and apps that teach drawing, and there's also software that enables you to create illustrations with a hand-drawn feel.

- On-screen or whiteboard (or as laminated cut-outs that can be stuck on a wall)? There are also interactive whiteboards, as well as software that gives you the look and feel of a whiteboard but with the benefit of being editable.
- If on screen, animated or static? Which option best supports your students to work towards your intended learning outcomes?
- What about photographs or videos? Consider copyright restrictions (you could create your own or look for Creative Commons licensed or other sources of copyright-free images).

Accessibility

Accessibility for any materials you create or activities you develop needs to be built into their design. How will your resources work, say, for some-one who relies on having note-takers in the session, or someone who lip-reads, someone partially sighted or someone with scotopic sensitivity? What about someone who has to miss the session – for example, due to illness – or simply someone who is too tired to take in a large volume of block text? While you may not be able to address all of these at once, you can build flexibility into your design so that activities and/or visuals may be easily adapted.

The Web Accessibility Initiative (WAI) develops resources and guidance to help make the Web more accessible for disabled users (see Henry, 2017 for more information). There are, of course, assistive technologies available, but the WAI site suggests many steps you can also take yourself to improve access to your online resources. It also has a list of tools that can analyse your content for accessibility (note that it's important to get specialist advice

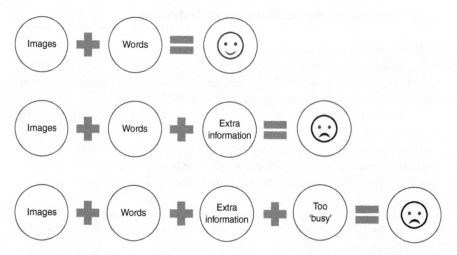

Figure V2   Mayer's tips on good design

about the platform that is being used to present content – if this has its own issues, then these will need to be addressed).

Examples of WAI guidance include levels of contrast between text and background, or what size and style font is most appropriate for what purpose. Where appropriate, you can also include audio commentaries or text-based alternatives to images, particularly where resources are designed to be used independently by learners. Such approaches are relevant whether you are creating a website or a slide presentation, or using an online function or an app such as a quiz or game (you can also assess existing materials for accessibility).

Practical design tips

Here are some further ideas for approaches that employ a range of media and modes to engage the senses. The examples shown use space, positioning, movement, colour and sound to communicate, rather than written or spoken words alone. We have included both low-tech and high-tech examples as it's important to employ variety in your teaching.

Non-linear representations
Sometimes you might find yourself moving

> *beyond the linear world of the written word, lists, and spreadsheets and entering the non-linear world of spatial relationships, networks, maps, and diagrams.*
>
> (Dave Gray in Tom, 2015)

You can also ask students to design and share their own visual representations. Note, however, that sometimes these can be very personal and not mean much to others. Providing explanations of visuals that they've created can help students to articulate their thought processes.

Card matching or sorting
A visual–tactile resource can be created by placing statements, scientific formulae, key terms and definitions, etc. on sets of cards for students to match or sort. Cards can be real or virtual (some quiz apps allow you to design online card-based activities). The possibilities for this approach are endless, an extension being that students create their own card sets. This links to active learning and constructivist theory, metalearning and collaborative learning.

Other student-created resources
Rather than simply have a group create a flipchart poster and present it back, you can put them up on the wall and encourage the students to

circulate and add to or comment on each other's. An electronic alternative is to have sets of students create individual slides on a shared slide show, or produce an electronic poster or an infographic. They could be presenting a solution, a precis, an example, arguments for/against, a definition, a diagram or an image, and so on.

Whiteboards

As students debate a topic or discuss how to approach a problem, note key words and points on the whiteboard/smartboard/screen to consolidate them and to refer back to later. Better still, get the students to volunteer to scribe these themselves. Mini whiteboards are a flexible resource, too, and can be used in a myriad of different ways.

Graphs and charts

So you've got the students to write examples of something on sticky notes, and you've collected them in and stuck them on the board. Ask them how to classify the examples. Can they be turned into a bar chart? A scatter graph? A Venn diagram? A map?

Statements on the wall

This involves putting up enlarged copies of key statements or expressions on the wall in different parts of the room. Students can be asked to (a) move them around according to different criteria – for example, true/false or unverifiable/verifiable or (b) position themselves by different statements according to other criteria (which they agree with the most and so on).

Comics

Comics can be a novel and entertaining way of communicating with students, and there are a number of apps and websites that provide the tools with which to do this. We have produced comics that outline assignment guidance and interactive ones where you can choose how the story ends. Students can also enjoy creating their own, on a given topic. For published examples, see the 'Graphic Guides' or 'For Beginners' series.

Videos

You can find out more about the use of videos in F is for Flexible. These can be ready-made or bespoke, teacher-created or learner-created. The important thing is to make their purpose transparent to students.

A final note about media. Over the course of a module, use a diverse but appropriate range and use them often so that students become comfortable with them. As well as conventional tools such as boards and screens, flip-chart paper and sticky notes, you and your students can also (with appropriate permission) write/draw on tabletops with dry wipe markers (or on paper table covers), or on windows with 'grease' pens. Take photos or videos to record the results, with written/spoken student commentaries where appropriate.

Any resources or activities that you create need to be clearly aligned with your intended outcomes and rooted in good practice. Hopefully, you will find that engaging your students thoughtfully through a range of different media, modes and senses not only enlivens your teaching, but also promotes deeper learning.

is for
WELLBEING

HOW TO SUPPORT OURSELVES AND OUR STUDENTS TO BE HAPPIER AND HEALTHIER

CHAPTER SUMMARY

There is increasing evidence that students and teachers in HE are becoming more anxious and less happy (Aronin and Smith, 2016; Coughlan, 2016; de Pury, 2016; Kinman and Wray, 2013). We begin this chapter with a look at why wellbeing is important for teaching and learning, and what factors might contribute to rising stress levels. We then suggest some creative ways to support our students and ourselves. One aspect that is often missing from the literature on student wellbeing is the importance of staff wellbeing. We therefore consider teachers first, before going on to look at students' views.

What do we mean by wellbeing?

When we begin to talk about wellbeing, there is a tendency to adopt a deficit model and to describe the symptoms of 'unwellbeing' with the emphasis often on mental health issues. When we seek to look at the factors that compose our wellbeing, the topic becomes more complicated, not least because we all differ in our needs and responses. Ry and Keyes (1995) describe psychological wellbeing as being related to autonomy, environmental mastery, personal growth, positive relations with others, purpose in life and self-acceptance. The World Health Organization (2004) talks about a

> state of wellbeing in which every individual realises his or her own abilities, can cope with the normal stresses of life, can work productively and fruitfully, and is able to make a contribution to her or his community.

A word about 'mental health'. The Disability Discrimination Act (DDA) classes mental health difficulties that impact on daily life for a year or more as a disability. We consider mental health to be a spectrum in the same way as physical health is, ranging from severe conditions requiring help from specialist psychiatric services to issues more commonly treated via GPs, to the WHO definition of wellbeing above. Placing oneself on this spectrum (and we are, of course, all on the spectrum) is a complex business that has as much to do with the perceptions of others and the external environment as it does with our own identities.

Why is teacher and student wellbeing important for teaching and learning?

It would be easy to begin this chapter with a familiar list of stress-inducing factors in the life of anyone involved in higher education. First, however, let's take a closer look at the link between wellbeing and learning.

To begin with, research by the Social Market Foundation (2016) suggests, perhaps not surprisingly, that higher student satisfaction correlates with lower non-continuation rates – that is, the happier you are, the more likely you are to stay. However, the converse is also true, added to which there has been a deeply worrying increase in student suicide figures in England and Wales over the last few years (Coughlan, 2016).

The news is not much more encouraging for those students who struggle but stick it out – a number of subject discipline-specific studies have found a significant correlation between high levels of anxiety and low level of academic performance (see, for example, Vitasari et al., 2010 (Engineering); Mihăilescu et al., 2016 (Medicine)). Students themselves are also well aware of the link between their state of health and their ability to cope with academic demands (Morris, 2011).

Academics' wellbeing

Students' wellbeing is important but teachers also matter. A report by the University and College Union states that the stress levels of academic staff in higher education present a *serious cause for concern* (Kinman and Wray, 2013: 34). Cannizzo and Osbaldiston (2016), in an analysis of the Australian academic experience, describe notions of work/life balance in the Academy as 'porous', with work carried out in 'non-work' time becoming increasingly common. Factors include a 'long hours' culture, the increasing use of ICT to enable flexible working, competing pressures regarding research and teaching and lack of funding and resources leading to an overload of work (Winfield *et al.*, 2003 in Cannizzo and Osbaldiston, 2016). Resource constraints can affect the design and use of the physical environment, too – for example, placing staff in open-plan offices to facilitate bigger teaching spaces (see Kinman and Garfield, 2015 for more on the impact of this). Meanwhile, changes in management approaches that place accountability on individual employees mean that there may be less uptake of flexible working opportunities and more emphasis on individual staff *working effectively* to manage their time. This is particularly true for those who are teaching on hourly paid or fixed term contracts and, according to a UK study by Barratt and Barratt (2011), disproportionately so for women – in part due to the *skewed allocation of types of work not strongly associated with promotion* (2011: 141). Staff who identified themselves as disabled also have poorer wellbeing than those of their colleagues who identify as able-bodied (Kinman and Wray, 2013).

Later, we look at ways to look after yourself in what may feel like, at times, an unsupportive environment. First, however, we examine the knock-on effects of putting in extra hours at work.

What happens when your work–life balance gets out of kilter? The following task is intended to highlight issues on a number of levels.

TASK 1

Meet Camila, a fictional teacher in a post-92 UK university. Read what she has to say, then complete the checklist below.

I love teaching. I work long, long hours, but the students make it all worthwhile. It's all about being available for them, letting them know you care. I have an open-door policy – they can drop in to see me in my office any time and I'll respond to e-mails as soon as I get them, day or night. I take a long time over my marking but the students really appreciate the feedback, and also the high-quality support materials I've developed. I'm research-focused too ... And it's so tempting to take on extra work – projects, funding bids, writing ... Spare time? What's that? There's no hope of a social life and frankly the family have to fend for themselves. It's exhausting, but that's how it is these days, isn't it?

Which of the following does Camila provide evidence of?

- a collegial approach to working life – we as professionals need to develop a community of practice just as we ask our students to do;
- professional boundaries;
- an approach which develops learners' resilience (more of this later);
- an awareness of the consistency of the student experience across different modules with different members of staff;
- a recognition that other colleagues may not be able or willing to put in the same number of hours over and above their working day, which may lead to a distortion in terms of outputs across the team;
- a sustainable approach to her work/life balance.

REFLECTIONS

As far as we're concerned, Camila didn't evidence any of the items in the list. It's commendable that she finds so much satisfaction in her job and is committed to supporting her students. However, the choices she makes about how she works mean that she is at risk not only of harming her own mental and physical health, but of impacting on the expectations of her students and subsequently the wellbeing of her colleagues, too.

Meanwhile, who cares for the teaching staff? The relentless drive regarding performative measures of teaching in higher education appears to leave little room for a supportive, creative and enabling professional work environment (Burke *et al.*, 2015; Skelton, 2007).

Strategies to support your own wellbeing

Here are just a few ideas that we've picked up as we have supported ourselves and others and been supported in hard times at the smart board.

Stop trying to be a superhero – recognise your limitations, work together and create a professional community where it's OK to shout for help.

You can't be a perfect teacher – it's an oxymoron (Saunders *et al.*, 2017). Teaching is a reflective process, not a static state of faultlessness or 'excellence', in spite of the discourses that currently abound in higher education policy.

Take responsibility for 'self-care on the job' (Jen Su, 2013), and look for tips for how to look after yourself in times of stress from sources such as the 'Mind' website (March, 2016) and 'self-help' books (for example, *Help! How to Become Slightly Happier and Get a Bit More Done* (Burkeman, 2011)).

It's not always your fault so don't beat yourself up over a poor evaluation. Instead, seek peer and institutional support to explore ways in which to address any serious issues raised, particularly those that occur as a result of a shortage of resources and time.

What helps support students' wellbeing?

Eight out of 10 students (78 per cent) say they experienced mental health issues in the last year (Gil, 2015). LGBT students, those from disadvantaged backgrounds and disabled students were identified as being most at risk. Worryingly, around half of those who identified as having mental health problems did not seek support. These findings by a National Union of Students survey sparked UK media headlines about a crisis in student mental health. How did we get to this point? John de Pury of Universities UK (2016) points to the increasing number of school leavers entering university (thus increasing the numbers of those with pre-existing mental health conditions), along with a wider national crisis in mental health, exacerbated by the chronic under-funding of services (see also Kawa, 2016). Furthermore,

> *For the wider cohort, transition – from home, from childhood, to new fields of knowledge, opportunity & identity – can mean dislocation, illness and, importantly, difficulty accessing appropriate services.*
>
> (de Pury, 2016)

Social factors are also at play, including the introduction of university tuition fees and the withdrawal of financial support, increased rates of family conflict and the effects of the recent economic recession (Royal College of Psychiatrists, 2011).

There has been a strand in the literature on student wellbeing that rejects models of student support as in the book entitled The *dangerous rise in therapeutic approach to higher education* (Ecclestone and Hayes, 2009). A more extreme voice has referred insultingly to *snowflake students* (Turner, 2017). We suggest in this chapter that teachers and learners need to be treated holistically, not only for the sake of their wellbeing but also because the strength of that wellbeing will impact on their learning. There is, however, the need to support students in developing resilience so that they are equipped to deal with the demands of academic and working life. There is an argument also for including taught sessions for students on managing one's mental health.

To illustrate some of the issues students face, we present here a selection of published comments from students and possible responses from us as their teachers.

> *University is where many students, including myself, often find mental health issues starting, due to the massive lifestyle change that can sometimes feel incredibly isolating.*
>
> (Christopher Tobin, student, in Murray, 2017)

Students who are new to higher education may be living away from home, cooking and caring for themselves perhaps for the first time, away from established social networks and with strangers. For some, they are in a new country and also dealing with a new culture and language. Others still may be finding it difficult to return to learning after a number of years working in industry or bringing up children. Transitions of any kind can be difficult and this is a major change. It is important to find out what your own organisation offers in the way of support for transition, so that you can signpost students to appropriate sources of help. Many will be internal to your organisation, but there are other places that students can go, such as the Student Minds website (2017).

> *I now worry less about those little things. I suppose I'm just happier.*
>
> (Student, anonymous, on mentoring scheme at Edinburgh University in Spiers, 2016)

One of many ways in which organisations have provided support for students is through peer-to-peer schemes. Peer-assisted learning schemes have been shown to help transition to university as well as improving skills and retention rates (Hammond *et al.*, 2010). Such schemes have also been shown to support students who come from different cultural backgrounds (Rowlett and Waldock, 2017). They can also create lasting friendship groups and help build a learning community (Lawson, 2015 and Zhao and Kuh, 2004).

> *University was pitched to me as 'the best years of your life' and there is definitely an anxiety among young people to live up to that expectation. For those of us who struggle with mental illness at university you can feel constant disappointment for not fitting the student stereotype.*
>
> (Aiofe Inman, student, in Gil, 2015)

Learners may come to you for help with many diverse problems and you can't support them alone. Some universities produce guides for staff about how to support distressed students, and there are a number of published resources about supporting students' mental wellbeing (for example, Universities UK, 2015). Being able to signpost reliable sources of information regarding mental health is vital – for example, the Expert Self Care (ESC) Student app (ESC, 2017) (as recommended by the Higher Education Policy Institute) and counselling services. Nevertheless, there is a consensus that, in spite of improving services, universities could be doing more (Royal College of Psychiatrists, 2011).

> *Try not to worry about being behind on work! Everyone is! Also if anyone gets anything constructive out of doing problem sheets the first time round then they are a better student than me.*
>
> Emma Wills, student (Wills, 2014)

Understanding new ways of learning and feeling that you're struggling to keep up can be very stressful and isolating for students. As teachers, we can influence or lobby our organisations to change some aspects that students identify as stressful. Examples of these include: the bunching of assessment deadlines; unclear assessment tasks and feedback; lack of opportunity to develop skills and understand new approaches; a lack of understanding of mental health issues and inaccessible staff.

> *Get rid of the lecturer. Find somebody who can actually teach. What does the lecturer do? He (sic) just stands in the front and goes blah, blah, blah and that's it ...*
>
> Alan, a student, in Madriaga and Goodley (2010:120)

Alan was a respondent in a year-long study of eight students with the label of Asperger's Syndrome during their transitions into a UK university. He no doubt spoke for many students.

A final reminder

Sometimes it might seem that supporting the wellbeing of students comes at the expense of the wellbeing of staff. We need to work with organisations to ensure that human resources are available to meet the needs of both.

is for
EXPECTATIONS

HOW TO NEGOTIATE THEM WITH STUDENTS

CHAPTER SUMMARY

In this chapter we look at what teachers and students expect from higher education and ways in which their views may diverge. The tasks and comments aim to support teachers in shaping expectations so that students understand effective learning and are realistic in their evaluations of teaching. The goal here is for students to see themselves as active stakeholders rather than consumers.

Since the expectations of both students and tutors are shaped by their understanding of what is happening when they are engaged in learning, we also look at the impact of the commodification of higher education and the way student expectations and evaluations are used to measure the success of a course or an institution.

Perceptions of higher education and its purpose

What should higher education provide? The UK government says this:

> *greater competition and choice that will promote social mobility, [it should] boost productivity in the economy, ensure students receive value for money from their investment in higher education and strengthen the UK's world-class capabilities in research and innovation.*
>
> (BIS, 2016)

Much has been written on the marketisation of the higher education system, on a global as well as a national level (for example, Furedi, 2015). Along with research outputs, the currencies of the higher education market are manifested in (among other things) the measurement of achievement, retention and graduate employment statistics on one hand and student satisfaction survey results on the other – currently parcelled together in the UK as the Teaching Excellence Framework (see Bagshaw, 2017 for more on this). All of these aspects are now seen as 'metrics' which can be given a value. Critics of these metrics argue that they don't actually measure 'teaching' per se, but rather the student experience (2017). The subsequent danger is a dominance of discourses in higher education using the performative language of assessment, outcomes, 'delivery' and content at the expense of discussions of teaching and learning as messy, creative, sometimes painful, dynamic, responsive, personal and non-linear (Burke *et al.*, 2015). In a sense, this book is our attempt to recapture the latter, promoting teaching and learning as processes rather than as a series of inputs and outputs.

Tempting as it is to wade in, let's leave the critics to their debates. Here, our concern is to do with the impact on student expectations and on teaching and learning.

The impact of marketisation on student expectations about teaching

As higher education providers become more competitive, the university experience may be seen less as the advancement of learning per se or the 'public good', as stated in the Robbins report (1963) and more as a transaction at the end of which a degree is obtained and can be used as currency to access more wealth and influence. What expectations does this raise in our students and what does it do to the process of teaching and learning?

As early as 400 BC, Socrates understood that treating education as a product was a mistake. Establishing such a relationship creates 'merchants of knowledge,' as he put it, who are willing to give students what they want rather than what they need in order to keep the money flowing. Introducing this market-based exchange, explained Socrates, had a corrupting effect on the teaching and learning process.

(Angulo, 2016)

The terms 'satisfaction' and 'value for money' now used in evaluations of our work can sit uneasily with the paradigms of socially constructed knowledge, active and facilitative teaching. Terms from consumer culture prove difficult to define in the context of education. The confusion that ensues is typified in this research finding: *while 85% of full-time undergraduates at UK institutions are satisfied with their course, just 37% of them perceive they get value for money* (HEA, 2016).

How can we respond as professional teachers keen to work in partnership with our learners and to draw on a research base that promotes a way of learning that may now be regarded as not 'cost effective'?

Working with students and their expectations

Given the wider context, it would seem sensible to work more overtly with our students about their expectations – both to help them gain the most from university by becoming active and informed learners and to avoid disappointing evaluations of work that are based on a misunderstanding of what we are about.

TASK 1

Here are some comments from teachers in our work in higher education. What perception of higher education is being enacted here? Please note that the somewhat deficit view of students will be addressed in the comments below.

- 'Students say, "I've worked out that this session is costing me X amount of money." What do I do with that?'
- 'They won't do the work if it's not counting towards their summative assessment.'
- 'If I set them a pre-session task, they don't do it, they say "just tell me how to pass".'
- 'Attendance is so low, especially in the morning.'

REFLECTIONS

University education was never free – for a long time tax payers paid for a tiny and already privileged few to attend university. Now, in the UK, the cost has shifted to personal loans and over the years the narrative has changed so that students have come to expect to get their 'money's worth' (Rawnsley, 2017). Wouldn't you? And what exactly does this mean? Here are six 'headline' topics (Barr, 2014), expressed in Figure X1 as the shopping list of Harry, a first-year student.

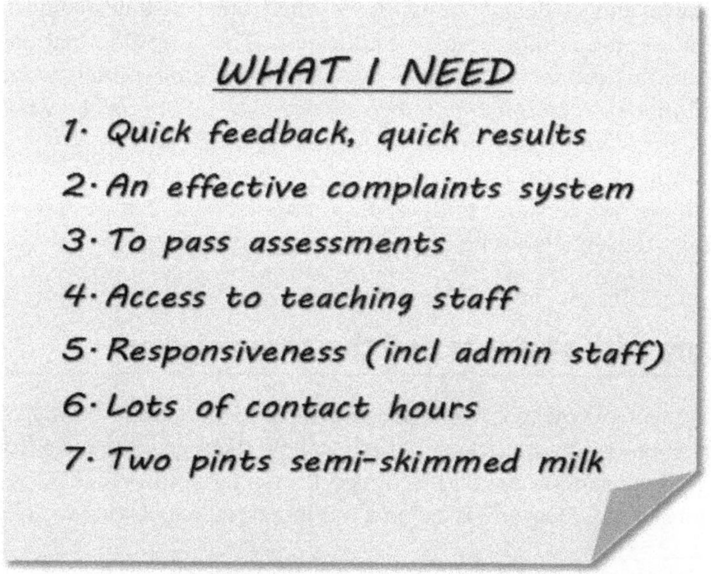

WHAT I NEED
1. Quick feedback, quick results
2. An effective complaints system
3. To pass assessments
4. Access to teaching staff
5. Responsiveness (incl admin staff)
6. Lots of contact hours
7. Two pints semi-skimmed milk

Figure X1   Harry's shopping list

Let's suppose that Harry is responsible for the student comments listed in the task above. First, it is worth noting that even if tuition fees are reduced or removed in the UK, such views may remain unchanged. This is partly because the marketisation of higher education pre-dates the introduction of tuition fees by several decades (Furedi, 2011: 1– 8). It's also because young people coming into higher education now are the product of schools where years of performativity pressures lead them to consider the 'exam' the most important part of any curriculum (see, for example, Taylor, 2016).

Another point to note is that students do not have the same sorts of consumer protection as might be suggested in the metaphor 'students as consumers' (Maringe, 2011). Finally, given the massification of higher education in the UK, the number of students classed as having 'disadvantaged' backgrounds entering university has increased significantly (Universities UK, 2015). Such students may simply not know what to expect and give up as borne out by the high non-continuation rates of learners in this category (O'Shea, 2016).

Meanwhile, we are in danger of forgetting Harry's perceived needs. The issues he raises above are addressed in other chapters of the book. What is just as interesting is what's missing. Here are a few ideas: study support, time management, a supportive community of practice, subject knowledge, the development of 'graduate' attributes, research skills, interesting taught sessions, access to resources, the development of critical thinking facilities with which to challenge the status quo ... One difference between our list and Harry's is that more of the items on our list require input from Harry, and not all of them relate directly to qualifications. This is where we can support students to understand what they need to do themselves to achieve their goals.

TASK 2

What does your department and organisation do to set student expectations of studying on the courses you teach? Could more be done?

REFLECTIONS

Check out your course publicity materials and handbooks if you are not familiar with them. Here students (and you) can read about what to expect from a course, so encourage them to engage with the material and revise it if necessary.

Ideas to help set expectations

This is not a comprehensive list, but an account of strategies that we or those we know have found helpful.

- At induction, ask students to write three expectations about the course on post-it notes (real or virtual). Present a collated version with comments linked to the published course details. Talk about whether expectations are realistic and how you can respond to realistic but unplanned for expectations. Use the gym analogy here (Enkerli, 2008) – just paying for membership doesn't make you fit.

- Include a 'What to expect from us' and 'What we expect from you' in course handbooks, which includes material on attendance, how to catch up, etc. Get the students to engage with the content by, for example, asking 'What surprises you?' What seems most challenging? Anything missing? Refer to this document frequently during sessions.

- Ensure regularly that students know where to go for support with different needs.

- See M is for Metalearning for ways to explain why not everything is about 'passing the test' and why active learning techniques are used. These may include study outside of taught sessions with the use of virtual learning environments, flipped learning etc. Use these approaches right from the beginning – for example, mixing the students up in sessions and setting the amount of time you expect them to spend on out-of-class tasks.

- Be explicit about your organisation's policies on employability. See O is for Occupations for more on this.

- Discuss the idea of 'spiky profiles' (EPALE, 2017), that is the idea that each student may have different strengths and weaknesses, so they can expect to be supported in different ways. Encourage student awareness of their own profiles and how they can seek support or challenges – from each other and from within the course team and the university.

There are many more things you can do to induct your students and make sure that they know what to expect from university. But remember that sometimes perhaps staff expectations of students need to be more flexible, and that the learning environment may also need to be changed in line with their own needs and hopes, and that this will be an ongoing process, not something that starts and stops at the beginning of a course.

Having addressed the beginnings (and middles) of courses, we now consider the endings.

Student evaluations

Ramsden (1992 in Fry *et al.*, 2009: 209) defines evaluation as

a way of understanding the effects of our teaching on students' learning. It implies collecting information about our work, interpreting the information and making judgements about which actions we should take to improve practice.

We evaluate our work using many different sources – our own reflections, our colleagues' observations and any other data we can triangulate and use to support development in our practice. Being able to respond appropriately to the feedback of learners is a key element of our profession (Eraut, 2004) – the key is to respond in a way that relates to improving learning – changing our 'performance' or simply being seen to respond may not do so.

Just as we offer help with learning to learn, most students need support in making evaluations if the information they offer is going to be useful for everyone. Critical evaluation is, after all, a skill we require of learners in higher education in many assessments. One way to do this is to look at National Student Survey-type questions used in the UK with learners, such as the one that asks if staff have made the subject interesting or the one that asks if feedback has been timely (an online search on National Student Survey questions plus year should lead you to them). Ask them to critically analyse the questions and consider what data they could elicit. Be aware that you are looking at the questions, not 'practising answers', as this is not allowed. This is a great way to look at metalearning – for example, look at what types of feedback have been received and how it has been used.

Here are a few suggestions to support the use of student evaluations:

1. Use mid-term evaluations and informal feedback which should mitigate against any nasty surprises in the NSS survey or final evaluations.
2. Evaluations should be linked to expectations and to what actually happened. We often use the final session of a module to do three things:

    • revisit initial expectations;
    • look together at what's been covered, making links to the assessment (maybe in a carousel where each station represents one session);
    • conduct an evaluation.

    This approach has the advantage of being useful both to the learners in that they have time to recall the work of the module and connect it to the assessment that will probably be uppermost in their mind, and to the teacher who can hear and see feedback on each aspect of the module.
3. Have a question about what students themselves contributed to the course in any evaluation you do so that learners remember that they have a responsibility to make the work successful, as much as you do.
4. Use creative approaches for mid-term or final evaluations – the one-minute paper where learners have a minute to reflect (Stead, 2005), the stop/start/continue idea where they suggest what they'd like to drop, what they'd like to introduce and what they'd like to keep about a module (Hoon et al., 2015).

5. Use a 'You said, we did' document in handbooks to show how you responded to the concerns of previous cohorts and for current mid-term evaluations.
6. Some research shows that students tend to give female teachers lower evaluation scores than male ones, even where the standard of teaching is the same (Boring *et al.*, 2016). It is worth alerting students to this phenomenon and asking them to monitor their responses to avoid bias.

Conclusion

We began this chapter with setting the context that shapes the expectations of today's learners and by exploring the issues this throws up for the teacher committed to facilitating an active, empowering and participatory experience in higher education for themselves and their students. We looked at the need to work with expectations from the outset, to consolidate them throughout the course and then to revisit them when learners are being asked to say whether these expectations have been met. As with all teaching, we'll never meet everyone's expectations all of the time – we're not in control of the context and as reflective practitioners we know that there is always a gap – but that's what we learn from for the next time.

is for
'WHY'

HOW TO QUESTION EVERYTHING

CHAPTER SUMMARY

In this chapter we briefly explore the definition of critical and creative thought before deciding that we don't want to limit the scope of ourselves and students' creativity by claiming that one list of skills encapsulates the ability to engage in critical analysis. The joy of critical reasoning is that we will all ask a different 'why' question depending on who we are, where we are and what we believe is important to us. To illustrate this, we introduce you to four theorists and their take on critical thinking and look at the myriad of ways in which you can use their ideas and those of others to develop the habit of asking 'why?'

What is critical thinking and why does it matter?

What do we mean by the terms 'creativity' and 'critical thinking'? Defining these terms is tricky since assigning a checklist of skills to them would be to limit the scope of what they can cover (OECD, 2016). The literature offers a wide range of definitions referring to many different skills from problem-solving to self-awareness. In some ways the definitions may depend on the student, the subject and the cultural context. For example, one student may question government policy while another finds enjoyment and challenge in critiquing the literature. Or one might benefit from comparing approaches to solving a particular problem, while another could do with assessing the impact of different degrees of accuracy in the solution. Let's start with an examination of why we want students (and ourselves) to be creative and critical thinkers.

TASK 1

Why we do we want our students to ask 'why' questions? (Surely, our lives would be a lot easier if they didn't ...)
    Jot down some ideas in response to this.

REFLECTIONS

We came up with the following answers to this question.

- Because educational theory tells us that is what will shift them from surface learning to deep learning (as described in Entwistle and Ramsden, 2015).
- Because higher education should be the place that ideas are challenged in order to create space for new ideas (for examples of new ideas from higher education that will change the world, see Parr, 2014).
- Because critical thinking skills will help them in the wider world and not just in employment (see Rezaei et al, 2013 for research on links between critical thinking skills and wellbeing).

Let's see if others agree.

What the historical and educational theorists say

Donald Schön: reflection in action

Closely linked to the concepts of critical thinking and creativity is the practice of reflection. Schön describes the practice thus:

> *The practitioner allows himself to experience surprise, puzzlement, or confusion in a situation which he finds uncertain or unique. He reflects on the phenomenon before him, and on the prior understandings which have been implicit in his behaviour. He carries out an experiment which serves to generate both a new understanding of the phenomenon and a change in the situation.*
>
> (Schön, 1987: 68)

Clearly, in order to reflect either in or after action there is a need to engage in critical thinking.

Ira Shor: the critical-democratic educator

Shor focuses on critical literacy and speaks passionately of the effect this can have on both teacher and student. He gives a powerful description of the way in which we could work together with our students to plan and facilitate learning.

> *Critical teaching is not a one-way development, not 'something done for students or to them' for their own good (Freire, 1989: 34). It's not a paternal campaign of clever teachers against defenseless students. Rather, a critical process is driven and justified by mutuality. This ethic of mutual development can be thought of as a Freirean addition to the Vygotskian zone. By inviting students to develop critical thought and action on various subject matters, the teacher herself develops as a critical-democratic educator who becomes more informed of the needs, conditions, speech habits, and perceptions of the students, from which knowledge she designs activities and into which she integrates her special expertise.*
>
> (Shor, 1999: 11)

Jane Adams: question established truths

Adams, born in the mid-nineteenth century, was, among many other things, a pioneering American social worker and philosopher.

> *She believed strongly in using current events to educate. However, she did not mean to 'teach current events' as teachers in our public schools often do. Rather she meant to take an event or issue of great current importance and encourage open enquiry and discussion.*
>
> (Palmer *et al.*, 2001:186)

Jane encouraged students to ask questions of established 'truths' such as those enshrined in religious beliefs and to use critical thinking to shine a light on concepts of social justice. She used stories to encourage students to imagine how the world could be rather than how it was – an inspirational woman and teacher.

Stephen Brookfield: stance and dance

Reflection for Brookfield involves more of a political and social analysis than perhaps Schön's less disruptive notion.

> *A key concept giving momentum to the idea of reflective practice involving both personal reflection and social critique is* **reflexivity**. *Reflexive practitioners engage in critical self-reflection: reflecting critically on the impact of their own background, assumptions, positioning, feelings, behaviour while also attending to the impact of the wider organisational, discursive, ideological and political context.*
>
> (Finlay, 2008)

Brookfield (2011) says dramatically, *if you can't think critically, your survival is in peril.* He goes on to make a strong case for the need for everyone to be able to identify the assumptions they are making, to check if these are valid and accurate, to look at their ideas and decisions from different perspectives and to make informed actions based on this reflection. For the teacher, Brookfield (1995) refers to *stance and dance* – the stance one needs is one of enquiry, the dance involves a complicated way of moving to respond and experiment to the context and one's critical analysis of it.

We also sought information from other sources, such as the Organization for Economic Development and Cooperation, which said:

> *There is a growing consensus that formal education should foster students' creativity and critical thinking skills to help them succeed in modern, globalised economies based on knowledge and innovation. Business surveys reveal that creativity and critical thinking skills are highly demanded by employers reflecting a rapidly changing employment landscape to which education systems need to adapt.*
>
> (OECD, 2016: 4)

And researchers into the Philosophy for Children movement. Philosophy for Children (P4C) is an approach that facilitates the development of critical thinking and ways to ask 'why' from a very early age. While the research quoted below refers to interventions in schools, this has also been successfully used in higher education (Daniel, 2014). The comments below indicate that critical thinking skills can help in all areas of life.

> *Teachers mostly reported that positive effects were observed in pupils' confidence in questioning and reasoning, both in P4C sessions and in other lessons. The teachers attributed positive changes in pupils' behaviour to P4C practice. Improvement in pupils' respect and behaviour are related to pupils' social and communication skills, cooperation, teamwork and resilience. In terms of social and emotional literacy, the self-reported benefits suggest that to some extent P4C can be a useful approach in overcoming the challenges of disruption in the classroom, and even bullying and other anti-social behaviours.*
>
> (Siddiqui *et al.*, 2017: 6)

TASK 2

What does critical thinking look like in your subject ...discipline?

REFLECTIONS

We can't look at every subject, but here are a few examples of ways to encourage critical thinking across the curriculum.

Example 1

> *a biology professor whose assignments force students to critically evaluate the significance of biology in the world around them by examining how accurately biology related science is depicted in news items and movies.*
>
> (OECD, 2016: 8)

Example 2

A maths teacher who

- encourages students to understand why something works rather than rote learning;
- looks at where the maths comes from and the situated historical nature;

(Continued)

(Continued)

- gets students to decide which degree of accuracy is appropriate for the situation;
- encourages students to decide if they need to take into account non maths factors;
- and lastly to consider why they are learning something (since sometimes we have to be honest and say it's part of the game).

Example 3

Diane, a Media and Public Relations teacher who, in a module on making media, uses these learning outcomes for a session on interviewing skills – each outcome prompts students to ask questions at every stage.
    At the end of the session, learners are expected to be able to:

- compare written profiles, evaluating good and bad points;
- examine video example of interviewing techniques, suggesting alternative methods;
- critique interviewing technique used in peer interviews.

So how can we all plan critical enquiry into the fabric of the session?

Here are some suggestions:

- Ask the students about the learning outcomes and encourage them to question both these and the rationale for your tasks – play with the learning outcomes and sometimes co-construct them with your students, aligning with the aims of the session. In some institutions this is taken further and students take part in course design. Here's an example of such work reported on in the OECD conference (OECD, 2016: 7).

Ben Koo (Tsinghua University, PR China) explained that students at this institution are asked to be active designers of the course content. Students are invited to engage in curriculum design at an early stage and they participate in the planning and delivering of courses. Creativity is fostered by asking participants to refine the delivery mechanism, as well as the content detail of the chosen subject. Critical thinking is fostered by asking students to provide feedback on peers' work. In the process, all students are asked to present and justify their projects' approaches.

- Explain to students why critical engagement is important for their learning and make sessions where they are expected to ask questions a habit rather than an unexpected surprise. Suggest frameworks for them to use when considering material such as that suggested in the excellent HEA piece on Critical Thinking (HEA, 2014).

You can also develop the art of critical thinking by the use of:

- open-ended design problems;
- analogy;
- textual analysis;
- self and peer evaluation using structured and constructive criticism;
- separate modules purely to teach the art of critical thinking;
- research either as part of a module assessment and/or as partners with academics;
- assessments which require personal projects unique to each student that will demand creativity.

It could be argued that everything we have said above simply describes the encouragement of 'thinking' through good teaching. If this resonates with you as a statement, then we feel our job here is done!

Z is for Zzzzzzz

HOW TO USE BREAKS AND PACE YOUR TEACHING

CHAPTER SUMMARY

Often when we teach, our heads are deep in our subject discipline. There is so much that we want to 'cover' or to impart to our students. The result can be a session so heavy in content that the students either lose interest or struggle to keep up. As one way to address this, in this chapter we look at why and how to use breaks and variety in creative teaching and creative learning.

> **TASK 1**
>
> As soon as you have read this task, get up if that works for you and move around the room, look out of the window, make yourself a drink, meditate for ten minutes or have a nap – after all, if you have read the chapters in order, you've made it to number 26 and you deserve a break.

> **REFLECTIONS**
>
> As you come back to read again, consider how you feel and if there are better ways for you to rejuvenate or maintain your interest – maybe you prefer to do a crossword, chat to a colleague, do some exercise. Think about whether any of your strategies are transferable to your students.

Rationale for the chapter

While breaks may be seen as simply the space between the material which really matters, they can be integral to learning. Here are some reasons why:

Breaks (and good time management) can be key to accessibility

As Slater says on running accessible events (2016):

> *Keeping to time is an accessibility requirement for many reasons. People may have planned toilet or rest breaks around particular speakers, need to take medication, or need to leave at a certain time for any number of reasons (including caring responsibilities or the end of a PA's shift). Sometimes this requires strict chairing!*

Research in neuroscience tells us that taking breaks improves our creativity

Thinkers and writers from Achille Mbembe to JK Rowling have described coming up with their best ideas while on a break, and discoveries in neuroscience suggest that walking away from a complex problem for a period allows the brain to break old patterns, clear itself, reset and come up with new connections.

> *It is the broken pattern that makes us sit up, take notice, and pay attention. In short, we think differently – and more resourcefully – when a break occurs.*
>
> (May, 2012)

Control studies from this discipline show that people perform tasks more creatively if they take rests or even if they are distracted from the job in hand for short periods. And creativity particularly blooms in such circumstances. Indeed *most people can engage in deliberate practice – which means pushing oneself beyond current limits – for only an hour without rest* (Jabr, 2013).

Our voices need a break sometimes too! The Natural Voice network recommends resting the voice after intensive use as well as going through a 'warm up' beforehand (Nielsen, 2012–17). 'Warming up' might be something you want to try with your students as well as for yourself, especially if it's going to be a discussion-rich session or the students are going to be giving presentations. This way of self-care is modelled for students, and the expectation is raised not only that everyone is expected to use their voice in sessions but that they should use it wisely.

More reasons to use breaks

- Breaks can give time for the reflective teaching and learning promoted elsewhere in this book.
- Unstructured time in sessions can allow students to form social bonds and to begin to form the communities of practice which we have referred to in other chapters.
- Breaks can give students time to accommodate or assimilate new knowledge, time to discuss and negotiate shared meanings and time to challenge and critique material informally (see K is for knowledge for more on this).
- Finally, breaks can mitigate against boredom. As part of their research, Mann and Robinson (2009) collated students' views of teaching methods and ranked them by boredom. The highest boredom rating was the session with PowerPoint slides and a handout provided.

Types of breaks and ideas about how to create them

'Official' breaks

- Negotiate when break times will be as part of the introduction to a session. It's a great way of showing students they are going to make active decisions about their learning from the word go. It also helps to mitigate against students taking comfort breaks or popping out to make phone calls at different times.

- Break earlier in the session rather than later when people have already begun to lose focus – don't be tempted to get through just one more slide if no one is really present to hear you. Research in an employment sphere says that when workers take breaks earlier in the day, they are more productive (Hunter and Wu, 2016).

- Vary your delivery by sending students off to get refreshments with reading material to look at in an extended break in a version of 'flipped learning'. Give them clear instructions about how you will be using their comments when you reconvene. Be aware that some will read more quickly than others so may not be ready when you reconvene. (You can mitigate this effect by making the material available before the session, explaining that you will also give reading time on the day and providing a range of 'break-time reading' in different mediums and of different lengths).

- In a shorter session, rather than having a full-blown coffee break with all the time it takes to go and come back again, simply allow the students to get up and stretch.

- Suggest to students that they take a break whenever they wish during an extended small group activity (again – be very clear about what needs to be ready for the plenary).

'Invisible' breaks (aka variety)

- Plan for a break at the end of the session – that is, 'finish' early. You can encourage students to use this time to come up and ask all the questions they did not think of, or were too lacking in confidence to ask, during the session.

- In a session based in a lecture-style room with hundreds of students, it would not be wise to suggest that people leave the room, but there are many ways to break up the session. In this situation, the break may be from having to focus on you and what you are saying. Try asking people to talk to the person on their left briefly about something you've just asked, suggest everyone stands and yawns before you resume, set a quiz. We've even seen a teacher do a short yoga session in a maths lecture to ensure that his students got a break, although this raises some issues about health, safety and inclusion.

- Introduce multisensory work. The senses most often required by our teaching are that of hearing (and listening if we are lucky!) and sight, yet our experience in the world involves constant multisensory stimulation.

> *For instance, visual and auditory information are integrated in performing many tasks that involve localising and tracking moving objects. Therefore, it is likely that the human brain has evolved to develop, learn and operate optimally in multisensory environments.*
>
> (Shams and Seitz, 2008: 411)

V is for Visuals has more content on this. Other ideas include passing round a tactile or scented object to reinforce learning. One teacher we know uses acupuncture needles in her sessions on complementary medicine. Clearly, there is a link here with the topic, but she says that her students always recall this part of the session better, having felt (and, of course, tweeted a photo of) their punctured limb. There are many ways to use the sense of taste too – providing drinks or snacks if this is appropriate in your context.

- Pause and allow students time to post questions on an online notice-board, or time to write their queries on post-its and stick them on the wall. You can then address one or more of the questions submitted.
- Ask the students simply to pause and reflect in silence for a minute or two. Don't take any questions during this and don't be afraid if the silence seems long.
- Get students out of their seats and encourage 'big' movements.

Here are four quick suggestions on how to do this by asking them to:

1. write on the board, or on windows with grease pens, or on flipchart posters or paper tablecloths;
2. wander round and have a look at what everyone else is doing;
3. find someone in the room they've never spoken to before and sit next to them;
4. queue up as if at a bus stop, then respond to a call out of a subject-related term. If it fits category A, the students step to the left. If category B, they step to the right. If both, they do a star jump. If neither, they stand still.

Be ready with alternatives to standing up/moving for those with mobility issues – if necessary, discuss these with the students in question beforehand.

Pacing and variety (over a module/course as well as within a single session)

- Have a simple 'starter' activity – make it optional so that those that want to take the time to 'arrive' in the room – for example, by making verbal contact with peers, can. This then functions like a warm-up.

- Teach little and often, revisiting the same topics at different levels or in different contexts as suggested by Bruner's spiral curriculum (1960).
- You don't have to 'deliver' content just by talking or asking the students to read something. Here are some alternatives.

    1. Accessing a text in different ways – for example, splitting it up into sections and giving different sections to different people, then getting them to share what they've learned using the jigsaw technique (Education World, 2017).
    2. Distributing highlighter pens and asking students to identify specific content or textual feature in material.
    3. Asking students to create a poster to illustrate what they are reading.
    4. Rather than having content 'up front', set a task first and then have the content in easily available form (i-pads, handouts) for the students to access and consult when they need it.
    5. Display content as if it were part of an exhibition, with posters on walls, interactive tasks around the room and questions for the students to answer.

And so we come to the end of the chapter which falls at the end of our book. You may not have read the chapters in order and we didn't write them that way, but this does seem an apt moment to say thank you for joining us in our alphabet, and now we are off for a well-earned break.

REFERENCES

Akerlind, GS (2004) A new dimension to understanding university teaching. *Teaching in Higher Education*, 9(3): 363–75.

Akinbode, A (2015) The quiet learner and the quiet teacher. *University of Hertfordshire Link*, 1(2).

Alsop, S (2005) *Beyond Cartesian Dualism Encountering Affect in the Teaching and Learning of Science*. Dordrecht, The Netherlands: Springer.

Angulo, AJ (2016) Don't turn students into consumers – the US proves it's a recipe for disaster. *The Guardian*, 6 July.

Argyris, C and Schön, D (1974) *Theory in Practice: Increasing professional effectiveness*. San Francisco, CA: Jossey-Bass.

Aronin, S and Smith, M (2016) One in four students suffers from mental health problems. *YouGov UK*, 9 August. Available online at: https://yougov.co.uk/news/2016/08/09/quarter-britains-students-are-afflicted-mental-hea/ (accessed 2 August 2017).

Asante, S (1996) *What is Inclusion?* Toronto: Inclusion Press.

Baars, S, Mulcahy, E and Bernardes, E (2016) *The Underrepresentation of White Working Class Boys in Higher Education: The role of widening participation*. London: LKMCo and KCL.

Baglieri, S and Knopf, J (2004) Normalizing difference in inclusive teaching. *Journal of Learning Disabilities*, 37(6): 525–9.

Bagshaw, A (2017) A beginner's guide to the Teaching Excellence Framework. *WONKHE*, 19 June. Available online at: http://wonkhe.com/blogs/a-beginners-guide-to-the-teaching-excellence-framework/ (accessed 30 July 2017).

Bailey, R (2013) Exploring the engagement of lecturers with learning and teaching agendas through a focus on their beliefs about, and experience with, student support. *Studies in Higher Education*, 38(1): 143–55.

Bamforth, SE, Robinson, CL, Croft, A and Crawford, A (2007) Retention and progression of Engineering students with diverse mathematical backgrounds. *Teaching Mathematics and its Applications*, 26(4): 156–66.

Bandura, A (1997) *Self-efficacy: The exercise of control*. New York: WH Freeman.

Barnett, R (2009) Knowing and becoming in the higher education curriculum. *Studies in Higher Education*, 34(4): 429–40.

Barr, N (ed.) (2014) *Shaping Higher Education: 50 years after the Robbins Report*. London: LSE.

Barrett, L and Barrett, P (2011) Women and academic workloads: Career slow lane or cul-de-sac? *Higher Education: The International Journal of Higher Education and Educational Planning*, 61(2): 141–55.

Barrett, T and Moore, S (2011) *New Approaches to Problem-based Learning: Revitalising your practice in higher education*. New York and London: Routledge.

Barrier, M (2005) Brad Bird, an interview by Michael Barrier. Available online at: www.michaelbarrier.com/Interviews/Bird/Bird_Interview.htm

Bart, M (2011) Shy students in the college classroom: What does it take to improve student participation? *Faculty Focus*, 2 August.

Bassett, P (2011) How do students view asynchronous online discussions as a learning experience? *Interdisciplinary Journal of E-Learning and Learning Objects*, 7.

BBC (2014) Thinking creatively: GCSE Bitesize Business Studies. Available online at: www.bbc.co.uk/schools/gcsebitesize/business/aims/publicsectorrev2.shtml (accessed 30 June 2017).

Beetham, H and Sharpe, R (eds) (2013) *Rethinking Pedagogy for a Digital Age: Designing for 21st century learning* (2nd edn). Abingdon and New York: Routledge.

Bekkering, H (2017) Learning styles and their place in the classroom. *The Guardian*, 13 March.

Benozzo, A and Colley, H (2012) Emotion and learning in the workplace: Critical perspectives. *Journal of Workplace Learning*, 24(5): 304–16. ISSN: 1366–5626. Available online at: http://eprints.hud.ac.uk/14014/

Bereiter, C and Scardamalia, M (2014) Knowledge building and knowledge creation: One concept, two hills to climb. In Tan, SC, So, HJ and Yeo, J (eds) *Knowledge Creation in Education*, pp. 35–52.

Berg, K (2010) Justifying physical education based on neuroscience evidence. *Journal of Physical Education, Recreation and Dance*, 81(3): 24–46.

Biggs, JB and Tang, CS (2011) *Teaching for Quality Learning at University: What the student does* (4th edn). Maidenhead: Open University Press.

BIS (2016) *Higher Education and Research Bill: Factsheet*. GOV.UK. Available online at: www.gov.uk/government/uploads/system/uploads/attachment_data/file/543500/bis-16-285-higher-education-research-bill-summary.pdf (accessed 4 August 2017).

Black, P and Wiliam, D (1998) Assessment and classroom learning. *Assessment in Education: Principles, Policy & Practice*, 5(1): 7–74.

Black, P, Harrison, C, Lee, C, Marshall, B and Wiliam, D (2004) Working inside the black box: Assessment for learning in the classroom. *Phi Delta Kappan Magazine*, 86(1): 8–21.

Blakemore, CL (2003) Movement is essential to learning. *Journal of Physical Education, Recreation and Dance*, 74(9): 22–5.

Blatchford, P, Chan, KW, Galton, M, Lai, KC and Lee, JC (eds) (2016) *Class Size: Eastern and Western Perspectives (Asia–Europe Education Dialogue)*. London and New York: Routledge.

Boeree, C (2001) *Jean Piaget 1896–1980*. Shippensburg University: Shippensburg.

Boring, A, Ottoboni, K and Stark, P (2017) Student evaluations of teaching (mostly) do not measure teaching effectiveness. *ScienceOpen Research*, 2016(1), 1–11.

Boud, D and Falchikov, N (2007) *Rethinking Assessment in Higher Education: Learning for the longer term*. London: Routledge.

Bourdieu, P and Passeron, JC (1994) *Introduction: Language and the relationship to language in the teaching situation*. In Bourdieu, P, Passeron, J-C and Saint Martin, M de, *Academic Discourse*. Cambridge: Polity Press, pp. 1–34.

Bradbury, A (2014) *Identity Performance and Race: The use of critical race theory in understanding institutional racism and discrimination in schools*. In Race, R and Lander, V (2014) *Advancing Race and Ethnicity in Education*. New York: Palgrave Macmillan.

British Council (2014) Massification of higher education in large academic systems. Available online at: www.britishcouncil.org/education/ihe/knowledge-centre/national-policies/report-massification-higher-education (accessed 30 July 2017).

Brookfield, S (1995) Becoming a Critically Reflective Teacher. San Francisco: Jossey-Bass

Brookfield, S (2005) *The Power of Critical Theory for Adult Learning and Teaching*. Maidenhead: Oxford University Press.

Brookfield, S (2011) *Teaching for Critical Thinking*. San Francisco, CA: Jossey-Bass.

Brookfield, S (2017) *Becoming a Critically Reflective Teacher* (2nd edn). San Francisco, CA: Jossey-Bass.

Bruner, J (1960) *The Process of Education*. Cambridge, MA: Harvard University Press.

Bunce, L, Baird, A and Jones, SE (2016) The student-as-consumer approach in higher education and its effects on academic performance. *Studies in Higher Education*, 0: 1–21.

Burke, P (2012) *The Right to Higher Education: Beyond the widening participation*. London: Routledge.

Burke, P, Stevenson, J and Whelan, P (2015) Teaching 'excellence' and pedagogic stratification in higher education. *International Studies in Widening Participation*, 2(2): 29–43.

Burkeman, O (2011) *Help! How to Become Slightly Happier and Get a Bit More Done*. Edinburgh: Canongate Books.

Burnett, C (2011) Medium for empowerment or a 'centre for everything': Students' experience of control in digital environments within a university context. *Education and Information Technologies*, 16(3): 245–58.

Burns, J (2017) Teach 'problem-solving' to produce engineers, schools urged, BBC News, 31 March. Available online at: www.bbc.co.uk/news/education-39422630 (accessed 2 August 2017).

Butler, D (2015) *Metacognition and Self-Regulation in Learning*. In Scott, D and Hargreaves, E (eds) *The SAGE Handbook of Learning*. London: Sage, pp. 291–309.

Butterwick, S and Lipson Lawrene, R (2009) Creating alternative realities – arts-based approaches to transformative learning. In Mezirow, J and Taylor, E (eds) *Transformative Learning in Practice: Insights from community, workplace, and higher education* (Jossey-Bass Higher Education Series). San Francisco, CA: Jossey-Bass.

Cannizzo, F and Osbaldiston, N (2016) Academic work/life balance: A brief quantitative analysis of the Australian experience. *Journal of Sociology*, 52(4): 890–906.

Cavanagh, M (2011) Students' experiences of active engagement through cooperative learning activities in lectures. *Active Learning in Higher Education*, 12(1): 23–33.

CBI (2016) *The Right Combination: CBI/Pearson Education and Skills Survey 2016*. London: Pearson.

Chanock, K (2000) Comments on essays: Do students understand what tutors write? *Teaching in Higher Education*, 5(1): 95–105.

Chinn, SJ (2001) Maths and dyslexia: A view from the UK. *Learning Works*. Available online at: www.learning-works.org.uk/chinns-uk-research-pdf (accessed 2 August 2017).

Chuah, S (2010) Teaching East-Asian students: Some observations. *The Economics Network*, October. Available online at: www.economicsnetwork.ac.uk/showcase/chuah_international (accessed 4 August 2017).

Clara, M (2017) Teacher resilience and meaning transformation: How teachers reappraise situations of adversity. *Teaching and Teacher Education*, 63: 82–9.

Clews, D (2010) *LOOKING OUT: Effective Engagement with Creative and Cultural enterprise: Arts HE and the Creative Industries*, Brighton: University of Brighton.

Clughen, L (2014) 'Embodied writing support': The importance of the body in engaging students with writing. *Journal of Writing in Creative Practice*, 7(2).

Coffield, F (2012) Learning styles: Unreliable, invalid and impractical and yet still widely used. In Adey, P and Dillon, J (eds) *Bad Education: Debunking myths in education*. Maidenhead: Open University Press.

Coffield, F, Moseley, D, Hall, E. and Ecclestone, K (2004) Should we be using learning styles? What research has to say to practice. London: Learning and Skills Development Agency.

Cohen, L (1992) *Anthem*. New York: Columbia Records.

Collier-Reed, B (2013) Considering two audiences when recording lectures as lecturecasts. *African Journal of Information Systems*, 5(3): 70–9.

Collins, S and Ting, H (2010) Actors and act-ers: Enhancing inclusion and diversity in teaching and teacher education through the validation of quiet teaching. *Teaching and Teacher Education*, 26(4): 900–5.

Connery, MC, John-Steiner, V and Marjanovic-Shane, A (2010) *Vygotsky and Creativity: A cultural-historical approach to play, meaning making, and the arts*. New York and Oxford: Peter Lang.

Cope, B and Kalantzis, M (2009) "Multiliteracies": New literacies, new learning. *Pedagogies: An International Journal*, 4(3): 164–95.

Cormier, D (2008) Rhizomatic education: Community as curriculum. Dave's Educational Blog, 3 June. Available at: http://davecormier.com/edblog/2008/06/03/rhizomatic-education-community-as-curriculum/ (accessed 30 July 2017).

Cottrell, L (2016) Joy and happiness: A simultaneous and evolutionary concept analysis. *Journal of Advanced Nursing*, 72(7),1506–17.

Coughlan, S (2016) Student suicide figures increase, BBC News Service, 25 May. Available online at: www.bbc.co.uk/news/education-36378573 (accessed 1 August 2017).

Cowan, J (2006) *On Becoming an Innovative University Teacher: Reflection in action* (2nd edn). Maidenhead: Open University Press.

Croft, A, Harrison, M and Robinson, C (2009) Recruitment and retention of students – an integrated and holistic vision of mathematics support. *International Journal of Mathematical Education in Science and Technology*, 40(1): 109–25.

Cronhjort, M, Filipsson, L and Weurlander, M (2017) Improved engagement and learning in flipped-classroom calculus. *Teaching Mathematics and its Applications: An International Journal of the IMA*, pp. 1–9.

Crossley, N (2001) Citizenship, intersubjectivity and the lifeworld. In Stevenson, N (ed.) *Culture and Citizenship*. London: Sage.

Csikszentmihalyi, M (1990) *Flow*. HarperCollins: New York.

Damasio, A (1994) *Descartes' Error: Emotion, reason and the human brain*. New York: Grosset/Putnam.

Daniel, M (2014) P4C in Preservice teacher education: Difficulties and successes encountered in two research projects. *Analytic Teaching* [S.l.], 19(1): 15–28.

Darn, S. (2010) Eliciting. British Council and BBC World Service. Available online at: www.teachingenglish.org.uk/article/eliciting (accessed 4 August 2017).

Davidson, L (2016) Blue sky thinking? The 10 business phrases most likely to make you scream. *Herald.ie*, 17 June. Available online at: www.herald.ie/news/blue-sky-thinking-the-10-business-phrases-most-likely-to-make-you-scream-34807763.html (accessed 29 July 2017).

Davies, WM (2009) Groupwork as a form of assessment: Common problems and recommended solutions. *Higher Education, 58*(4): 563–84.

Davis, LJ (2006) *The Disability Studies Reader* (2nd edn). New York and London: Routledge.

De Pury, J (2016) Universities and mental health. *Universities UK,* 3 March. Available online at: www.universitiesuk.ac.uk/blog/Pages/universities-mental-health.aspx (accessed 30 July 2017).

Desurvire, H, Caplan, M and Toth, J (2004) Using heuristics to evaluate the playability of games. *CHI '04 Extended Abstracts on Human Factors in Computing Systems,* 1509–12.

Devlin, M (2008) An international and interdisciplinary approach to curriculum: The Melbourne Model (keynote address). Universitas 21 Conference, Glasgow University, Scotland.

Dewey, J (1933) *How We Think.* New York: Heath.

Dewey, J (1966) *Democracy and Education: An Introduction to the Philosophy of education.* New York: The Free Press.

Dewey, J and Dewey, E (1915) *Schools of Tomorrow.* New York: EP Dutton.

Dickerson, C, Jarvis, J and Stockwell, L (2016) Staff–student collaboration: Student learning from working together to enhance educational practice in higher education. *Teaching in Higher Education,* 21(3): 249–65.

Dumont, H, Istance, D and Benavides, F (eds) (2012) The Nature of Learning: Using research to inspire practice: Practitioner guide from the innovative learning environments project. OECD, Centre for Educational Research and Innovation. Available online at: www.oecd.org/edu/ceri/50300814.pdf (accessed: 31 July 2017).

Dunn, K (2017) In defence of alchemy – thoughts on the future of student engagement. Sheffield Institute of Education Blog, 14 July, Sheffield Hallam University.

Dweck, C (2017) *Mindset.* London: Robinson.

Earl, L (2003) *Assessment as Learning: Using Classroom Assessment to Maximise Student Learning.* Thousand Oaks; CA: Corwin Press.

Ecclestone, K and Hayes, D (2009) *The Dangerous Rise of Therapeutic Education.* New York: Routledge.

Education World (2017) *The Jigsaw Technique.* Educationworld.com. Available online at: www.educationworld.com/a_curr/strategy/strategy036.shtml (accessed 1 August 2017).

Edyburn, D (2010) Would you recognize universal design for learning if you saw it? Ten propositions for new directions for the second decade of UDL. *Learning Disability Quarterly,* 33(1): 33–41.

Enkerli, A (2008) Student engagement: The gym analogy (updated: credited). *Disparate,* 21 November. Available online at: http://blog.enkerli.com/2008/11/21/student-engagement-the-gym-analogy/ (accessed 1 August 2017).

Entwistle, N (2001) Styles of learning and approaches to studying in higher education. *Kybernetes,* 30(5/6): 593–603.

Entwistle, N. and Ramsden, P. (2015) *Understanding Student Learning.* New York: Routledge.

EPALE (2017) *Spiky profile – EPALE – European Commission.* Available at: https://ec.europa.eu/epale/en/glossary/spiky-profile (accessed 1 August 2017).

Equality Act 2010. Available at: www.legislation.gov.uk/ukpga/2010/15/contents (accessed 4 August 2017).

Equality Challenge Unit (2015) Equality in higher education: Statistical report. Part 2: students. Available at: www.ecu.ac.uk/wp-content/uploads/2015/11/Equality-in-HE-statistical-report-2015-part-2-students.pdf (accessed 4 August 2017).

Equality Challenge Unit (2016) Use of language: Race and ethnicity. Available at: www.ecu.ac.uk/guidance-resources/using-data-and-evidence/use-language-race-ethnicity/ (accessed 4 August 2017).

Eraut, M (2004) The practice of reflection. *Learning in Health and Social Care*, 3(2): 47–52.

Ernest, P (1994) Constructing mathematical knowledge: Epistemology and mathematics education. *Studies in Mathematics Education*. 4: 297.

Ernest, P (1999) Is mathematics discovered or invented? *Philosophy of Mathematics Journal*, 12 (2).

Expert Self Care (2017) 'ESC Student' – supporting students' health and wellbeing, *ESC*. Available at: www.expertselfcare.com/health-apps/esc-student/ (accessed 1 August 2017).

Farrell, L (2001) Negotiating knowledge in the knowledge economy: Workplace educators and the politics of codification. *Studies in Continuing Education*, 23(2): 201–14.

Fedesco, H (2014) The impact of (in)effective listening on interpersonal interactions. *International Journal of Listening*, 29(2): 1–4.

Fernandes, A, Huang, J and Rinaldo, V (2011) Does where a student sits really matter? – The impact of seating locations on student classroom learning. *International Journal of Applied Educational Studies*, 10(1): 66–77.

Finlay, L (2008) *Reflecting on Reflective Practice*. PBL Paper 52. The Open University. Available online at: www.open.ac.uk/opencetl/sites/www.open.ac.uk.opencetl/files/files/ecms/web-content/Finlay-(2008)-Reflecting-on-reflective-practice-PBPL-paper-52.pdf

Flor, R.K, Bita, A, Monir, KC and Zohreh, ZZ (2013) The effect of teaching critical and creative thinking skills on the locus of control and psychological well-being in adolescents. *Procedia – Social and Behavioral Sciences*, 82: 51–6.

Foucault, M (1977) Discipline and punish, panopticism. In Sheridan, A. (ed.) *Discipline and Punish: The Birth of the Prison*. New York: Vintage Books, pp. 195–228.

Foucault, M (1998) *The History of Sexuality/Vol. 2, The Use of Pleasure* (2nd edn). London: Penguin.

Freire, P (1970) *Pedagogy of the Oppressed*. New York: Seabury.

Freire, P (1998) *Pedagogy of Freedom: Ethics, Democracy, and Civic Courage*, Critical Perspectives Series. Lanham, MD: Rowman & Littlefield.

Freire, P and Faundez, A. (1989) *Learning to Question*. New York: Continuum.

Fry, H, Ketteridge, S and Marshall, S (2009) *Teaching and Learning in Higher Education*. London: Routledge.

Furedi, F (2011) Introduction to the marketization of higher education and the student as consumer. In Molesworth, M, Scullion, R and Nixon, E (eds) *The Marketisation of Higher Education and the Student as Consumer*. London and New York: Routledge.

Gil, N (2015) Majority of students experience mental health issues, says NUS survey, *The Guardian*, 14 December.

Glass, CR and Westmont, CM (2014) Comparative effects of belongingness on the academic success and cross-cultural interactions of domestic and international students. *International Journal of Intercultural Relations*, 38: 106–19.

Goffman, I (1956) *The Presentation of the Self in Everyday Life*. New York: Anchor Books.

Gottschall, J (2012) *The storytelling animal: how stories make us human*. Boston: Houghton Mifflin Harcourt.

Gray, C and Klapper, J (2009) Key aspects of teaching and learning in languages. In Fry, H, Ketteridge, S and Marshall, S. *A Handbook for Teaching and Learning in Higher Education* (3rd edn). New York: Routledge.

Grundy, S (1987) *Curriculum: Product or Praxis?* Lewes: Falmer Press.

Gu, M (2001) *Education in China and Abroad: Perspectives from a Lifetime in Comparative education* (Vol. 9). Comparative Education Research Centre.

Guanci, G (2010) Best practices for webinars. *Creative Nursing*, 16(3): 119–21.

Guo, M (1994) Elicitation pedagogy: A method of second language teaching in China. *The American Journal of Semiotics, 11*(3/4), 103–14.

Hadzigeorgiou, Y (2006) Humanizing the teaching of physics through storytelling: The case of current electricity. *Physics Education*, 41(1): 42–6.

Hall, T, Meyer, A and Rose, D (2012) *Universal Design for Learning in the Classroom*. London, New York: The Guildford Press.

Hammond, JA, Bithell, CP, Jones, L and Bidgood, P (2010) A first-year experience of student-directed peer-assisted learning. *Active Learning in Higher Education*, 11(3): 201–12.

Hanson, R (2009) *Buddha's Brain: The Practical Neuroscience of Happiness, Love, and Wisdom*. Oakland, CA: New Harbinger Publications.

Hargreaves, E (2015) Pedagogy, fear and learning. In Scott, D and Hargreaves, E (eds) *The SAGE Handbook of Learning*. London: Sage, pp. 310–20.

Harrison, N and Peacock, N (2010). Cultural distance, mindfulness and passive xenophobia using Integrated Threat Theory to explore home HE students' perspectives on internationalisation at home. *British Educational Research Journal*, 36(6): 877–902.

Hatfield, J, Horsman, T and Szumko, J (2015) Navigating the essay: Making writing multi-sensory. *Journal of Writing in Creative Practice*, 7(2): 311–39.

Higher Education Authority (HEA) (2014) *Critical Thinking*. York: HEA. Available online at: www.heacademy.ac.uk/system/files/resources/critical_thinking.pdf (accessed 3 August 2017).

HEA (2016) a Students demand better value for money. HEA. Available online at: www.heacademy.ac.uk/about/news/students-demand-better-value-money (accessed 3 August 2017).

HEA (2016) HEA comments on the destinations of leavers statistics. HEA. Available online at: www.heacademy.ac.uk/about/news/hea-comments-destination-leavers-statistics (accessed 3 August 2017).

HEA (2017) Framework for internationalising higher education. HEA. Available online at: www.heacademy.ac.uk/individuals/strategic-priorities/international ising-higher-education (accessed 3 August 2017).

Heaslip, G, Donovan, P and Cullen, J (2014) Student response systems and learner engagement in large classes. *Active Learning in Higher Education*, 15(1): 11–24.

Heron, TE and Heward, WL (1982) Ecological assessment: Implications for teachers of learning disabled students. *Learning Disability Quarterly*, 5(2): 117–25.

Herrington, A and Herrington, J (2005) *Authentic Learning Environments in Higher education*. Hershey, PA and London: Information Science Publishing.

Higher Education Opportunity Act (HEOA) (2008) Public law, 110–315. Available online at: www2.ed.gov/policy/highered/leg/hea08/index.html

Hinchcliffe, GW and Jolly, A (2011) Graduate identity and employability. *British Educational Research Journal*, 37(4): 563–84.

Hockings, C (2010) Inclusive learning and teaching in Higher Education: A synthesis of research. York: HEA.

Holloway, D (2013) Mental health and emotional aspects. In Griffiths, G and Stone, R (eds) *Teaching Adult Numeracy: Principles and Practice*. Maidenhead: Open University Press/McGraw-Hill, pp. 11–24.

Holt, J (1964) *How Children Fail*. New York: Pitman.

Hoon, A, Oliver, E, Szpakowska, K and Newton, P (2015) Use of the 'Stop, Start, Continue' method is associated with the production of constructive qualitative feedback by students in higher education. *Assessment & Evaluation in Higher Education*, 40(5): 755–67.

Hooper, M (2016) Supporting thriving communities: The role of universities in reducing inequality. University Alliance. Available online at: www.unialliance.ac.uk/supportingthrivingcommunities (accessed 4 September 2017).

Horobin, H (2015) The subtle stereotyping of other in transnational physiotherapy education. In Centre for Racial Equality in Scotland and the University of Edinburgh 2nd International Conference 2015, John MacIntyre Conference Centre, University of Edinburgh, 24–6 June.

Hoskins, S and Mitchell, J (2015) Research-based learning – taking it a step further. York: HEA.

Hunter, EM and Wu, C (2016) Give me a *better* break: Choosing workday break activities to maximize resource recovery. *Journal of Applied Psychology*, 101(2): 302–11.

Ibabe, I and Jauregizar, J (2010) Online self-assessment with feedback and metacognitive knowledge. *Higher Education: The International Journal of Higher Education and Educational Planning*, 59(2): 243–58.

Ironside, PM (2004) 'Covering content' and teaching thinking: Deconstructing the additive curriculum. *Nurse Education*, 43(1): 5–12.

Jabr, F (2013) Why your brain needs more down time. *The Scientific American*, 15 October.

Jackson, C (2015) Affective dimensions of learning. In Scott, D and Hargreaves, E (eds) *The SAGE Handbook of Learning*. London: Sage, pp. 353–62.

Jacob, J (2015) Interdisciplinary trends in higher education. *Palgrave Communications*, 1.

Jacobs, R (2011) Aesthetic development in higher education. An interdisciplinary dialogue. *Practice and Evidence of Scholarship of Teaching and Learning in Higher Education*, 6(2): 232–48.

Jaques, D (2000) *Learning in Groups: A Handbook for Improving Groupwork* (3rd edn). London: Kogan Page.

Jeanne, H (1990) Enriching prior knowledge: Enhancing mature literacy in higher education. *Journal of Higher Education*, 61(4): 425–47.

Jen Su, A (2013) Put on your oxygen mask first: 6 tips for self-care on the job. *Huffington Post*, 25 March.

Jenkins, A, Healey, M and Zetter, R (2007) *Linking Research and Teaching in Disciplines and Departments*. York: Higher Education Academy.

Jindal-Snape, D, Davies, D, Collier, C, Howe, A, Digby, R and Hay, P (2013) The impact of creative learning environments on learners: A systematic literature review. *Improving Schools*, 16(1): 21–31.

Jonassen, DH and Rohrer-Murphy, L (1999) Activity theory as a framework for designing constructivist learning environments. *Educational Technology Research and Development*, 47(1): 61–79.

JOPERD (2010) Physical activity and academic achievement. *Journal of Physical Education, Recreation and Dance*, 81(7): 5.

Joseph, G (2010) *The Crest of the Peacock: Non-European roots of mathematics*. Princeton, NJ and Oxford: Princeton University Press.

Kanigel, R (2014) Helping students step outside their comfort zone. *International Educator*, 23(1): 48–51.

Kara, H (2015) *Creative Research Methods in the Social Sciences: A practical guide*. Bristol: Policy Press.

Kardong-Edgren, S (2013) Bandura's self-efficacy theory ... something is missing. *Clinical Simulation in Nursing*, 9(9), E327–E328.

Katai, Z and Toth, L (2010) Technologically and artistically enhanced multi-sensory computer-programming education. *Teaching and teacher education*, 26(2), pp.244–251.

Katai, Z, Toth, L and Adorjani, AK (2014) Multi-sensory informatics education. *Informatics in Education*, 13(2): 225–40.

Kaur, S and Manan, SA (2013) Developing interdisciplinary teaching: A vignette of a postgraduate course. *Procedia – Social and Behavioral Sciences*, 90: 755–63.

Kawa, P (2016) Improving student mental health – recognition must lead to real action. *WONKHE*, 19 October. Available online at: http://wonkhe.com/blogs/policy-watch-student-mental-health/ (accessed: 1 August 2017).

Kentish, B (2017) University tuition fees in England now the highest in the world, new analysis suggests. *The Independent*, 28 March.

Kidd, W and Czerniawski, G (2011) *The Student Voice Handbook: Bridging the academic/practitioner divide*. Bingley: Emerald Group Publishing.

Kidron, A and Kali, Y (2015) Boundary breaking for interdisciplinary learning. *Research in Learning Technology*, 23.

Kinman, G and Garfield, I (2015) The open-plan university – noisy nightmare or open ideas hub? *The Guardian*, 16 October.

Kinman, G and Wray, S (2013) Higher stress: A survey of stress and well-being among staff in higher education. UCU. Available online at: www.ucu.org.uk/media/5911/Higher-stress-a-survey-of-stress-and-well-being-among-staff-in-higher-education-Jul-13/pdf/HE_stress_report_July_2013.pdf (accessed 14 September 2017).

Knight, PT (2001) Complexity and curriculum: A process approach to curriculum-making. *Teaching in Higher Education*, 6(3): 369–81.

Knowles, M (1980) *The Modern Practice of Adult Education: From Pedagogy to Andragogy* (rev. and updated edn). Chicago: Follett Publishing.

Kolb, DA and Fry, R (1975) Toward an applied theory of experiential learning. In Cooper, C (ed.) *Theories of Group Process*. London: John Wiley.

Kontra, C, Goldin-Meadow, S and Beilock, S (2012) Embodied learning across the life span. *Topics in Cognitive Science*, 4(4): 761–39.

Kontra, C, Lyons, D, Fischer, S and Beilock, S (2015) Physical experience enhances science learning. *Psychological Science*, 26(6): 737–49.

Kovacs, K (2016) The case against oversimplified accountancy. *Inside Higher Education*, 6 December. Available online at: www.insidehighered.com/news/2016/12/06/study-higher-ed-accountability-should-be-based-multiple-metrics-not-one (accessed 3 August 2017).

Krathwol, DR, Bloom, BS and Masia, BB (1956) *Taxonomy of Educational Objectives: The classification of educational goals/handbook II, Affective domain*. New York: David McKay.

Krathwol, DR, Bloom, BS and Masia, BB (1964) *Taxonomy of Educational Objectives: The Classification of Educational Goals/Handbook II, Affective Domain*. New York: David McKay.

Kress, G (2010) *Multimodality: A social semiotic approach to contemporary communication*. London and New York: Routledge.

Kuhnke, E (2012) *Body language for dummies* (2nd ed.). Chichester: Wiley.

Langer, E and Moldoveanu, M (2000) The construct of mindfulness. *Journal of Social Issues, 56*(1): 1–9.

Laurillard, D (2012) *Teaching as a Design Science: Building pedagogical patterns for learning and technology*. New York and London: Routledge.

Lave, J and Wenger, E (1991) *Situated Learning: Legitimate peripheral participation*. Cambridge: Cambridge University Press.

Lawson, D (2015) Mathematics support at the transition to university. In Grove, M, Croft, T, Kyle, J and Lawson, D (eds) *Transitions in Undergraduate Mathematics Education*. Birmingham: University of Birmingham, pp. 39–56.

Lazzari, M (2009) Creative use of podcasting in higher education and its effect on competitive agency. *Computers and Education, 52*(1): 27–34.

LeDoux, JE (2000) Emotion circuits in the brain. *Annual Review, Neuroscience*. 23: 155–84.

Lefstein, A and Snell, J (2014) *Better than Best Practice: Developing teaching and learning through dialogue*. London: Routledge.

Lévi-Strauss, Claude (1966) *The Savage Mind*. Chicago: University of Chicago Press.

Lewis, CS (1955) *The Magician's Nephew*. London: The Bodley Head.

Lillis, T and Scott, M (2007) Defining academic literacies research: Issues of epistemology, ideology and strategy. *Journal of Applied Linguistics, 4*(1): 5–32.

Lipnevich, A and Smith, J (2009) Effects of differential feedback on students' examination performance. *Journal of Experimental Psychology: Applied,*15(4): 319–33.

Lippman, P (2015) Designing collaborative spaces for schools. *The Education Digest*, 80(5): 39–44.

Lunn, J (2008) Global perspectives in higher education: Taking the agenda forward in the United Kingdom. *Journal of Studies in International Education*, 12(3): 231–54.

Madriaga, M and Goodley, D (2010) Moving beyond the minimum: Socially just pedagogies and Asperger's Syndrome in UK higher education. *International Journal of Inclusive Education*, 14(2): 115–31.

Mager, RF (1962) *Preparing Objectives for Programmed Instruction*. San Francisco, CA: Fearon.

Maley, A and Mukundan, J (2007) *Poems for Young Asian readers*, Vol. 7. Malaysia: Pearson Longman.

Mallettt, R and Runswick-Cole, K (2014) *Approaching Disability: Critical issues and perspectives*. Abingdon: Routledge.

Mann, S and Robinson, A (2009) Boredom in the lecture theatre: An investigation into the contributors, moderators and outcomes of boredom amongst university students. *British Educational Research Journal*, 35(2): 243–58.

Maringe, F (2011) The student as consumer: Affordances and constraints in a transforming higher education environment. In Molesworth, M, Nixon, E and Scullion, R (2011) *The Marketisation of Higher Education: The student as consumer*. London: Routledge, pp. 142–54.

Masika, R and Jones, J (2016) Building student belonging and engagement: Insights into higher education students' experiences of participating and learning together. *Teaching in Higher Education*, 21(2): 138–50.

Maslow, AH (1964) *Religions, Values and Peak-Experiences*. London: Penguin Books.

Maslow, A (1970) *Motivation and Personality* (2nd edn). New York: Harper & Row.

Mason, J (2002) *Researching Your Own Practice: The discipline of noticing*. London: RoutledgeFalmer.

Mason, J and Johnston-Wilder, S (2004) *Fundamental Constructs in Mathematics Education*. New York: RoutledgeFalmer.

Masterman, L (2013) The challenge of teachers' design practice. In Beetham, H and Sharpe, R (eds) *Rethinking Pedagogy for a Digital Age: Designing for 21st Century Learning* (2nd edn). Abingdon and New York: Routledge.

Maughan, C (2011) Why study emotion? In Maharg, P and Maughan, C (eds) *Affect and Legal Education: Emotion in Learning and Teaching the Law (Emerging Legal Learning)*. Burlington, VT: Ashgate.

May, M (2012) Stuck on a problem? Then take a break. *The Globe and Mail*, 23 October.

Mayer, RE (2001) *Multimedia Learning*. New York: Cambridge University Press.

McCarey, M, Barr, T and Rattray, J (2007) Predictors of academic performance in a cohort of pre-registration nursing students. *Nurse Education Today*, 27(4): 357– 64.

McDowell, L, Wakelin, D, Montgomery, C and King, S (2011) Does assessment for learning make a difference? The development of a questionnaire to explore the student response. *Assessment & Evaluation in Higher Education*, 36(7): 749–65.

McDuff, N and Barefoot, H (2016) It's time for real action on the BME attainment gap. WONKHE. Available online at: http://wonkhe.com/blogs/analysis-time-for-real-action-on-bme-attainment/ (accessed 4 August 2017).

McGrath, L and Nichols, K (2017) Of writing and wardrobes. Sheffield Institute of Education Blog, 15 June. Sheffield Hallam University.

McGregor, J (2007) Understanding and managing classroom space. *Curriculum Briefing*, 5(2).

Mendell, M and Heath, G (2005) Do indoor pollutants and thermal conditions in schools influence student performance? A critical review of the literature. *Indoor Air*, 15(1): 27–52.

Mergler, N and Schleifer, R (1986) Actual minds, possible worlds (book review). *MLN*, 101(5): 1279–83.

Meyer, J and Norton, L (2004) Editorial: Metalearning in higher education. *Innovations in Education and Teaching International*, 41(4): 387–90.

Mezirow, J (1991) *Transformative Dimensions of Adult Learning*. San Francisco, CA: Jossey-Bass.

Mezirow, J (1997) Transformative learning: Theory to practice. *New Directions for Adult and Continuing Education*, 74: 5–12.

Mezirow, J and Taylor, E (2009) *Transformative Learning in Practice: Insights from community, workplace and higher education*. San Francisco, CA: Jossey-Bass.

Mihăilescu, AI, Diaconescu, LV, Ciobanu, AM, Donisan, T and Mihailescu, C (2016) The impact of anxiety and depression on academic performance in undergraduate medical students. *European Psychiatry*, 33: S284.

Miller, M (2016) *The Ethnicity Attainment Gap: Literature Review*. Widening Participation Research and Evaluation. Sheffield: TUoS

Miller, M (2016) Widening Participation Research and Evaluation *The Ethnicity Attainment Gap: Literature Review*. Sheffield: TUoS

Mills, M (2013) Collaborative presentations using Google Docs-12. In Ferris, S and Wilder, H (2013) *The Plugged-In Professor: Tips and Techniques for Teaching with Social Media* (Chandos Publishing Social Media Series). Burlington, VT: Elsevier Science, pp. 151–63.

Moll, L, Amanti, C, Neff, D and González, N (1992) Funds of knowledge for teaching: Using a qualitative approach to connect homes and classrooms. *Theory into Practice*, 31: 132–41.

Montessori Schools Association (2008) *Guide to the Early Years Foundation Stage in Montessori Settings*. London: Montessori St Nicholas Charity. Available online at: www.cotswoldmontessori.co.uk/upload/Guide%20to%20EYFS%20in%20Montessori%20Settings.pdf

Montessori, G and Gerald, L (2004) *The Montessori Method: The Origins of an Educational Innovation, Including an Abridged and Annotated Edition of Maria Montessori's The Montessori Method*. Lanham, MD and Oxford: Rowman & Littlefield.

Montgomery, C (2011) Educating Multiliterate Graduates for a Globalised World: The Role of Interdisciplinarity, The Informal Curriculum and Boundary Crossings. Northumbria Research Conference Proceedings, 5–6 May. Newcastle-upon-Tyne: Northumbria University.

Morris, C (2011) Open minds: Towards a 'mentally well' university in taking wellbeing forward in higher education: Reflections on theory and practice. University of Brighton Press Centre for Learning and Teaching.

Murray, J (2017) Is Theresa May really serious about mental health provision for students?, *The Telegraph*, 16 January.

Neary, M, Saunders, G, Hagyard, A and Derricott, D (2014) *Student as producer: Research-engaged teaching, an institutional strategy*. York: Higher Education Academy.

Neary, M and Winn, J (2009) *The Student as Producer: Reinventing the Student Experience in Higher Education. The Future of Higher Education: Policy, Pedagogy, and the Student experience*. London: Continuum.

Nicholson, A (2015) Research-informed teaching: A clinical approach. *The Law Teacher*, 1–16.

Nielsen, M (2012–17) *Look After Your Voice*. Available online at: https://naturalvoice.net/about/look-after-your-voice (accessed 5 August 2017).

Neuroscience News (2015) Learning with all the senses. *Neuroscience News*, 5 February.

Newman, G (2015) A decade into the Melbourne Model, young graduates give their assessment. *The Sydney Morning Herald*, 4 October.

Nguyen, J and Carvalho, H (2014) A simple approach for teaching a complex topic by asking students to participate in an engaging narrative to improve attention and retention. *The FASEB Journal*, 28(1): 531–4.

Ning, H and Downing, K (2012) Influence of student learning experience on academic performance: The mediator and moderator effects of self-regulation and motivation. *British Educational Research Journal*, 38(2): 219–37.

Noddings, N (2003) *Happiness and Education*. Cambridge: Cambridge University of Chicago Press.

Nunes, T, Schliemann, A and Carraher, D (1993) *Street Mathematics and School Mathematics*. Cambridge: Cambridge University Press.

Obenland, C, Munson, A and Hutchinson, J (2012) Silent students' participation in a large active learning science classroom, *Journal of College Science Teaching*, 42(2): 90–8.

O'Connor, J and Robertson, E (2000) Brahmagupta. In MacTutor History of Mathematics Archive: University of St Andrews, Scotland.

O'Connor, KW, Schmidt, G and Drouin, M (2016) Suspended because of social media? Students' knowledge and opinions of university social media policies and practices. *Computers in Human Behavior*, 65: 619–26.

O'Day, R (2009) Universities and professions in the early modern period. In Cunningham, P, Oosthuizen, S and Taylor, R (eds) *Beyond the Lecture Hall: Universities and community engagement from the Middle Ages to the present day*. Cambridge: University of Cambridge Faculty of Education and Institute of Continuing Education, pp. 79–102.

O'Donovan, J and Maruthappu, M (2015) Distant peer-tutoring of clinical skills, using tablets with instructional videos and Skype: A pilot study in the UK and Malaysia. *Medical Teacher.* 37(5): 463–69.

OECD (2016) Fostering and assessing students' creativity and critical thinking in higher education. Summary report International seminar OECD Centre for Educational Research and Innovation (CERI) 20–1 June, Paris.

Orr, J (1993) Computer-aided engineer: Present or perish. *Computer-Aided Engineering*, 12(1): January.

Oughton, H (2013) The Social Context of Numeracy. In Griffiths, G and Stone, R (eds) *Teaching Adult Numeracy – Principles and Practice*. Maidenhead: Open University Press/McGraw-Hill.

O'Shea, S (2016) Avoiding the manufacture of "Sameness": First-in-family students, cultural capital and the higher education environment. *Higher Education: The International Journal of Higher Education Research*, 72(1): 59–78.

Oxford University Press (2017) *Oxford Living Dictionaries: English*. Available online at: https://en.oxforddictionaries.com/ (accessed 4 August 2017).

Palmer, JA, Bresler, L and Cooper, DE (2001) *Fifty Major Thinkers on Education: From Confucius to Dewey* (Routledge Key Guides). London: Routledge.

Parekh, B and Runnymede Trust, Commission on the Future of Multi-Ethnic Britain (2000) The future of multi-ethnic Britain: Report of the Commission on the Future of Multi-Ethnic Britain. London: Profile.

Parr, C (2014) 20 new ideas from UK universities that will change the world. *Times Higher Educational Supplement*, 9 June.

Perillo, L. (2009) *Transcendentalism*. In Perillo, L (2009) *Inseminating the Elephant*. Washington, DC: Copper Canyon Press.

Phillipson, N and Wegerif, R (2016) *Dialogic Education: Mastering core concepts through thinking together*. Abingdon: Routledge.

Piaget, J (1952) *The Origins of Intelligence in Children*. New York: Norton.

Pinto, M (2014) 7 Things a quiet student wishes their teacher understood. *Huffington Post*, 25 October.

Piro, JM (2008) Foucault and the architecture of surveillance: Creating regimes of power in schools, shrines, and society. *Educational Studies*, 44(1): 30–46.

Postholm, M (2013) Classroom management: What does research tell us? *European Educational Research Journal*, 12(3): 389–402.

Pritchard, A and Woollard, J (2010) *Psychology for the Classroom: Constructivism and social learning* (Psychology for the Classroom Series). London: Routledge.

Pryor, J and Torrance, H (1997) Formative assessment in the classroom: Where psychological theory meets social practice. *Social Psychology of Education*, 2(2): 151–76.

QIA (2003) Multi-sensory learning. Available at: http://learning.gov.wales/docs/learningwales/publications/140801-multi-sensory-learning-en.pdf (accessed 14 August 2017).

Quality Assurance Agency (2016) Subject Benchmark Statement: Art and Design. Available at: www.qaa.ac.uk/assuring-standards-and-quality/the-quality-code/subject-benchmark- statements (accessed 2 August 2017).

Rawnsley, A (2017) You don't need a double first to see university funding is in chaos. *The Guardian*, 9 July.

Razbully, S and Bamber, P (2008) Cross curricula planning and the global dimension at Liverpool Hope. Seminar given at Education for Sustainable Development and Global Citizenship ITE Network Inaugural Conference, 10 July.

Redondo, E, Fonseca, D, Sánchez, A and Navarro, I (2013) New strategies using handheld augmented reality and mobile learning-teaching methodologies, in architecture and building engineering degrees. *Procedia Computer Science*, 25: 52–61.

Reeve, J (2014) How can adopting the materials and environment of the studio engage Art & Design students more deeply with research and writing? An investigation into the Reframing Research technique. *Journal of Writing in Creative Practice*, 7(2): 267–81.

Rennie, J (2010) Rethinking literacy in culturally diverse classrooms. In Pullen, DL and Cole, DR *Multiliteracies and Technology Enhanced Education: Social practice and the global classroom*. Hershey, PA: Information Science Reference.

Rezaei, AR (2015) Frequent collaborative quiz taking and conceptual learning. *Active Learning in Higher Education*, 16(3): 187–96.

Rezaei, KF, Kalantar, AB, Monirb, C and Zohrehb, ZZ (2013) The effect of teaching critical and creative thinking skills on the locus of control and psychological well-being in adolescents. *Procedia – Social and Behavioral Sciences*, 3 July, pp. 51–6. Available online at: www.sciencedirect.com/science/article/pii/S1877042813012901 (accessed: 14 October 2017).

Richards, J (2001) *Curriculum Development in Language Teaching*. Cambridge: Cambridge University Press.

Richmond, D (2013) Getting the quiet students involved. Available at: https://debrichmondblog.wordpress.com/2013/03/03/getting-the-quiet-students-involved/ (accessed: 2 August 2017).

Riley, P (2013) Teaching, learning, and living with iPads. *Music Educators Journal*, 100(1): 81–6.

Robbins, L (1963) *Higher Education: Report of the Committee Appointed by the Prime Minister under the Chairmanship of Lord Robbins 1961–63 (The Robbins Report)*. London: HMSO.

Robeznieks, A (2015) Improving health includes holding 'walking meetings'. *Modern Healthcare*, 45(34).

Robson, S (2015) Innovative Pedagogy Series: *Promoting Pedagogic Research and Professional Dialogue about Teaching: Rebalancing notions of academic excellence in higher education*. York: HEA.

Rodionova, Z (2016) The 10 best degree subjects if you want to make a lot of money after university. *The Independent*, 13 April.

Rogers, C and Freiberg, HJ (1994) *Freedom to Learn* (3rd edn). New York: Merrill.

Rogers, C, Lyon, H and Tausch, R (2013) *On Becoming an Effective Teacher: Person-centred teaching, psychology, philosophy, and dialogues with Carl R. Rogers and Harold Lydon*. London: Routledge.

Rogerson-Revell, P (2007) Humour in business: A double-edged sword: A study of humour and style shifting in intercultural business meetings. *Journal of Pragmatics*, 39(1): 4–28.

Rowlett, P and Waldock, J (2017) Sheffield Hallam University, LTA conference abstract, June.

Royal College of Psychiatrists (2011) *Mental Health of Students in Higher Education*. London: RCP.

Rubin, M, Denson, N, Kilpatrick, S, Matthews, K, Stehlik, T and Zyngier, D (2014) "I am working-class". *Educational Researcher*, 43(4): 196–200.

Ry, C and Keyes, C (1995) The structure of psychological wellbeing revisited. *Journal of Personality and Social Psychology*, 69(4): 719–72.

Ryan, J and Viete, R (2009) Respectful interactions: Learning with international students in the English-speaking academy. *Teaching in Higher Education*, 14(3): 303–14.

Ryan, J (2011) Academic shock: Thoughts on teaching international students. *The Guardian*, 18 May.

Sadoski, M and Paivio, A (2001) *A Dual Coding of Reading and Writing*. Mahwah, NJ: Lawrence Erlbaum Associates.

Sambell, K, McDowell, L and Montgomery, C (2013) *Assessment for Learning in Higher Education*. Abingdon and New York: Routledge.

Sanchez, T (2014) *Stories of Selected Heroes/Heroines who Define us as Americans*. Lanham, MD and Plymouth: University Press of America.

Saunders, D and Blanco Ramírez, G (2017) Against 'teaching excellence': Ideology, commodification, and enabling the neoliberalization of postsecondary education. *Teaching in Higher Education*, 22(4): 396–407.

Savin-Baden, M (2008) *Learning Spaces: Creating opportunities for knowledge and creation in academic life*. Maidenhead: Society for Research into Higher Education and Open University Press.

Schmidt, H, Rotgans, J and Yew, E (2011) The process of problem-based learning: What works and why. *Medical Education*, 45(8): 792–806.

Schön, DA (1983) *The Reflective Practitioner: How professionals think in action*. New York: Basic Books.

Scott, D and Hargreaves, E (2015) An introduction and a theory of learning. In Scott, D and Hargreaves, E (eds) *The Sage Handbook of Learning*. London: Sage.

Scott, S (2007) *Shyness and Society: The illusion of competence*. New York: Palgrave Macmillan.

Sen, NB (1968) *Wit and Wisdom of Gandhi, Nehru, Tagore*. Delhi: New Book Society of India.

Shafak, E (2010) The politics of fiction. Available online at: www.ted.com/talks/elif_shafak_the_politics_of_fiction#t-110906 (accessed 14 September 2017).

Shakespeare, W (author), Wells, S and Taylor G (eds) (1997) *The Complete Plays: Romances*. London: The Folio Society.

Shams, L and Seitz, A (2008) Benefits of multisensory learning. *Trends in Cognitive Sciences*, 12(11): 411–17.

Sharples, M, Adams, A, Ferguson, R, Gaved, M, McAndrew, P, Rienties, B, Weller, M and Whitelock, D (2014). *Innovating Pedagogy 2014: Open University Innovation Report 3*. Milton Keynes: The Open University.

Shiltz, E (2006) Two chariots: The justification of the best life in the *Katha Upanishad* and Plato's *Phaedrus*. *Philosophy East and West*, 56(3): 451–68.

Shor, I (1999) What is critical literacy? *Journal for Pedagogy, Pluralism and Practice*, 4(1): 1–26.

Siddiqui, N, Gorard, S and See, BH (2017) *Non-cognitive Impacts of Philosophy for Children*. Project Report, School of Education, Durham University, Durham.

Siemens, G (2004) Connectivism: A learning theory for the digital age. Available online at: www.elearnspace.org/Articles/connectivism.htm (accessed 12 September 2017).

Singh, G and Cowden, S (2016) Intellectuality, student attainment and contemporary higher education. In Steventon, G, Cureton, D and Clouder, L (2016) *Student Attainment in Higher Education: Issues, controversies and debates*. New York: Routledge.

Skallerup Bessette, L (2016) Assessment as care, assessing of care. University of Mary Washington, 30 November. Available online at: http://umwdtlt.com/assessment-as-care-assessment-of-care/ (accessed 2 August 2017).

Skelton, A (ed) (2007) *International Perspectives on Teaching Excellence in Higher Education*. Abingdon and New York: Routledge.

Skemp, R (1989) *Mathematics in the Primary School*. London: Routledge.

Skinner, BF (1974) *About Behaviorism*. New York: Random House.

Slater, J (2016) Accessibility of events. Unpublished manuscript. Sheffield Hallam University.

Smith, M (1992) Modularisation – its versatility and value. *Nurse Education Today*, 12(2): 137–41.

Smith, MK (1999) The cognitive orientation to learning. The encyclopedia of informal education. Available at: http://infed.org/mobi/the-cognitive-orientation-to-learning/ (accessed 2 August 2017).

Smith, MK (2001, 2010) David A. Kolb on experiential learning, *The Encyclopaedia of Informal education*. Available online at: http://infed.org/mobi/david-a-kolb-on-experiential-learning/

Social Market Foundation (SMF) (2016) Staying the course. SMF and Hobsons. Available online at: www.smf.co.uk/wp-content/uploads/2016/09/Social-Market-FoundationStaying-the-Course-FINAL-1-1.pdf (accessed 2 August 2017).

Solomon, R (1995) Some notes on emotion, 'East West'. *Philosophy East and West*, 45(2): 171–202.

Somekh, B and Lewin, C (2011) *Theory and Methods in Social Research* (2nd edn). London: SAGE.

Soria, K and Stubblefield, R (2015) Knowing me, knowing you: Building strengths, awareness, belonging, and persistence in higher education. *Journal of College Student Retention: Research, Theory & Practice*, 17(3): 351–72.

Speirs, N (2016) Student comments: Important things to know about the mentor/mentee relationship. University of Edinburgh. Available online at: www.ed.ac.uk/student-recruitment/widening-participation/projects/peer-mentoring/student-comments (accessed 14 September 2017).

Springer, L, Stanne, M and Donovan, S (1999) Effects of small-group learning on undergraduates in science, mathematics, engineering, and technology: A meta-analysis. *Review of Educational Research*, 69(1): 21–51.

Spurr, D, Griffiths, G and Stone, R (2013) Adult numeracy learners. In Griffiths, G and Stone, R (eds) *Teaching Adult Numeracy: Principles and practice*. Maidenhead: Open University Press/McGraw-Hill, pp. 45–60.

Stan, E (2012) About praise and its efficiency in education. *Journal of Educational Sciences and Psychology*, II(LXIV)(1): 28–34.

Stead, DR (2005) A review of the one-minute paper. *Active Learning in Higher Education*, 6(2): 118–31.

Steele, CM and Aronson, J (1995) Stereotype threat and the intellectual test performance of African-Americans. *Journal of Personality and Social Psychology*, 69: 797–811.

Steinzor, BH (1950) The spatial factor in face to face discussion groups. *The Journal of Abnormal and Social Psychology*, 45(3): 552–5.

Stephens, Greg J, Silbert, Lauren J and Hasson, Uri (2010) Speaker-listener neural coupling underlies successful communication (Psychological and Cognitive Sciences: Neuroscience) (Author abstract Report). *Proceedings of the National Academy of Sciences of the United States*, 107(32), 14425-14430.

Stevenson, J (2012) *Black and Minority Ethnic Student Degree Retention and Attainment*. The Higher Education Academy.

Stolz, SA (2015) Embodied learning. *Educational Philosophy and Theory*, 47(5): 474–87.

Strauss, V (2013) Howard Gardner: Multiple intelligences are not learning styles. *Washington Post*, 16 October.

Stroud, S (2007) Orientational meliorism in Dewey and Dogen, Charles S. Peirce Society. *Transactions of the Charles S. Peirce Society*, 43(1): 185–215.

Student Minds (2017) A short history of student minds. Available online at: www.studentminds.org.uk/history-of-student-minds.html (accessed 2 August 2017).

Taneja, Aakash (2014) Enhancing student engagement: A group case study approach. *Journal of Information Systems Education*, 25(3): 181–7.

Tanner, CK (2008) Explaining relationships among student outcomes and the school's physical environment. *Journal of Advanced Academics*, 19(3): 444–71.

Taylor, R (2016) The effects of accountability measures in English secondary schools: Early and multiple entry to GCSE Mathematics assessments. *Oxford Review of Education*, 42(6): 629–45.

Tertiary Education Quality and Standards Agency (TEQSA) (2010) *Australian Universities Quality Agency: Report of an Audit of the University of Melbourne*. Melbourne: AUQA.

Tom (2015) Essential guide to visual thinking for e-learning. The Rapid E-Learning Blog, 10 February. Available online at: http://blogs.articulate.com/rapid-elearning/essential-guide-visual-thinking-e-learning/ (accessed 2 August 2017).

Tran, T (2015) Is graduate employability the "whole-of-higher-education-issue"? *Journal of Education and Work*, 28(3): 207–27.

Turner, C. (2017) Universities warned over 'snowflake' student demands. *The Telegraph*, 8 January.

Tyler, RW (1949) *Basic Principles of Curriculum and Instruction*. Chicago: University of Chicago Press.

United Nations Educational, Scientific and Cultural Organisation (UNESCO) (2012) *A Place to Learn Lessons: Lessons from research on learning environments*. Quebec: UNESCO Institute for Statistics.

Universities UK (2015) *Patterns and Trends in UK Higher Education 2015*. London: Universities UK.

Universities UK (2016) *Higher Education in England: Provision skills and graduates*. London: Universities UK.

Urdang, S, Urdang, J and Urdang, L (eds) (1967) *The Random House Dictionary of the English Language*. New York: Random House.

Vitasari, P, Wahab, MNA, Othman, A, Herawan, T and Sinnadurai, SK (2010) The relationship between study anxiety and academic performance among engineering students. *Procedia-Social and Behavioral Sciences*, 8: 490–97.

Von Glasersfeld, E (2001) Radical constructivism and teaching. *Prospects*, 31(2): 161–73.

Vygotsky, L and Cole, M (1978) *Mind in Society: The development of higher psychological processes*. Cambridge, MA: Harvard University Press.

Walk, S (2008) Joy in school educational leadership. September, 66(1). *The Positive Classroom*, pp. 8–15. Available online at: www.ascd.org/publications/educational-leadership/sept08/vol66/num01/Joy-in-School.aspx

Wampole, C (2016) *Rootedness: The ramifications of a metaphor*. Chicago: The University of Chicago Press.

Warwick, J (2016) Characterizing student expectations: A small empirical study. *PRIMUS*, 26(5): 406–23.

Watkins, C. (2015) Metalearning in classrooms. In Scott, D. and Hargreaves, E. (eds) *The SAGE Handbook of Learning*. London: Sage, pp. 321–30.

Weale, S (2017) Teachers must ditch 'neuromyth' of learning styles, say scientists. *The Guardian*, 13 March.

Webb, J, Schirato, T and Danaher, G (2002) *Understanding Bourdieu*. London: Sage.

Weller, S (2016) *Academic Practice*. London: Sage.

Wenger, E, McDermott, R and Snyder, W (2002) *Cultivating Communities of Practice: A guide to managing knowledge*. Boston, MA and London: Harvard Business School/Oxford University Press/McGraw-Hill.

West, S (2017) From Colgate lasagna to crystal Pepsi: Visit the Museum of Failure. *The Guardian*, 19 April.

Whiteside, A and Garrett Dikkers, A (2015) Leveraging the social presence model: A decade of research on emotion in online and blended learning. In Tettegah, S and McCreery, M (2015) *Emotions, Technology, and Learning (Emotions and Technology)*. Cambridge, MA: Academic Press (Elsevier).

Williams, J (2013) *Consuming Higher Education: Why learning can't be bought*. London: Continuum.

Wills, E (2014) Dealing with stress at university. Imperial College Blog. Available online at: wwwf.imperial.ac.uk/blog/student-blogs/2014/08/09/dealing-with-stress-at-university/ (accessed 2 August 2017).

Wilson, M and Gerber, LE (2008) How generational theory can improve teaching: Strategies for working with the 'millennials'. *Currents in Teaching and Learning*, 1(1): 29–44.

Wingate, U (2015) *Academic Literacy and Student Diversity: The case of inclusive practice*. Bristol: Multilingual Matters.

Winterson, J (2012) *Why be Happy When You Could be Normal?* New York: Random House.

Witney, D and Smallbone, T (2011) Wiki work: Can using wikis enhance student collaboration for group assignment tasks? *Innovations in Education and Teaching International*, 48(1): 101–10.

Wolfram, C (2014) The UK needs a revolution in the way maths is taught: Here's why. *The Guardian*, 23 February.

Wolk, S (2008) Joy in school. *Educational Leadership*, 66(1): 8–15.

World Health Organization (2004). *Promoting mental health: concepts, emerging evidence, practice (Summary Report)*. Geneva: World Health Organization.

Wrigglesworth, J (2016) What's the meaning of International Students? Sheffield Institute of Education Blog, 15 June. Sheffield Hallam University.

Zhao, C-M and Kuh, G (2004) Adding value: Learning communities and student engagement. *Research in Higher Education*, 45(2): 115–38.

INDEX